EUREKA STOCKADE

*So we must fly a rebel flag,
As others did before us,
And we must sing a rebel song,
And join in rebel chorus.
We'll make the tyrants feel the sting,
O' those that they would throttle;
They needn't say the fault is ours,
If blood should stain the wattle.*

EXCERPT FROM
'Freedom on the Wallaby'
— HENRY LAWSON, 1891

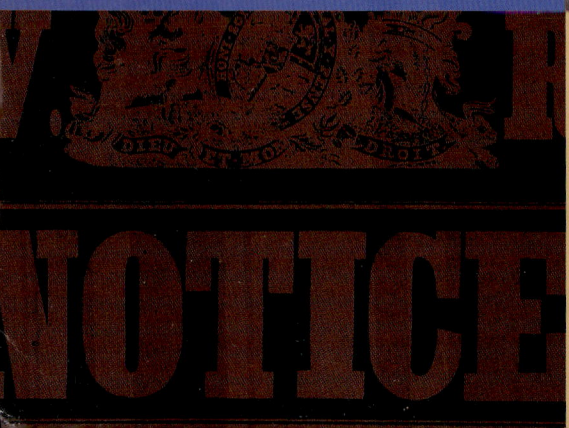

The Five Mile Press Pty Ltd
950 Stud Road
Rowville Victoria 3178 Australia
Phone: +61 3 8756 5500
Email: publishing@fivemile.com.au

First published in 2004
Text © Geoff Hocking

All rights reserved

Designed by Geoff Hocking
Edited by Emma Borghesi

Printed in China

TITLE PAGE:
The Eureka Stockade
Photograph painted by Beryl Ireland
(LA TROBE PICTURE COLLECTION,
STATE LIBRARY OF VICTORIA)

National Library of Australia
Cataloguing-in-Publication data

Hocking, Geoff.
Eureka Stockade: a pictorial history
Includes index.
ISBN 1 74124 426 9

1. Gold Miners - Victoria - History - Pictorial works.
2. Eureka Stockade (Ballarat, Vic.) - Pictorial works.
3. Gold miners - Victoria - Ballarat - History - Pictorial works.
4. Riots - Victoria - Ballarat - Pictorial works.
I. Title.

Every attempt has been made to trace and acknowledge copyright. Where an attempt has been unsuccessful, the publisher would be pleased to hear from the copyright owner so any omission or error can be rectified.

EUREKA STOCKADE

A Pictorial History

The events leading to the attack in the
pre-dawn of 3 December 1854

GEOFF HOCKING

The Five Mile Press

'Roll up, Eureka's heroes, on
    that grand Old Rush afar,
For Lalor's gone to join you in
    the big camp where you are;
Roll up and give him welcome
    such as only diggers can,
For well he battled for the rights
    of miner and of man…'

— HENRY LAWSON

Author's Note:
Some of the text in this work has been previously published in *The Red Ribbon Rebellion — Decade of Dissent.*
Published by New Chum Press 2001 © Geoff Hocking

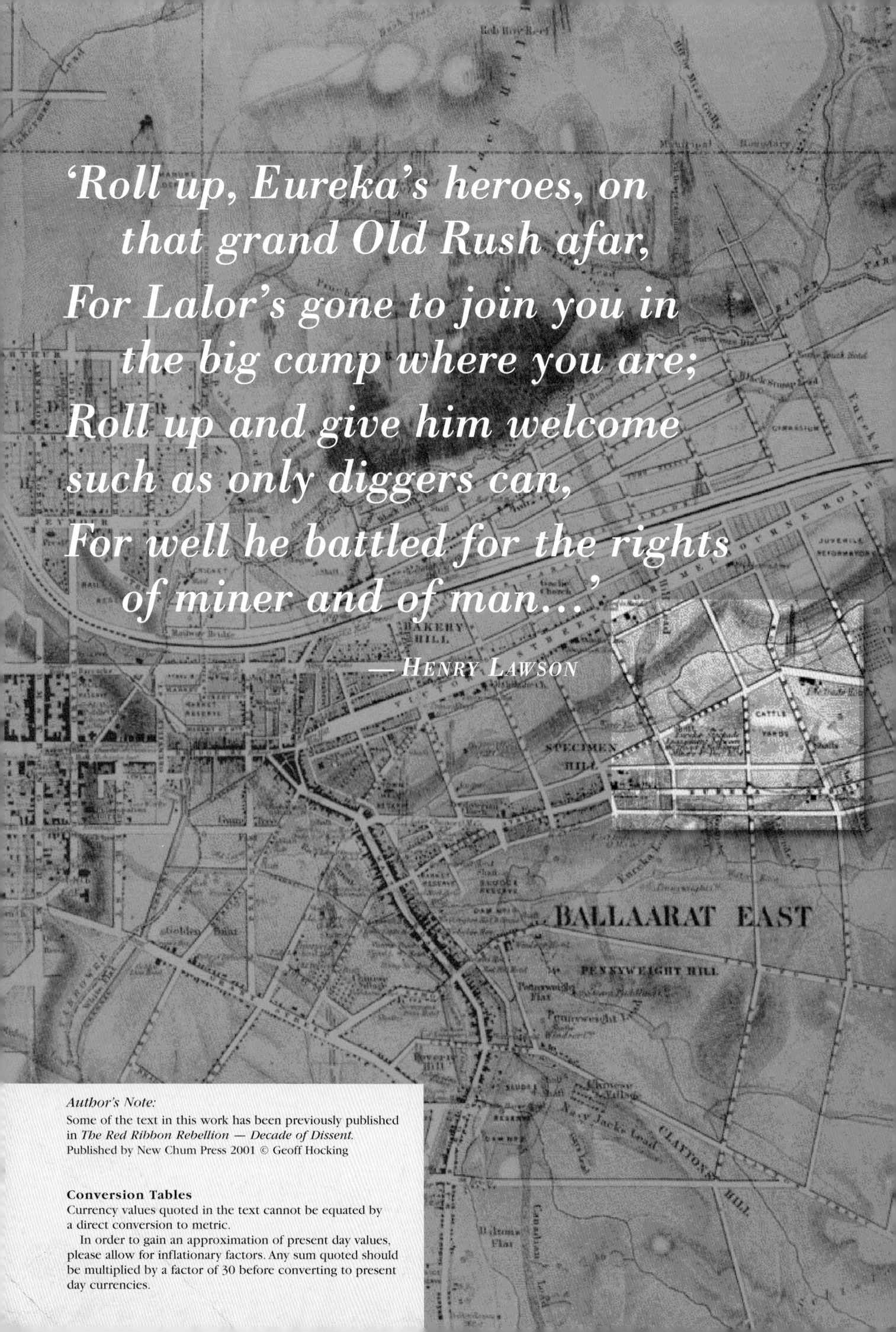

Conversion Tables
Currency values quoted in the text cannot be equated by a direct conversion to metric.

In order to gain an approximation of present day values, please allow for inflationary factors. Any sum quoted should be multiplied by a factor of 30 before converting to present day currencies.

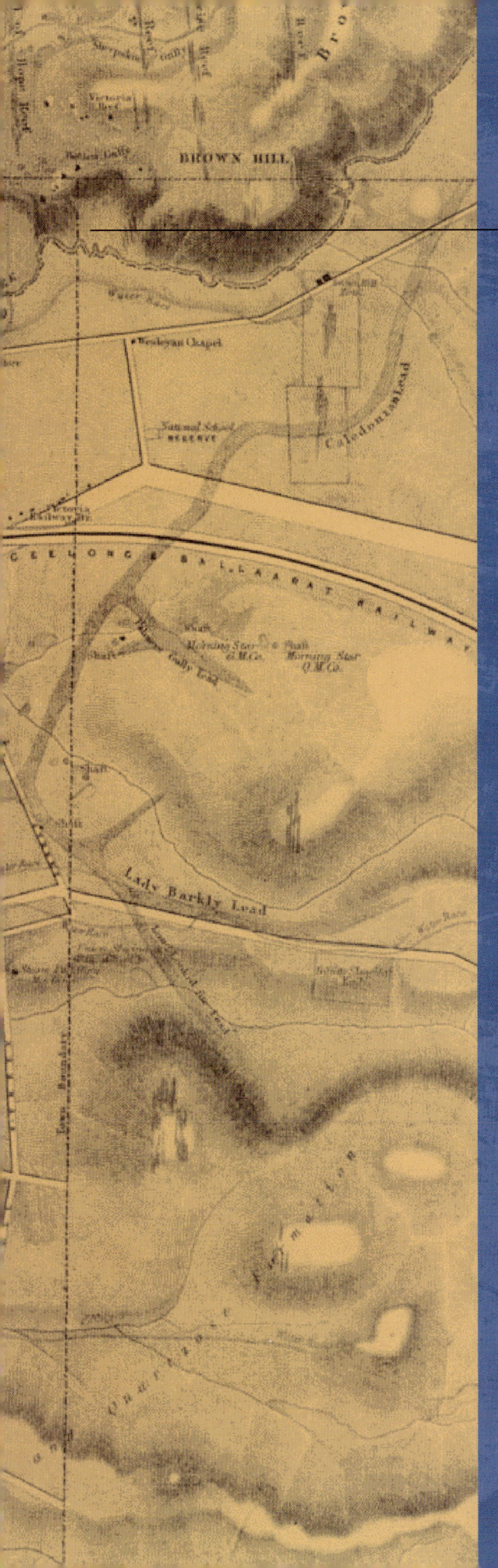

Contents

Introduction — 7
A Rush from the Crown — 8
Before the Ballarat Field — 10
The Journey Begins — 17
Gold in the Ballarat Hills — 27
The Road to Sedition — 50
Red Ribbon Rebellion — 65
A New Governor — 76
Joe! Joe! Joe! — 85
The Troubles Begin — 97
3 December 1854 — 132
Prisoners of the Crown — 164
Treason against Victoria — 166
In Memoriam — 178
Ballarat after the Battle — 197
Bibliography — 204
Notes — 204
Index — 206

4TH DECEMBER, 1854 — 'Recent events at the Mines at Ballaarat render it necessary for all true subjects of the Queen, and all strangers who have received hospitality and protection under her Flag, to assist in preserving Social Order and maintaining the Supremacy of the Law.

The question now agitated by the disaffected is not whether an enactment can be amended or ought to be repealed, but whether the Law is or is not to be administered in the name of Her Majesty. Anarchy and confusion must ensue unless those who cling to the institutions and the soil of their adopted country step prominently forward.

His Excellency relies upon the loyalty and sound feeling of the colonists.

All faithful subjects, and all strangers who have had equal rights extended to them, are therefore called upon to enrol themselves and be prepared to assemble at such places as may be appointed by the civil authorities in Melbourne and Geelong, and by the magistrates in the several towns of the Colony.' — CHAS. HOTHAM

EUREKA!

Introduction

THE SURPRISINGLY SHORT BUT BLOODY battle at the gravel pits on the Eureka diggings, which began just before dawn on Sunday morning, 3 December 1854, was a dramatic conclusion to months of heated agitation on the Ballarat diggings.

Following years of fruitless petitions and deputations to the colonial administration in defiance of insufferable taxation, refusal of suffrage and denial of property rights; and after centuries of hatred, discrimination and sectarian mistrust (that began with the British occupation of the Emerald Isle and the subjugation of its people generations before), this denouement was finally played out under the azure blue flag of the Southern Cross on the Victorian diggings.

The battle at the Eureka Stockade, a crude embattlement of broken drays, fallen logs and stakes driven into the ground, lasted for less than half an hour, yet 22 diggers and six troopers of the 40th Regiment lay mortally wounded or already dead.

After the smoke had settled and the sun rose to cast its long golden fingers over the dusty battleground, the 40th Regiment went about the gruesome business of upholding the Queen's laws — with ruthless vengeance.

Wounded diggers were bayoneted where they lay, tents were set alight, and as the troops ranged far and wide across the diggings more than 100 men were arrested, with 13 sent for trial charged with treason. Amongst those brought to trial were the Italian Raffaello Carboni, the American negro John Joseph, Dutchman Jan Vennick and several of the leaders of the Ballarat Reform League, a loosely formed organisation which had sought to represent the concerns of the diggers to the colonial governor.

The Ballarat Reform League had previously failed to convince Charles Joseph La Trobe, the first governor of the Colony of Victoria, of the rights of their cause, and had pinned their hopes on his replacement, military man Sir Charles Hotham. Hotham, however, was faced with the task of restoring the finances of a colonial economy left in ruins by the dilettante La Trobe and saw the goldfields as the easiest means by which he could restore the coffers of the Treasury back to fiscal health. Rather than ease the burden of taxation on the diggers, he increased it. He demanded that the troops be increasingly diligent in the collection of the much-disputed licence fee, and imposed weekly 'licence hunts' on all the goldfields and set the diggings on the inexorable course towards revolution.

Unlike Bendigo, where more than 14,000 heavily armed miners rallied under their red banner 15 months earlier and demanded that Commissioner Panton represent their concerns to the governor (he agreed, and so they all went back to their tents without a shot being fired), Ballarat was riddled with corruption from the liquor-licensing court to the camp commander, where the rule of British law was to brook no challenge from the seditious Irish, 'the French Red Republican, the German political metaphysician, the American Lone Star Member [or] the British Chartist'.[1]

OPPOSITE:
The Victorian *Government Gazette*
Published 4 December 1854

Fond of issuing proclamations, the Governor of the Colony of Victoria, Sir Charles Hotham, called upon all who had enjoyed the hospitality of the Crown to enrol in his special forces and protect the towns against insurrection in this bulletin published in the *Gazette* the day after the battle at the Eureka Stockade.
   He seemed to have missed the point entirely.

ABOVE:
Giving out Licenses
Engraving from The Three Colonies of Australia: New South Wales, Victoria, South Australia; their Pastures, Copper Mines, and Gold Fields, *by Samuel Sidney, published in 1852*

(LA TROBE UNIVERSITY LIBRARY COLLECTION, BENDIGO)

A Rush from the Crown

GOLD WAS FOUND IN A CALIFORNIAN creekbed in January 1848, by James Marshall, a carpenter engaged in constructing a water mill for landowner Captain John Sutter on his extensive holdings at Coloma, east of Sacramento. The news was carried to the port of San Francisco by the storekeeper at Sutter's Fort, the Mormon leader Sam Brannan, who rode exuberantly through the port city shouting, 'Gold! Gold! Gold from the American River,' as he waved a glass jar filled with nuggets over his head.

California caught gold fever. However, for reasons of geography, and the inability of ship-owners to find crews to sail their vessels back to the east coast, the initial excitement stopped there. It was some months before the news of the discovery could be carried back across the mountains, over the great plains of the mid-west to reach New York in June. Much to the displeasure of the British government, this news was also carried across the Atlantic, on board the steamship *Europa,* to reach London on 10 October 1848, almost ten months after California had gone quite 'mad'.

The British were wary of the 'wily yankee' and his grandiose schemes, and were still smarting over the loss of that colony to the great American republic. The editor of the *Times*, after perusing the American papers carried to London by the *Europa*, advised his readers to view the news from America 'with great caution'. The British were fearful that any great rush of its subjects to chase after gold in California would only serve to swell a persistent anti-British sentiment in the United States.

In a Europe that was already reeling from one revolutionary battle after another, the last thing that the British wanted was to encourage its own people to travel to parts of the globe where the Crown had no influence, to be seduced by notions of freedom, franchise and democracy. However, it was the discovery of gold, both in California, and two years later in the colonies of New South Wales and Victoria, that ushered in a nascent spirit of independence in the Australian colonies, and saw the acceptance of all of the demands made in the People's Charter which had been drafted in 1838, and denied time and time again by the British parliament. Even in the far-flung corners of the empire, the empathy of the common man for his fellows was palpable; when a small group of rural workers from Dorset who had attempted to form a farm labourer's union were arrested, convicted and transported to the penal colony of New South Wales in 1834, thousands of Sydney-siders lined the streets to bid them welcome. Known as the Tolpuddle Martyrs, these five simple, honest men were just another link in the unbreakable chain of the human spirit that led to the protests against the government forces on the goldfields and the battle of wills at Eureka.

The news of the Californian discovery could not be stifled in London. From there it spread all around the globe. By the time the residents of the Colony of New South Wales learned of the rush to Californian gold (which had captured the imagination of more than half of the civilised world), almost a full 12 months had passed since the first nuggets had been collected from the gravel bed in John Sutter's mill-race.

The rush to be rich was on in full force. Ships leaving from the eastern seaboard of Australia bound for the Californian coast were soon filled with old hands and new migrants alike. Many had hardly set foot on Australian soil before they took ship again, this time away from the rule of the Crown and into the heartland of the democrats.

It was in California that those who were instrumental in making the discoveries of gold in Australia learned the art of gold-seeking; it was also in California that many of the same men had studied the ways of the republican, and it was from California that many of those who were prominent players in the Australian insurrection had first breathed in the heady draught of true freedom.

Opposite:
Hutchings' California Scenes — Methods of Mining
The rush to the diggings on the west coast of America brought thousands across the seas from Australia's east. It was, in fact, easier to get to California from Sydney than it was from New York. From America's east, eager diggers would be forced to travel via the Panama isthmus, or attempt a perilous land crossing, which concluded with the almost impassable Rocky Mountains.

Before very long, the California diggings rang to the sounds of the Australian vernacular, and the Van Demonians and 'Sydney Ducks' soon made their mark.

With the discovery of gold in Australia in 1851, the rush to California came to an end, and traffic soon flowed from America's west coast to New South Wales. Before long, the Australian colonies rang to the sound of an American drawl as well.
(BANCROFT LIBRARY COLLECTION, UNIVERSITY OF CALIFORNIA, BERKELEY)

HUTCHINGS' CALIFORNIA SCENES.—METHODS OF MINING.

SINKING A SHAFT
Is represented in the above engraving. These are sunk to ascertain if there is *pay dirt* upon the bed rock, or in any strata of gravel above it; or to find the basin or hollow in the rock upon a hill before commencing to tunnel. Sometimes all the pay dirt is thus hoisted by the windlass. These shafts are frequently very deep; one at Weaverville, Trinity Co., is 625 feet in depth.

CANALS.
The above is intended to represent a Canal, by means of which the water of a river or creek, after winding among the hills for many miles, supplies the mining districts with water. They are built at great cost, and are a great public convenience, for without them the mines would be comparatively useless. The time may come when the whole of the water from our mountain streams will be needed for mining and manufacturing purposes, and will be sold at a price within the reach of all.

The Hydraulic Telegraph.
The above represents the manner of constructing the "Hydraulic Telegraph," as it is named. A small flume is placed upon poles or high tressels, through which the water is conveyed from the canal or ditch to a wooden funnel at the end, to which is attached telegraphs are generally from 50 to 130 feet which the water escapes, thus creating the ing down banks of earth into the sluice.

SLUICING.
To the right a company of miners are "sluicing;" those at the upper end are throwing in the pay dirt, and the man at the lower end is tending the sluice. Several lengths of sluice-boxes, or troughs with the ends out, supported by tressels, form the sluice; across the bottom, inside, are riffles or false bottoms, to save the gold; a stream of water being turned down, the gold is separated from the dirt, which is washed out

GROUND SLUICING.
This illustrates one of the many methods of ground sluicing. A trench first dug down the hill-side, into which a small stream of water is turned; miners are stand across or in the stream, and with their picks loosen the gravel and dirt, while the force of the water carries it into a sluice below. Sometimes a stream of water is made to run by the side of a bank, it falls into the water, and by undermining or picking down the bank, it falls into the water, which it is removed, and the pay is afterward carefully washed.

The above is an illustration of a gold-saving machine, recently invented by Mr. Jas. Patterson of Placerville, by whom a similar one is patented, in which the finest particles of scale or flour gold are saved. The rocks are seen rolling over the end, while the dirt gold and water pass thro' a tom apron into the machine, where the gold is separated by means of quicksilver, and being washed over patent riffles.

James Wilson Marshall
discoverer of gold in California
Houseworth, Photographer.

TURNING THE RIVER.
This view represents the building of a dam across the river, to turn it into a flume. From ten to twenty men form themselves into a joint stock company, for the purpose of draining and working the bed of the river. Sometimes several companies will unite, and by their enterprise build a flume several miles in length, into which the whole stream is turned. Wheels are placed in the flume to pump out the remaining water, or elevate rocks or dirt from below, after which the dirt is washed in a sluice, tom or cradle. The "Sailors' Claim" on Feather River, cost over $200,000, and employed three hundred men daily.

PANNING OUT.
above represents the primitive method of mining. A pan filled rth is set into the water, and by shaking it from side to ride, is washed out, and the gold gradually sinking to the bottom an, is there saved. This method is still used by every com- wash out the product of the days' labor; while the Chinaican uses the pan or bowl exclusively.

TUNNELING.
els are drifted into the hills, to save the labor of washing down the whole. The strata of gravel or pay dirt lying upon the bed rock is generally the richest, and is taken out as represented above. Sometimes tunnels are run ck, to drain the water off, and work the inside of the hill to advantage. The Table Mountain Tunnel near Jamestown, is 900 ft through solid rock, upon which, 3,756 days labor have been expended.

ROCKING THE CRADLE
The earth to be washed is carried in buckets to the emptied into the sieve or hopper, when water from poured upon it; as the cradle is rocked from side to as it, water falls through the sieve up in an apron slop the back of the cradle, and passing over the bottom out at the end,—while the gold remains on the end of the cradle. Chinamen are the principal with this machine.

according to Act of Congress, in the year 1855, by Jas M. Hutchings in the Clerk's Office of the U.S. District Court for the Northern District of California   Published by J. M. Hutchings

Before the Ballarat Field

'During the ten years that the province of Port Phillip had been settled it had been daily progressing in population and wealth. Vast interest had been silently growing up, and new classes were beginning to emerge into importance. All depended on the land.

The first wealth of Port Phillip was acquired by pastoral pursuits, and nearly every person was either directly or indirectly engaged in squatting.'

— McCombie, *History of Victoria*

THE BALLARAT DIGGINGS GREW ON THE outskirts of William C. Yuille's station, to the north-east of Buninyong, Victoria's oldest inland settlement. By the time gold was discovered, almost the entire central highlands of the Colony of Victoria had been overrun with sheep. Settlers had followed Major Mitchell's tracks out from Sydney, taking up the rolling, grassy country that he had described so rapturously as his 'Australia Felix', after he had hurried back from his expedition of discovery to Sydney in 1836.

The first expedition into the region, after Mitchell, set out from Corio Bay in August 1837, before any settlement had even begun at Geelong. The party of Thomas Learmonth, surveyor D'Arcy, Dr. Thompson, manager of the Derwent Company of Tasmania David Fisher, the East India Company's Captain Hutton, and Henry Anderson set their sights on a mount that could be seen in the distance as they came over Bellpost Hill. After they had reached and eventually ascended the slopes of Mount Buninyong they were able to see the good open grasslands that lay to the north-west, the waters of Lake Burrumbeet and the distant Pyrenees and Grampians ranges. This party of explorers were intent on finding good country for the expansion of their grazing interests; they had no inkling of what lay beneath those hills.

Above:
Mount Buninyong
Engraving by Samuel Calvert, published 1873

This engraving was exhibited in the International Exhibition, 1873. It shows settlers amongst the large trees at the base of Mount Buninyong, and in the company of a small group of the original inhabitants of the district.
(BY PERMISSION, NATIONAL LIBRARY OF AUSTRALIA)

Before the Ballarat Field

MOUNT BUNINYONG

Spelling 'Ball-aa-rat'

The local Aborigines had a name for the grassy valley in which gold was discovered. They called it 'a resting place', and when they pronounced its name the second syllable was drawn out to sound 'Ball - aa - rat'.

The first Europeans are said to have transcribed it to read Ballaarat, though the spelling Ballarat was commonly used from the 1850s. The *Ballarat Times* is an example. Both spellings appear in documents and pictures and sometimes even together. Several of the illustrations in this book use the spelling Ballaarat.

The occasional usage of Ballaarat in the text is a direct transcription from original material, otherwise, the spelling is the more commonly used contemporary spelling – Ballarat.

In the days of gold, and after, the valley of Ballarat was anything but a resting place for Europeans and Aborigines alike.

The country drew them into the west and the party split up to cover as much ground as possible; however, their navigation skills were not as good as had been anticipated and they got quite lost, even missing the provision cart that was sent out to meet them on their return.

Eventually, they found their way back to the coast, having fasted all the way. Another expedition set out the following year. This time Thomas Learmonth was joined by his brother Somerville, Mr. Aitken, Henry Anderson and William Yuille. This second journey of exploration set out from Aitken's house on the road between Port Phillip and Mount Macedon, at Mount Aitken. They headed north towards Mount Alexander, then followed the course of the Loddon River, traversing all of the country that was to become, two decades later, the source of great wealth for all of the colony.

The Learmonth brothers, together with Anderson and Yuille, settled in the country which later encompassed the Ballarat, Buninyong and Sebastopol diggings. The Learmonths built their homestead on the future site of the Buninyong Gold Mining Company's ground at Buninyong; Anderson settled at Winter's Flat where the Yarrowee and Woolshed creeks ran together; Yuille took all that country that is known today as Ballarat West, Ballarat East and Sebastopol.

Yuille's station extended from Buninyong to Yuille's swamp, 16 kilometres to the north, known today by the more attractive name of Lake Wendouree. When William Cross Yuille and his cousin Archibald took up their holding in 1838, they could not know of the wealth that lay beneath the surface, or in the creekbeds that wound across the landscape; their interest lay in the golden fleece thickening on the backs of their flocks.

Captain John Hepburn (who gave his name to the area now known as Hepburn Springs) first crossed the same central highlands in 1838. He described the country he passed in a letter to a Mr. John Betts of Birmingham, who advised him in reply: 'John, look closely into all the streams; dig, and wash the earth; search diligently for gold, for I am sure your feet are passing over immense wealth every day.'[1] Although Hepburn did not find any gold in the streams, he did discover the skull of an escaped prisoner in the 'brink of a waterhole at the junction of the creeks known as Barker's and Forest creeks'. The prisoner was one of a party of eight who had escaped from a work party near Yass. These escapees were more than likely the first Europeans to walk on the golden ground; it was a pity their minds were set on murder and mayhem and not on the rewards of honest toil.

Six of the absconders were murdered as they slept, by their mates George Comerford and Thomas Dignum, after they had started to bicker over the lack of food and in which direction they were to tramp. The murdered men were tossed on

THE LATE MR. W. C. YUILLE.

Above:
Squatter William C. Yuille
Yuille made his first journey into the region north-west of Port Phillip in 1838. He set out from Mt Aitken, headed for Mt Alexander, then followed the Loddon River west towards Buninyong. Before two decades were over, the area around Mt Buninyong had become one of the richest places on earth.
(LA TROBE PICTURE LIBRARY, STATE LIBRARY OF VICTORIA)

Before the Ballarat Field

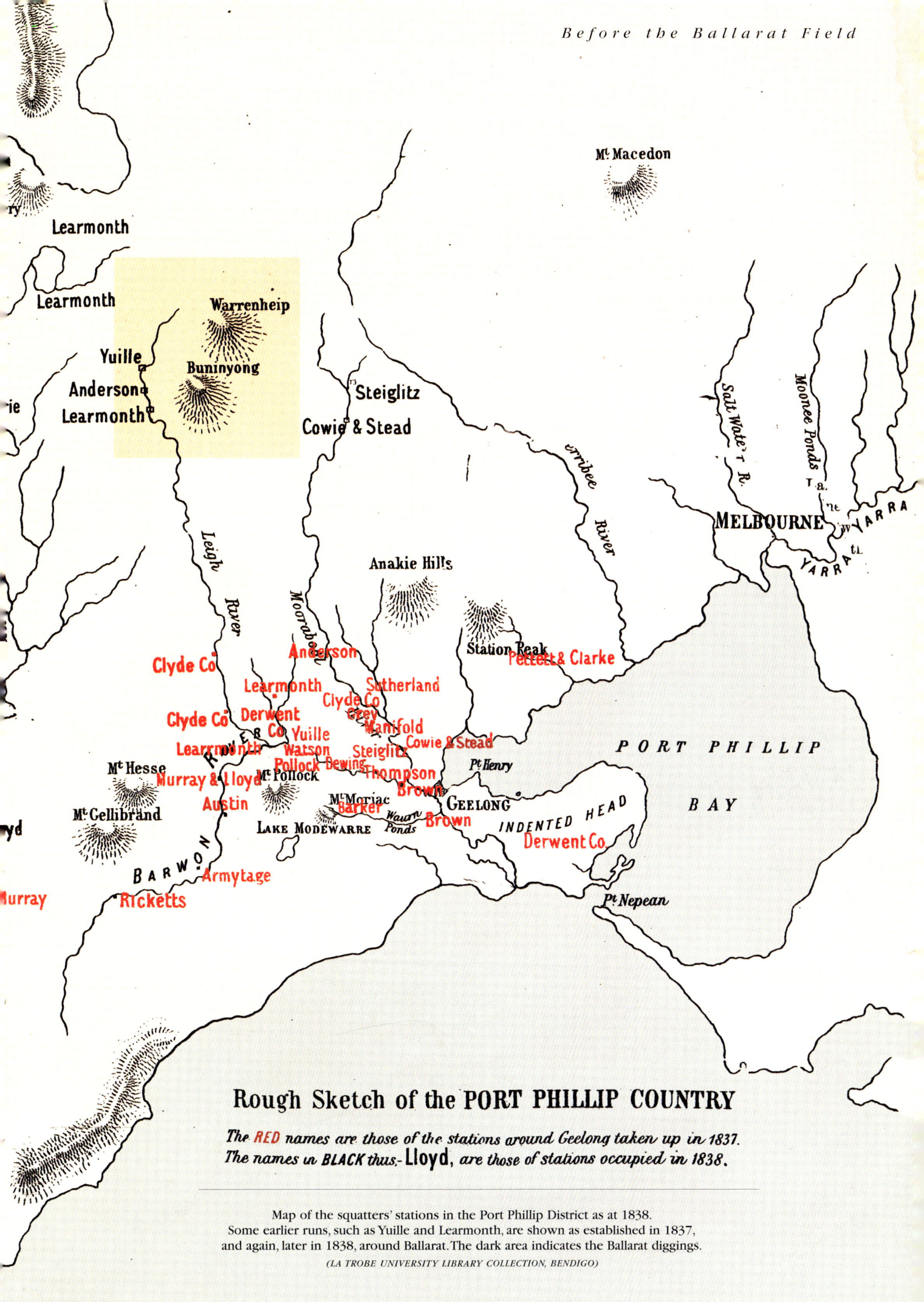

Rough Sketch of the PORT PHILLIP COUNTRY

The RED names are those of the stations around Geelong taken up in 1837.
The names in BLACK thus:- Lloyd, are those of stations occupied in 1838.

Map of the squatters' stations in the Port Phillip District as at 1838.
Some earlier runs, such as Yuille and Learmonth, are shown as established in 1837,
and again, later in 1838, around Ballarat. The dark area indicates the Ballarat diggings.

(LA TROBE UNIVERSITY LIBRARY COLLECTION, BENDIGO)

a large bonfire in an attempt to destroy the evidence of this callous deed. When the pair made their way to Port Phillip, robbing settlers and homesteads as they went, they were finally arrested and brought to trial. The court could not believe the tale of horror that was recounted and decided to make the journey to the waterhole at the junction of Barker's and Forest creeks. The evidence of the fire and burnt bodies were there for all to see.

Hepburn had buried the skull in the dry bed of the waterhole, but the next time he passed through the area he noted that the hole was full of water. He wrote:'If I had been fortunate enough to have found gold then, I should most certainly have never acquired my present position, but I was not to be the Hargraves'.[2]

Bonan Yong — the settlement

The first inland settlement began in Bonan Yong (later anglicised, Buninyong) in 1841 when timber splitters and sawyers George Gab, George Innes and George Coleman built crude slab and bark huts for themselves and their families. Before long, Gab had constructed a rooming house which offered accommodation for the travellers who were passing through the district. Jamieson's Hotel was later built on this site. In 1844, the first doctor in the district, Dr. Power, built his hut behind the Buninyong Hotel. The settlement then comprised a blacksmith's shop and a store and a second hut built by Gab which he used as a hotel. Buninyong was growing apace. It became a

---

ABOVE:
Ballaarat from Mount Buninyong
Drawn by S.T. Gill
Lithograph published by James Blundell & Co., Melbourne 1855
The rolling pasture of Mitchell's 'Australia Felix' attracted the sheep herders who established their stations, dotted across the undiscovered goldfields.
(REX NAN KIVELL COLLECTION, NK9843/2
BY PERMISSION, NATIONAL LIBRARY OF AUSTRALIA)

popular place for bullock teamsters to build and leave their wives and families while they were on the road. The growing township afforded these early settlers some protection against Aboriginal marauders and others who sought to live outside the law.

In 1847, the Reverend Thomas Hastie arrived to establish the first school and church in the region. The buildings were constructed entirely from local labour as a gift to the growing community. Hastie regularly travelled around the squatting runs, visiting members of his human flock. Hastie recalled his impression of the landscape he came to know well when on one such occasion he was visiting a shepherd in his hut out on the Creswick road:

> I often passed the spot on which Ballarat is built … and there could not be a prettier spot imagined. There was, in general, plenty of grass and water, and I have often seen the cattle in considerable numbers lying in quiet enjoyment after being satisfied with the pasture. There was a beautiful clump of wattles where Lydiard street now stands, and on one occasion, when Mrs. Hastie was with me, she remarked, 'What a nice place for a house, with the flat in front and the wattles behind!'[3]

Hastie recalled that the shepherd complained of the silence of the bush. He told him that 'the solitude was so painful that he could not endure it, for he saw no one from the time the shepherds went out in the morning till they returned at night … [Hastie] was the only person he had seen who was not connected with the station'.[4]

Journalist, and co-owner of the *Ballarat Star*, William Bramwell Withers, in his book *History of Ballarat* (published in 1870), wrote of the district in the days before the diggers swarmed across the landscape, as being:

> … a pleasantly picturesque pastoral country. Mount and range, and table land, gullies and creeks and grassy slopes, here black and dense forest, there only sprinkled with trees, and yonder showing clear reaches of grass, made up the general landscape.
>
> A pastoral quiet reigned everywhere.[5]

At the time that gold was first discovered, the settlement consisted of a blacksmith's shop, a grocer's store, a church, and several cottages and huts that housed around 50 families. Buninyong was at the centre of a popular trail for travellers and carters en route from the coastal port of Geelong up to the stations north of the ranges.

That was before the roaring days — before the days of gold.

ABOVE:
Bunynong [sic] *Hill, Near Ballarat*
Engraving from The Three Colonies of Australia: New South Wales, Victoria, South Australia; their Pastures, Copper Mines, and Gold Fields, *by Samuel Sidney, published in 1852.*
(LA TROBE UNIVERSITY LIBRARY COLLECTION, BENDIGO)

V R

THE MELBOURNE MORNING HERALD EXTRAORDINARY.

Vol. XI.   MELBOURNE, MONDAY EVENING, NOVEMBER 11, 1850.   No. 1508.

GLORIOUS NEWS!
SEPARATION AT LAST!!

We lose not a moment in communicating to the PUBLIC the Soul-stirring Intelligence that

SEPARATION HAS COME AT LAST!!
The Australian Colonies' Bill,
WITH THE AMENDMENTS MADE IN THE LORDS, ON THE 5th JULY,
WAS AGREED TO IN THE COMMONS ON THE 1ST AUG.,
AND ONLY AWAITS THE QUEEN'S SIGNATURE TO BECOME
THE LAW OF THE LAND.
The long OPPRESSED, long BUFFETED Port Phillip, is at length an
INDEPENDENT COLONY,
Gifted with the Royal name of VICTORIA, and endowed with a flourishing revenue and almost inexhaustible resources.
Let all classes of Colonists then lose not a moment in their hour of triumph in celebrating the Important Epoch in a suitable manner, and observing one
GENERAL JUBILEE.

The "Public Rejoicings" Committee lately nominated by the Citizens of Melbourne, will assemble without delay; let one and all co-operate with them heart and hand in giving due effect to the enthusiastic ovations of our

New-born Colony!

The Journey Begins

Separation rejoicings – opening of Princes Bridge by C.J. Latrobe Esq. Nov. 15th 1851.

11 November 1850

BY 5 JULY 1850, THE SOUTHERN district of the Colony of New South Wales, south of the Murray River, had been granted separation from its colonial governance from Sydney. The Colony of Victoria was finally able to govern itself when separation was announced in the headlines of the *Melbourne Morning Herald* in its edition marked 'Extraordinary' of 11 November, 1850: 'Glorious News! Separation At Last!!'

It had been just over a decade since Captain Lonsdale had sailed through the heads of Port Phillip Bay aboard HMS *Rattlesnake*, to take control of the 'illegal' settlement that was growing at the mouth of the Yarra Yarra River.

This southern corner of the Colony of New South Wales had long been occupied by all kinds of adventurers — whalers, traders, and settlers from Van Diemen's Land, who were taking the earliest opportunity of establishing a foothold in this 'Australia Felix', as the earliest explorer Major Thomas Livingstone Mitchell had dubbed the region, on his return to Sydney from his trek to discover the 'confluence of the Murray and the Darling rivers' in 1836.

It seems that Mitchell had 'got lost' and diverted from his course, casting his eye over the richly pastured, rolling hillsides that were central Victoria at that time. He did pop-up at Bridgewater Bay on the south-west coast and observe the Hentys on their well-established property, and he did rush to the top of Mount Macedon on the very day that Lonsdale entered the bay, observing 'nothing at all' happening in the great 'south countrie' that he was to take full credit for discovering.

The fact that there were already hundreds of settlers who were well-established around Port Phillip Bay was of little interest to Mitchell as he rushed back to Sydney to publish 'his discovery'. Mitchell left his men, and the long boat they had carted across the waterless highlands, stuck with a broken axle in the very creek where gold was discovered on the Mount Alexander diggings — the richest alluvial goldfield in the world, and the site of the Victorian diggers' early protest against the government and its excessive taxes.

At that time, most of the population of the southern colony were ticket-of-leave men and women who had made their way across Bass Strait to escape the harsh regime that prevailed in Van Diemen's Land. There were also scores of other 'Van Demonians' whose departure from the island prison was not necessarily approved by the authorities there, nor welcomed in Port Phillip.

ABOVE:
Separation rejoicings on opening of Princes Bridge by C.J. Latrobe [sic] Esq. Nov. 15th 1851
Watercolour drawing by William Strutt
(STATE PARLIAMENTARY LIBRARY, VICTORIA)

OPPOSITE:
Melbourne Morning Herald, 11 November 1850
The separation of the Colony of Victoria from New South Wales is granted — at last!
(LA TROBE PICTURE COLLECTION, STATE LIBRARY OF VICTORIA)

'Australia Felix'

In 1836, explorer Major Thomas Livingstone Mitchell named the region of the central Victorian Highlands 'Australia Felix'. He was so excited by his discovery of the great 'south countrie' that he pronounced the 'rich soil, flowery plains and green hills' as 'ready for the immediate reception of civilised man; and destined to become eventually a portion of a great empire'.

He was not to know the impact that thousands of miners were to have on the pretty valleys when they invaded in 1851.

A decade after Mitchell's discovery, and only a short while after Captain Lonsdale's replacement by District Commissioner Charles Joseph La Trobe, exciting reports from New South Wales were to challenge the concept of a new economy based on agriculture and a new aristocracy created with land grants to free settlers and built on the backs of the labouring classes.

There had been many reports of gold found in the hills and creeks of both New South Wales and Victoria over the years, but the mass exodus of 'settlers' to California in 1849 had encouraged the New South Wales government to post a reward for the discovery of payable gold in that colony, and to hopefully reverse the migration across the Pacific.

Australian gold

As if to answer the governor's call, up stepped Edward Hammond Hargraves. Hargraves had migrated from his birthplace in Gosford, England, to the Australian colonies in 1832, at the age of 14 years. He had been raising cattle on the Manning River, and had also worked on a property near Bathurst in central New South Wales before he decided to go to California. Bathurst was the first inland settlement to be established after the Blue Mountains had been crossed in 1813 by explorers Blaxland, Lawson, and another squatter whose political ideas would later seek to influence the administration of the diggings, William Charles Wentworth.

When disappointed at the poor returns on the sale of 70 cattle that he had nurtured through the drought years of 1847–48, Hargraves returned to his farm and announced that he was going to try his luck on the Californian goldfields. Like thousands of other colonists keen for adventure, Hargraves joined the rush to California in 1848, and while he was never too keen on actually doing any digging he did learn the art of gold-finding. He also learnt that to be known as the discoverer of a new goldfield would bring fame, wealth and position to that lucky individual — and Hargraves had determined that he should be that individual.

While working in the creeks around Sacramento he was struck by the similarity of that terrain to that he had known around Bathurst. He became convinced that gold would be found in those creeks and gullies at home and left California in 1851, bound for glory. As he stood on the gangplank ready to board the ship bound for Australia, he turned to take one last look at California, and an American digger cried out to him: 'There's no gold in the country you're going to, and if there is, that

ABOVE:
Charles Joseph La Trobe
Oil on canvas by Sir Francis Grant, c. 1855

Several Victorian colonists subscribed to commission this portrait of the former governor a year after he had departed. This impressive painting showing a fine man resplendent in his military uniform may have served to remind them that he wasn't so bad after all — even after everything he had done to the colony.
(LA TROBE PICTURE COLLECTION, STATE LIBRARY OF VICTORIA)

EDWARD HAMMOND HARGRAVES.
The Discoverer of Gold in Australia.

darned Queen of yours won't let you dig it.' In proud defiance, Hargraves took off his hat and struck a pose, replying, 'There's as much gold in the country I am going to as there is in California; and Her Most Gracious Majesty the Queen, God bless her, will make me one of her gold commissioners.'

On board that same ship that conveyed Hargraves back to Australia was James Esmond, another veteran of the Californian rush, who was to discover the first gold in Victoria at Clunes. These men had brought back from America the knowledge that could fire every man's imagination. The discoveries they made brought men their economic independence, and encouraged them to seek their own destiny free from servitude. Hargraves and Hiscock had brought back from America the very seeds of revolution, which they cast into the waters flowing along the gravel-strewn creekbeds of the colonies.

It was Hargraves's discovery of gold in the Colony of New South Wales, and the subsequent discoveries in the central highlands across the newly separated Colony of Victoria in 1851, that brought irrevocable change to the fortunes of all in the colonies.

ABOVE:
Edward Hammond Hargraves
The Discoverer of Gold in Australia
Engraving from Picturesque Atlas of Australasia, 1888

A common mistake is made in the spelling of Edward Hammond Hargraves's surname. On the Bendigo diggings there was a Commissioner Hargreaves, and one of the main streets there is named after him. Hargraves Street in Castlemaine is named after the gentleman shown in this engraving.
(PRIVATE COLLECTION)

The first gold in Australia

There had been numerous discoveries of gold across the Colony of New South Wales prior to the finds that ushered in the big rush to the diggings in 1851. Before the great rush, the Colony of New South Wales extended as far south as Port Phillip Bay, taking in all of the region that was renamed Victoria after separation was granted on 1 July 1851.

1823 — Gold had been found as early as 1823 when a convict working on a road gang near Bathurst received a flogging for having a lump of gold in his possession. The hapless fellow was suspected of having stolen a gold watch, and melting it down into a nugget. Whichever way the gold came into his possession, his back was scarred just the same.

1839 — Count Paul de Strzelecki found gold in the Australian Alps when he was exploring the territory in 1839. He was advised to keep the discovery quiet; the government was fearful that a restless convict community would be impossible to control if they knew of the discovery.

1840 — Gold was found in Campbell's Creek on the Strathlodden Run in what later became part of the Mount Alexander diggings. A nephew of squatter William Campbell had filled his pannikin with pure gold, but was also advised to keep his mouth shut 'lest people should come and turn up the soil and shepherds abandon their flocks'.

1844 — When Reverend W.B. Clarke showed Governor George Gipps some gold he had found near Hartley (NSW), Gipps exclaimed, 'Put it away, Mr Clarke, or we shall have our throats cut.'

1846 — Some gold was found at Montecute in South Australia; yet it wasn't until miners returned to Adelaide after they had rushed to Victoria in 1852 that any real effort was put into the creeks around that city.

1849 — The first small rush began in the Pyrenees when Thomas Chapman, a shepherd boy, found gold at Glenmona Station 160 kilometres north-east of Melbourne. When the news of Chapman's discovery was reported in the *Argus* on 6 February, the Superintendent of Port Phillip, Charles La Trobe dispatched some troopers to the area to prevent any trespass on the squatter's land. They were surprised to find 30 or 40 men already at work.

Hargraves makes his mark

Gold was discovered, early in 1851, when Edward Hargraves panned out some nuggets at the junction of Lewis Ponds and Summerhill Creeks, just out of Bathurst, in central-western New South Wales. Hargraves, a veteran of the Californian goldrush of 1849, knew what he was looking for, and with the assistance of young John Lister, the son of the landlady of the Wellington Inn, who had shown him to the creek, Hargraves panned in the gravel of the creekbed and found some small nuggets gleaming in the bottom of his dish — just as he had expected.

Hargraves described the moment on 12 February 1851 when he first found Australian gold:

> This is a memorable day in the history of New South Wales. I shall be a baronet, you [Lister] will be knighted, and my old horse will be stuffed, put into a glass-case and sent to the British Museum!
>
> At that instant I felt myself to be a great man. I was as mad, perhaps at the moment, as Don Quixote was his life through; for the good youth afterwards told me, he expected I should obtain for him the honour I had promised'.[1]

When Hargraves's find was made known in the pages of the *Sydney Morning Herald* on 15 May 1851, the rush to New South Wales that followed had the same effect on Victoria as California had on the population of the Australian east coast three years earlier. Although Hargraves was not made a baronet, he was made a gold commissioner and rewarded £1,000 for his discovery.

At the same time, Hargraves had also instructed brothers William and Charles Tom in the method of gold-panning, and they had given him samples of their finds from the nearby Ophir Creek to show to the colonial secretary. While Hargraves may not have been the only fellow to discover New South Wales gold, he was the one who knew how to promote his discovery, and to promote himself. Lister and the Toms received nothing at all for their part in the discovery for a further 40 years, when they were finally recognised and rewarded by the government.

It was later in the year, coinciding with the Victorian discoveries, that Bathurst made its biggest find. An Aboriginal shepherd boy working for Dr. Kerr found a nugget in the Murroo creek that weighed in at two hundredweight. The *Bathurst Free Press* became very excited:

> Bathurst is mad again. The delirium of gold fever has returned with increased intensity. Men meet together, stare stupidly at each other, talk incoherent nonsense and wonder what will happen next. A hundredweight of gold is a phrase scarcely known in the English language.[2]

It was not long, however, before this euphoria dissipated into anger, resentment and eventually rebelliousness when New South Wales governor, Sir Charles FitzRoy, introduced a licence fee for the right to dig for gold. On the Bathurst creeks, the diggers had found a new kind of freedom; as

---

ABOVE:
Edward Hammond Hargraves, Discoverer of Gold in New South Wales
Oil painting by Thomas Balcombe, 1851
(STATE LIBRARY OF NEW SOUTH WALES COLLECTION)

OPPOSITE:
Hargraves Discovers Gold
Young John Lister showed Hargraves to Lewis Ponds Creek, a tributary of Summerhill Creek near Bathurst, where he proceeded to dig in the gravel bed and panned out some nuggets, the first gold in New South Wales.
Engraving from *Picturesque Atlas of Australasia*, 1888
(PRIVATE COLLECTION)

The Journey Begins

HARGRAVES DISCOVERING GOLD.

James Bonwick observed, they went about as they liked, where 'The wild, free and independent life appears the great charm. They have no masters. They go where they please and work where they will.'[3] In a colony built on the backs of transported convicts and ruled by military decree, it must have been difficult for the governor to concede such freedom to those who had once been his servants, some little more than his slaves.

To the south, in the Colony of Victoria, Superintendent of Port Phillip Charles Joseph La Trobe, who had replaced Lonsdale in 1839, witnessed an instant decline in the population of his new colony. A Gold Discovery Committee was formed and a reward soon posted for the discovery of gold in Victoria, while the good burghers of Melbourne hoped to bring the labouring classes back to their masters in Port Phillip.

Just four weeks after Hargraves's find had been announced in New South Wales, the *Port Phillip Gazette* announced the following:

TWO HUNDRED GUINEAS REWARD
The committee appointed by the general meeting held in Melbourne on the 9th instant, is now prepared to offer a reward of
TWO HUNDRED GUINEAS
to any person who shall discover to them a
GOLD MINE
or DEPOSIT within 200 miles of Melbourne capable of being worked to advantage, this amount to be independent of any reward the Government may be disposed to grant.
WILLIAM NICHOLSON, MAYOR CHAIRMAN

The committee did not know that gold had already been discovered in Victoria, but it was not long before their notice had its effect. Gold had been found in the Merri Creek earlier in 1851, and on 15 July Louis John Michel and his prospecting party announced their discovery of a gold mine at Anderson's Creek, also in the hills to the east of Port Phillip. However it was the reports coming from a group of men working in the Pyrenees Ranges to the north, where Learmonth and Yuille had got lost searching for good grazing land in 1837, that encouraged others to also cast their eyes to the ground.

Off to the diggings!

In March 1851 some specimens of gold had been discovered at Clunes; by June some gold was also taken from the Loddon River at Burnbank. The most significant find was at Clunes, towards the end of June, when James Esmond was the first to work a claim on Donald Cameron's station.

Esmond walked from the Pyrenees Ranges to Geelong to give his report to the *Geelong Advertiser* that he had discovered gold at Clunes. By this time there was no sense in holding back; the reward offered was a substantial sum and there were plenty of other eager prospectors out in the ranges, their eye cast on the same prize.

The following report was published in the *Geelong Advertiser* on 7 July 1851:

> To date we have been backward in publishing rumours of mineralogical discoveries, but,

Above:
James Esmond
A veteran of the Californian goldrush (a '49er), Esmond found the first gold at Clunes on his return to Victoria in 1851.

satisfied now with the testimony before us, we announce the existence of a goldfield in the Pyrenees. This is a preface to a glorious run of prosperity in Victoria.

Esmond was duly rewarded with a grant of £1,000.

He later played a prominent part in the battle at the Eureka Stockade, appointed as Lalor's captain. Curiously enough, he was not sent for trial. Maybe his prominent position as the discoverer of the Pyrenees diggings saved him, and the government, from that embarrassment.

On 8 August 1851, gold was found at Buninyong, Victoria's oldest inland settlement. It was, however, the announcement on 8 September of the discovery of alluvial gold on Dr. Barker's sheep run in the foothills of Mount Alexander, found a couple of weeks earlier on 20 July (not far from the spot where Hepburn had discovered the prisoner's skull), that fired the imagination of the entire colony, and eventually the world.

It soon became clear that gold was 'literally strewn' across the central highlands of Victoria and all it needed was to be there to be made rich. It was only in September 1851 that the boundaries of the colony were officially proclaimed by the governor, and in that month the rush to the diggings really began. By the end of the month, there were over 500 men on Ballarat. Within weeks, the Port Phillip settlement was almost deserted. Once again La Trobe was left with a capital in decline.

The 'squattocracy', who also made up the membership of the Legislative Council, demanded that the governor do something to bring the workers back to their farms, the shepherds to their flocks, labourers to their workshops and skivvies back into their parlours. La Trobe's new aristocracy was collapsing in the face of a nascent spirit of independence, paid for in gold.

The squatters and the government had long kept the land out of the grasp of the working man, refusing to allow any purchase of property by any

First gold in Victoria

Following young Thomas Chapman's short-lived rush to the Pyrenees, the imagination of many in the colony was inspired to also seek for gold.

There were plenty of characters about who had more than a passing interest in keeping their eye to the ground in the hope that they too may be the first to spy a flash of yellow, such was the feverish infection that was spreading around the globe from California.

Once Hargraves's find was announced to an eager and waiting world, the rush to New South Wales took off; for the few able-bodied men left in Victoria their interest soon also lay in the creekbeds and the gullies.

1851

March — Gold was discovered at Clunes.

10 June — A discovery was recorded from Burnbank, a tributary of the Loddon river.

July — Gold was discovered in the hills around Warrandyte to the east of Melbourne. Louis John Michel and a small party of prospectors, including Henry Frencham, found some gold at Anderson's Creek.

20 July — Three shepherds discovered some nuggets of gold while panning in the creekbed near their hut, at what has since become known as Specimen Gully on Dr. Barker's sheep run on the south-western side of Mount Alexander. Although they kept their secret as long as they could, fear that they may be dismissed, or at worst, arrested, forced John Worley to send samples to Melbourne for assessment. The announcement of their find was made in the *Argus* on 8 September.

8 August — While out, presumably, searching for a lost cow, store-keeper and blacksmith Thomas Hiscock picked up a piece of gold-studded quartz near Buninyong, Victoria's oldest inland settlement. Hiscock's discovery ushered in the great rush to Ballarat.

October — Margaret Kennedy and a Mrs. Farrell were camped by the Bendigo Creek while their husbands were away, working for squatters Fenton and Gibson. The two women had been down to Mount Alexander and studied the methods of panning there. When they returned to their camp, they hitched up their skirts, stepped into the creekbed and soon filled their billy cans with gold. Their find started the Bendigo rush, although Henry Frencham, who was further down the creek at the same time, also laid claim to that starting that rush.

except the new aristocrats, but now the diggers were simply taking it as they pleased. Gold was the new currency and the labouring classes were best fitted to make the most of it. They swarmed across the squatters' runs, camping in hordes, turning over the land and changing the face of the landscape forever.

The rush to gold made poor men rich and many rich men the poorer as they saw the lands they had held for so long overrun by gold-seekers. The world was truly turned 'topsie-turvey'; the common man was in his ascendancy, the aristocrat was in decline. Yet the squatters and the bureaucrats were never going to give up their position of privilege without a fight. The government of the day was pressed to do something to bring the colonies back to order.

Just like earlier attempts by the British to discredit the Californian diggings and to stem the flow of migration away from the United States and back to its colonies, the news of Australian gold could not be kept hidden from Queen Victoria's subjects. There was, however, a considerable passing of time between Hargraves's discovery and the news breaking in mother England.

In mid-1851, the first shipment of Australian gold was loaded from Moore's Wharf on the Sydney Rocks and £81,000 of gold was carried to the old country. The colonists saw this shipment as the turning point in Australia's history; they saw this as the moment when Australia changed from a place where nobody really wanted to be sent to that place where everyone wanted to be.

It was not until later in the year that several ships arrived back in the English ports at around the same time, carrying the exciting news from the colonies. Along with the extraordinary cargo of nuggets, they also carried the news that not only had a rich goldfield opened up around Bathurst, but that gold had also been found south of the Murray at Buninyong; in the creeks around Creswick; in the gravel beds at Ballarat; and that nuggets were just lying, strewn across the ground, in the foothills of Mount Alexander, the granite outcrop that Major Thomas Mitchell had named the day that he spied Lonsdale sail into the heads to establish the rule of British law at Port Phillip.

The germ of revolution

There had been a shortage of labour in the colonies following the British government's acceptance of the demands of the Australasian Anti-Transportation League, who had formed in 1846, to seek an end to the practice of sending convicts to the colonies. The established settlers and emancipists who made up the league wanted to develop the Australian colonies as a desirable destination for free emigration. They were keen to rid themselves of the convict stain and sought to encourage migration of the 'right kind of people' who could help build a suitable colonial society. They had not foreseen the effect that the gold discoveries would bring to their settled lives. They could not foresee the changes to the dynamics of their young society that thousands of free-wheeling adventurers would create. As the first ships took their golden cargo back across the seas to

ABOVE:
A Cradler
The '49ers brought back to Australia many techniques of gold-seeking developed on the Californian diggings. The discoverer of the Clunes goldfields, James Esmond, claimed to be the first to use a rocking-cradle in Victoria.
Engraving from The Three Colonies of Australia: New South Wales, Victoria, South Australia; their Pastures, Copper Mines, and Gold Fields, *by Samuel Sidney, published in 1852*
(LA TROBE UNIVERSITY LIBRARY COLLECTION, BENDIGO)

startle mother England, the Australian newspapers heralded a new era for the colonies. The *People's Advocate* commented:

> A high and noble destiny awaits the long despised Australia, and she must now be treated by her haughty mistress, not as a child, but as an equal. In every point a great change must be, or Australia will know how to vindicate her *rights*.

In this simple opinion is expressed the very germ of revolution. Britain was not at all enamoured of the notion of democracy. Mother England had only begrudgingly allowed limited franchise at home and its system of governance was still firmly entrenched in the halls of privilege, patronage and petty officialdom.

The English Crown had lost the American colonies to a rebel insurgency, and had witnessed, at close proximity, the French revolution and the Austro–Hungarian struggles, and were constantly battling with insurgency from within their own Emerald Isle. Yet the Crown remained secure in the firm belief that the empire would hold against all comers, and that in the end the blood that ran through the veins of all Englishmen would bind them together.

The Englishman abroad, however, toiling for himself with the sun on his back and free under azure blue skies, was a different fellow to that at home. Freedom beat servitude any day, and the Australian diggings was just the place for an Englishman to taste his freedom. The wealth torn from the soil gave the same man the desire to be treated as an equal by those who sought to lord it over him at home, and in that desire was born the fire of rebellion. All a revolution needed was a spark, and the Crown, with its representatives in the Australian colonies, could not help itself but to eventually strike that spark.

ABOVE:
Gold Digging in Australia 1852: Fair Prospects
Watercolour by S.T. Gill, 1852
Two mates examine the washings from their dish, hoping for a 'fair prospect'.
(BY PERMISSION, NATIONAL LIBRARY OF AUSTRALIA)

"The enormous ant-hive swarms like a railway cutting, where the crown of a hill is carried down to fill a valley … far away to the right and left, are the tents, thickly clustered and pitched, and, far beyond, the lofty white-barked trees form a background … This is Ballarat!" — DAVID BLAIR, *History of Australia*, 1879

THE AUSTRALIAN GOLD-FIELDS.
BALLARAT.

WE have already published some description of these vast plains on the northern shore of Port Phillip Bay, which extend thirty miles from east to west, and twenty-five miles from the mountains to the sea; and our former remarks were accompanied with an Engraving representing the marvellous view from Mount Alexander over the expanse of level country, relieved here and there by the rugged eminences of what appear to be extinct volcanoes. A panorama of the whole district may be seen from Mount Aitkin, a lofty volcanic hill rising in the southern skirts of the mountain chain, not very far from Mount Macedon; and to look out from this eminence at sunset is to witness one of the most extraordinary spectacles in the world. The towers of Melbourne can just be descried on a rise in the plain about twenty-five miles to the south-east; a breathless silence reigns over the desolate expanse, which stretches far and wide, here and there swelling into rocky knolls and chequered with the shadows of passing clouds. In the midst rises Mount Cotterell, sweeping out of the plain with a long low outline, like an ocean wave after a storm. In the middle ground, or near the base of the mountains, several isolated volcanic hills rise out of the plain, and terminate in craggy crests, like those upon the curl of a broken wave. To the west, the expanse is shut in by the bold granitic hills of Station Peak, or Anaki, on crossing which, in a western direction, we come to the confines of another vast plain extending almost without interruption for 200 miles from east to west, commencing near Geelong. From this, too, there rise several hills of the same volcanic character, steep and abrupt on one side, and on the other sweeping down to the more level country, as though they were islands in some great lonely sea. One of them, however, to range, instead of from the plain, and has a to show its volcanic origin. This is Mount Bo are the great gold-fields of Ballarat. To the r and almost girt round with rocky granite hil tract which, from the beauty of the scenery vegetation, might well be called "the garde dome-shaped lava hills rise, in pairs, out o country, to the height of 200 ft. or 300 ft. but clothed with the richest pasturage, they isolated, and have obtained the characteristic n the country is finely wooded with clumps and between. The soil, both on plain and hill, coloured earth, formed from decomposing

THE GOLD-FIELDS OF AUSTRALIA: BALLARAT.

and there rocky headlands or spurs advance from the flanking hills into the flats, forcing the creek to sweep away to the opposite hills, and perhaps crossing its channel as rocky bars. Should the valley be highly auriferous, the rich deposits will generally be found, first, along the rocky bed of the creek, especially where it is crossed by one of these bars; secondly, on the sides and tops of the swelling hills which flank the valley; thirdly, in the "gullies" which branch off from the main valley; and, fourthly, in the alluvial flats, not diffused over their entire area, but following a definite line or band which winds through them in a certain direction, which, however, can only be determined by opening the ground, and is probably in the direction of the original channel of the valley, before the beds of clay and gravel had been deposited. There are vast tracts to which this description is applicable: but the richest are those where gold was first discovered—namely, the valleys of Forest and Fryer's Creeks, Bendigo, and Ballarat; and these still form the great centres of the mining population of Victoria.

The *Melbourne Argus*, at the time of the discovery of gold at Ballarat, said:—"If Fortunatus had thrown the contents of his cap over the lands of Ballarat, the yield of riches would not have been increased. Here surface workings are abandoned and the substrata are delved into for riches which will repay a thousandfold the labour expended on them. The yield is immense and seemingly inexhaustible; the gold lies in 'pockets' in the blue slaty clay, and may be picked out with a knife-point. So rich, indeed, is it that many have abandoned cradle-workings for tin dishes, which have yielded two to three ounces in one washing. Many will make fortunes, hundreds a competency, and the vast majority will do well. Nature has spread out a vast magazine of riches for the enterprise of Geelong to stretch forth her hand and take it, and strong and earnestly have her sons set about the pleasant task. I little thought when I first started to Boninyong that it would fall to my lot to chronicle facts which, if embodied in romance or made the elements of a fairy tale, would have excited a smile of incredulity."

These facts were that, at Ballarat, 143 cradles and 567 men had produced in 712 days 4010 ounces, or £12,030 worth of gold. At that time the gold-fields at Ballarat were occupied by white tents, which stood on the slopes of the hills or in the green flats, and watch-fires threw a strange lurid glare on the p assembly soon gathered there; and the Gove arranged and assorted, afterwards produced a s regular streets of canvas arose, and not a few roughly-hewn planks, were erected around Butchers' shops, doctors' tents, refreshment-b dealers' shanties, forges, each with its rough made the place strangely picturesque, but y irregular in appearance. Now this phase, too, h is likely to become one of the most important miners form companies and employ labour an mining itself has become a recognised, if not dustry, yielding average profits or fair wage digging has come to, we cannot do better tha report of the market and operations in this dis advices from Victoria:—

Gold in the Ballarat Hills

IN AUGUST 1851, BLACKSMITH Thomas Hiscock found gold at Buninyong, 16 kilometres from what was to soon become the great Ballarat goldfields. Hiscock had migrated from his birthplace in Berkshire, England, with his wife and two sons in 1842. They spent their first few years in the colony at Trawalla, 160 kilometres north-east of Geelong. In 1844, they moved to Buninyong, the settlement which was then at the centre of a number of squatters' sheep runs.

At Buninyong, Hiscock opened a blacksmith and wheelwright's shop and a general store. His business was ideally placed as the settlement was a favourite camping place for bullock teamsters, who passed through the district on their way from the port of Geelong as they travelled up country.

Thomas Hiscock was completely unaware of James Esmond's find at Clunes when, accompanied by his son, 17-year-old Thomas Hiscock jnr. and their neighbour's son, John Thomas, they began to look for gold in the hills and gullies around their home.

Like so many others in the colony, they too were aware of the reward offered for the discovery of gold in Victoria. Although only John Thomas had any real knowledge of gold, his late father Edward had been a lapidary in London, and John had often seen the precious metal worked by his father. They set out day after day, when they could, with their eyes cast upon the ground. They had little luck on the first sojourns into the bush as, having no real knowledge of geology, they didn't know for what or where they should look.

It was on 2 August 1851, when the three were working their way along the road heading out west from Buninyong, that Thomas Hiscock snr. was heard to cry out the unforgettable exclamation of 'Gold!' Searching along slightly higher ground than the others, he called out to John Thomas, who was nearest to him at that time, 'I have found gold at last.' After days of searching and

LEFT:

The Gold-Fields of Australia, Ballarat
The *Illustrated Times, 8 July 1865*

The gold rush was reported all around the world; newspapers, particularly in the United Kingdom, played a large part in encouraging large-scale immigration to the antipodes.

(REX NAN KIVELL COLLECTION, U4951
BY PERMISSION, NATIONAL LIBRARY OF AUSTRALIA)

getting excited by the flash of yellow, only to be disappointed by yet another deposit of mica (or 'fool's gold'), the two youths were not inclined to believe him and just carried on with their search. When Thomas snr. scrambled down to show them a piece of quartz richly splashed with flashes of gold, they were easily convinced. Even though the next day was a Sunday, the three gold-seekers were back at work and after a few days they had washed out a considerable amount of gold.

The first 2.5 ounces of Victorian gold was sent to Mr. Patterson, a jeweller in Geelong, and he was the first to work the hundreds of thousands of ounces to be taken from the Buninyong and Ballarat diggings.

The Hiscocks were quite content to keep their search confined to the area around their home; the fact that they could pick up alluvial gold around Buninyong was good enough for them. It wasn't until some draymen bound for Clunes were passing through Buninyong that Hiscock learned of Esmond's claim. He then realised that his was just one of a number of discoveries that would lure thousands of men into the district.

Even though some excitement followed the Clunes discovery, the area was quite isolated and it was no mean feat for a prospective digger to carry what gear he could cobble together all the way up from Geelong into those gullies. The rush did not really start until Hiscock's discovery was announced. No doubt eager to claim his part of the reward, Hiscock wrote to the editor of the *Geelong Advertiser* and his find was made known to the world on 10 August 1851.

Gold – the first rush

Once the discovery of gold was announced around the settlement of Buninyong, men on their way to Clunes decided to travel no further. They didn't bother to make the last 43 kilometres to Esmond's diggings and instead decided that Hiscock's was good enough for them, and so the rush was on. Before the end of the first week, hundreds of gold-seekers had made their way into the district, taking up claims along the creeks. Nor was it long before the government officials arrived to collect their taxes.

Within days, scores of men began to arrive in the district. They fanned out from Buninyong, following the creeks the full 16 kilometres until they reached what became known as Golden Point: Ballarat.

The licence

Just as Governor FitzRoy had done in New South Wales, the Victorian government also moved

ABOVE:
A monument to the discovery of gold at Buninyong in 1851 by Thomas Hiscock. Hiscock's find ushered in the rush to Ballarat, then on the edge of squatter Yuille's sheep station.
Photographic carte-de-visite by J.W.H. Austin, Durham Lead, c. 1880

(PRIVATE COLLECTION)

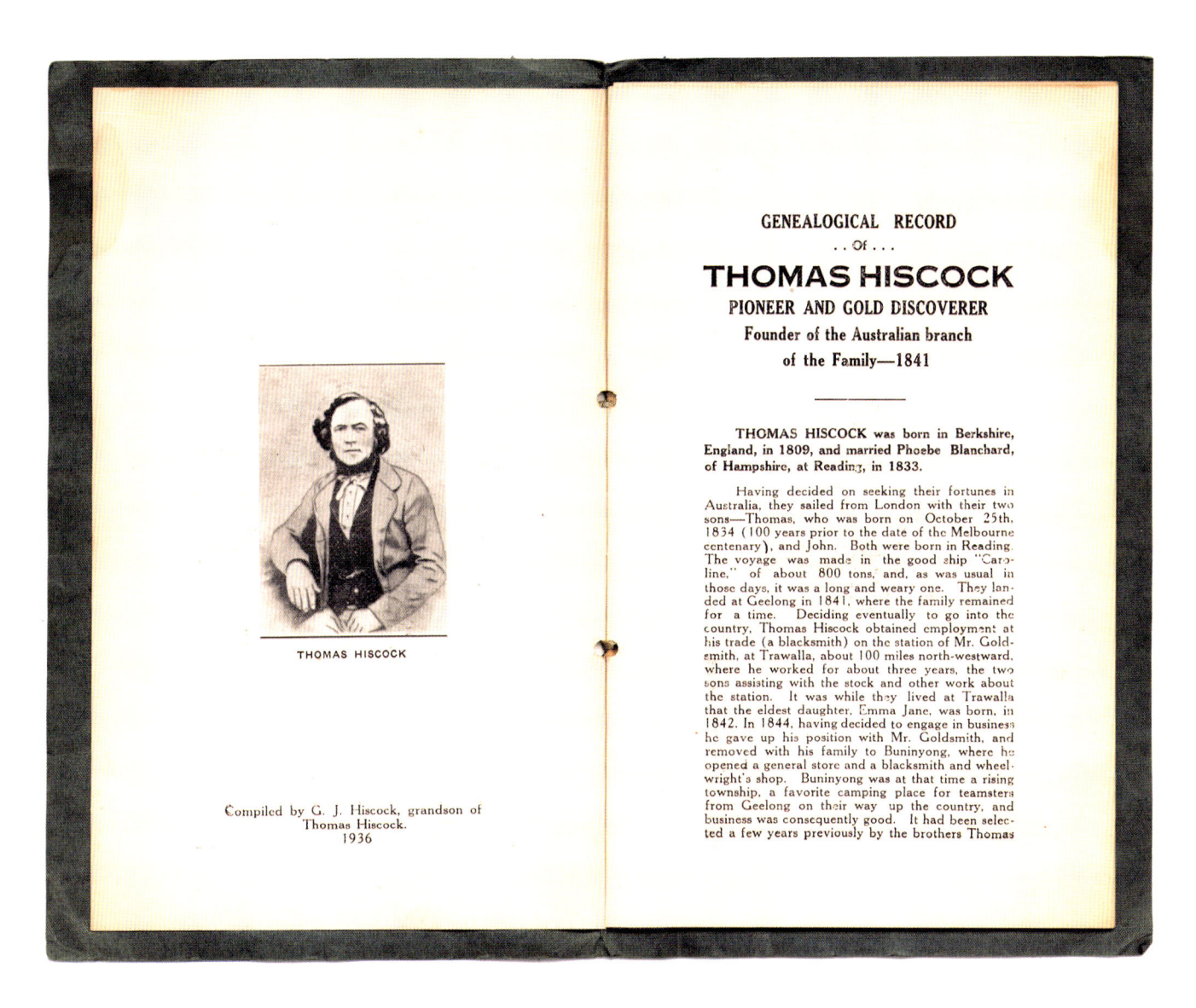

quickly in an attempt to take control of the goldfields, and to collect the funds it believed necessary to provide for its management. On 15 August 1851, Lieutenant-Governor La Trobe issued and signed into law his first proclamation:

> Whereas by law all mines of gold and all gold in its natural place of deposit within the Colony of Victoria, whether on the lands of the Queen or any of Her Majesty's subjects, belong to the Crown; and whereas information has been received by the Government that gold exists upon and in the soil of the colony, and that certain persons have commenced or are about to commence searching and digging for their own use, without leave or authority from Her Majesty.

La Trobe was claiming for the Crown (the Treasury) the ownership of all gold in the soils of Victoria. His proclamation continued:

> Now I, Charles Joseph La Trobe, Esq., Lieutenant-Governor aforesaid, on behalf of her Majesty, do hereby publicly notify and declare that all persons who shall take from any land within the said colony, any gold, metal, or ore containing gold, or who, within any waste lands which have not yet been alienated by the Crown, shall dig for and disturb the soil in search of such gold, metal, or ore, without having been duly authorised in that behalf by Her Majesty's Colonial Government, will be prosecuted criminally and civilly as the law allows, and I further notify and declare such regulations as upon

ABOVE:
Family History and Genealogical Record of Thomas Hiscock, Pioneer and Discoverer of Gold in Victoria
Published by Hiscock & Sons Pty Ltd, 'Standard' Office, Benalla, 1936
(PRIVATE COLLECTION)

further information may be found expedient, will be speedily prepared and published, setting forth the terms on which licenses will be issued for this purpose, on the payment of a reasonable fee, given under my hand, etc.[1]

Three days later (18 August 1851) came the second proclamation:

[The Governor with the advice of the Executive Council] has been pleased to establish the following provisional regulations, by which licenses may be obtained to dig and search for and remove [gold].

1. From and after the 1st day of September next, no person will be permitted to dig, search for, or remove gold, on or from any land, whether public or private, without first taking out or applying for a license in the form annexed.

2. For the present, and pending further proof of the extent of the gold deposits, the license fee has been fixed at one pound ten shillings per month, to be paid in advance, but it is understood that the rate is subject to future adjustment as circumstances may render expedient.

3. The licenses on the spot can be obtained from the commissioner who has been appointed by His Excellency the Lieutenant-Governor to carry these regulations into effect, and who is authorised to receive the fee payable thereon.

4. No person will be eligible to obtain a license, or the renewal of a license, unless he shall produce some certificate of discharge from his last service, or prove to the satisfaction of the commissioner that he is not a person improperly absent from hired service.[2]

While the government attempted to cover all contingencies with this proclamation, it is the last clause [4] that the government shows its true intentions. Clause 4 clearly attempted to drive the working classes back to their tasks and the criminal classes off the diggings completely — unless a digger could prove his bona-fides he was outside the law from the start, and the commissioners and troopers did their best to keep as many in that state as possible.

The first commissioner soon arrived on the diggings and began to collect licence fees. At that time the Buninyong yield was pretty poor indeed. Few of the diggers were able to pay the government what was demanded; most who could resented having to give what little they had over to the government. Most of the diggers simply vanished among the trees when the commissioner rode into view.

'New-chums' were often arrested as soon as they arrived on the diggings, greeted by the troopers as

ABOVE:
Charles Joseph La Trobe
La Trobe's first proclamation, on 15 August 1851, warned all who may wish to abandon their employ and join the ranks of the gold-seekers that the government was taking a very keen interest in their efforts.

La Trobe warned that the government was preparing to impose upon them the first of the licence fees that would ultimately lead to the state of unrest ending in the Eureka insurgency.

(LA TROBE UNIVERSITY LIBRARY COLLECTION, BENDIGO)

they crossed a rise or turned a bend in the road that led to the 'field. Many were immediately arrested for being without the required licence and driven to 'the Camp' to be chained to the logs where they were treated as felons, regardless of their 'bona-fides'.

For many, their first impression of the diggings was coloured by the actions of the troopers, and the laws, as they were enforced, hardened them against the officials. It was this kind of rough 'British Justice' that caused so much dissent amongst men who were at heart 'honest, hard-working and loyal'.

The licence fee was introduced on 1 September and before long the men on Ballarat were doing their best to avoid it. When Commissioner Armstrong made his patrol over the Buninyong diggings, several of the first diggers there hid away in Mother Jamieson's Inn. This may have been the first indication the Ballarat diggers were not going to be a pushover for the government officials, nor hand over their hard-won cash too easily.

Two of the men who were in the inn were the Irishmen John Dunlop and James Regan who, after slipping away into the bush, made their way along the White Horse Range on Yuille's Ballarat station until they came to a small hill on the northern edge of the run.

There they began to pan the creekbed where, towards the end of the month, they had panned out the first gold taken from a tributary of the Yarrowee creek. This was one gully away from the famed Golden Point, from which more than 20,000,000 ounces of gold was to be found in the next few years. In the first few months between September and December 1851, 30,323 ounces were carried by escort to Melbourne from Golden Point.

ABOVE:

Mount Macedon from the Black Forest
Drawn by S. T. Gill
Lithograph published by James Blundell & Co., Melbourne 1855

The road to the Bendigo and Forest Creek diggings wound around the base of Mount Macedon. Travellers going both ways were more than pleased when they had passed through the forest into open country, for it meant they had managed to avoid the brigands and the bushrangers who lurked there.

There are countless incidents when travellers were attacked, and left naked, tied to trees, with all their worldly goods taken into the custody of the 'Van Demonians'. It soon became the practice for diggers to band together, often in the company of draymen, for the journey through the Black Forest.

(REX NAN KIVELL COLLECTION, NK9843/1
BY PERMISSION, NATIONAL LIBRARY OF AUSTRALIA)

The Buninyong and Ballarat diggings were really one and the same; they shared the same topography and they were forever linked in the minds of all who travelled there as the one goldfield. Consequently, Thomas Hiscock was rewarded as the discoverer of the Ballarat diggings with a sum of £1,000. A further £476.4.0 was collected from the public purse and added to this reward.

There were two other claimants for the discovery of the Ballarat (Golden Point) diggings, but the committee charged with responsibility for determining the founders of the goldfields believed that both of these parties (Brown, and Regan and Dunlop) had first been attracted to Hiscock's diggings, and subsequently only made their discoveries further along the same range.

The *Geelong Advertiser* wrote that 'the discovery of Ballarat was but a natural consequence of the discovery at Buninyong, and agreed to recommend that the sum of £1,000 be given to Mr. Thomas Hiscock as the substantial discoverer of the Ballarat deposit'.

Gold in the Bendigo Creek

By October, gold was reported in the Bendigo Creek just by a chain of waterholes near to where James 'Bendigo' Mouat had his hut.

Two women, Mrs. Margaret Kennedy and her companion Mrs. Farrell, had camped by the creek while their husbands were away in the service of squatters Gibson and Fenton. Aware of the discovery of gold, announced in September on squatter Dr. Barker's Ravenswood Run, they made the journey to Forest Creek (Mount Alexander) to witness the method of gold-seeking there.

On return to their camp, they hitched up their skirts and set about having a go at panning.

They soon filled a pannikin with nuggets and before long were stashing more in their spare stockings. They began to fear for their lives as it soon became known that they were getting gold in the Bendigo Creek.

Surprisingly, the valley in which Bendigo now stands was quite a busy spot at that time, and there

ABOVE, LEFT:
Margaret Kennedy, along with her friend Mrs. Farrell, is credited with the discovery of Bendigo gold in October 1851.
(COURTESY OF JAMES LERK, BENDIGO)

ABOVE, RIGHT:
Henry Frencham, also claimed to be the discoverer of the Bendigo field. Frencham had also been in the party of gentlemen who found the first gold at Anderson's Creek (Warrandyte) just to Melbourne's north in July 1851.
(COURTESY OF JAMES LERK, BENDIGO)

DIGGERS ON WAY TO BENDIGO.

were a large number of all kinds of men passing through. Shepherds were going from run to run, with one eye on their flocks and another on the ground, as well as travellers, prospectors, and even several journalists who themselves were out looking for the next big 'find'.

There were several others who also claimed to have been the first to discover gold on the Bendigo field:

Squatters Fenton and Gibson were also out prospecting nearby and the man with the 'curly moustache', Mr Henry Frencham, who had been with Louis John Michel at Anderson's Creek (Warrandyte), had discovered specks of gold as he worked his way from the north-east along the creek from the White Hills towards the spot where Kennedy and Farrell were encamped.

When Frencham came upon Kennedy and Farrell hard at their work and was made aware of their success, he hastily dispatched one of his party to ride down to Forest Creek and report to Captain Harrison that gold had been found to the north of the Big Hill in Bendigo's Creek.

Frencham attempted to claim the reward for the discovery of the Bendigo field, as did several others, but in the end it was quite impossible to tell exactly who made the first discovery as there were just too many doing exactly the same thing at the same time with the same degree of success.

However, Mrs. Kennedy and Mrs. Farrell went down in history as the discoverers of the Bendigo field, remembered as the women who were getting quart-pots of gold from the Bendigo Creek.

The licensing commissioners soon followed and made their claims on behalf of the governor.

The first protest in Ballarat

One of the first meetings gathered to protest at the government licence fee took place near Golden Point on 25 August 1851, just two weeks after the discovery of the field was made known. A Mr. Connor and his party had come up from Geelong

ABOVE:
Diggers on Way to Bendigo
Drawn by S.T. Gill
Lithograph published by James Blundell & Co., Melbourne 1855
(REX NAN KIVELL COLLECTION, NK9843/2
BY PERMISSION, NATIONAL LIBRARY OF AUSTRALIA)

to Buninyong and set out for the Point. They had been working the ground since they had arrived on 20 August and had little success. When the commissioners arrived on 19 September, they asked for directions to Connor's party; by this time he had enjoyed better luck and showed a pannikin of gold to the commissioner, boasting that there was plenty enough to pay his fee.

Digger George Sutherland wrote in his book *Tales of the Goldfields* that the commissioner, Armstrong, announced 'the license-fee was to be enforced, and that, as half of September was still to run, each man would be required to pay fifteen shillings'.[3] This infuriated most of the other diggers who had not shared in Connor's success and a meeting was quickly convened to protest at what they believed was a breach of faith by the government. They petitioned the commissioners, pleading that few of the men on the Point at that time had got enough gold to pay their expenses — at that time it was known as Poverty Point, only one gully away from the richest field of all — Golden Point.

The following day Connor was called in by the commissioner and asked to pay his fee for the rest of the month.

A second meeting was held outside a bark hut in full hearing of the commissioners. One of the diggers, Herbert Swindells, was in full force standing upon a stump as he addressed the crowd. As Swindells denounced the conduct of the commissioners, he flourished a pistol over his head, threatening that 'before he was done with this business, he would shoot someone'.[4]

Resolutions were passed agreeing that no one would pay the fee for September; two were chosen as delegates to present their case to the commissioner and state their grievances. Mr. Oddie was chosen, as he was a moderate and circumspect gentleman, as well as the vocal and fluent

---

At the Diggings
Engraving, published by D. Urquhart, Melbourne, from a drawing by William Strutt

Strutt's observations of Victorian life, from the opening of Princes Bridge, the investiture of the first parliament through to the daily activity of the goldfields have left an enduring, and accurate, legacy of fine drawings.

In this lively drawing, Strutt has recorded the events that were the common experience of all the diggers. 'New chums' arrive to a scene of bustling activity; diggers are panning, cradling, and washing out pay dirt, while a party of men are working together at the bottom of a shaft.

In the background a gold escort can be seen hurrying by, taking gold back to the Treasury in Melbourne, while to the left, a pair of ever watchful troopers can be seen galloping across the field, in the never-ending search for more unlicensed diggers.

(REX NAN KIVELL COLLECTION NK9844/29
BY PERMISSION, NATIONAL LIBRARY OF AUSTRALIA)

BELOW:
Gold-Washing at Ballarat
Engraving from The Three Colonies of Australia: New South Wales, Victoria, South Australia; their Pastures, Copper Mines, and Gold Fields, *by Samuel Sidney, published in 1852*
(LA TROBE UNIVERSITY LIBRARY COLLECTION, BENDIGO)

Swindells, a determined orator, whom they felt could well present their case.

The commissioners, who had already heard the vocal tirade of the meeting given from 'the stump', gave the delegates an abrupt hearing, leaving them in no doubt as to the intention of the Crown. Oddie and Swindells left in no good humour. This was not improved when they learned that Connor, although he had been among those who had petitioned against the licence, had paid up, not wishing to lose his claim by default. As he left the commissioners' camp he was pelted with clay by his fellow diggers who were determined to hold their resolve against the tax. Connors was covered in clay from head to foot and several of the diggers also dealt him a few salutary blows for his trouble. Disappointed at the result of their attempt to change the commissioners' mind, most of the diggers then rushed to the licence hut to pay their tax so they too would not lose their claims.

True to his own invective, Swindells held out until he was the last man to apply for his licence, which was refused by the commissioners as he had led the protest. Unable to then either dig for gold or remain on the diggings, he was in a very unfortunate position, until the other diggers took up a collection on his behalf and 12 ounces of gold was subscribed. He somehow lost the lot within the next 24 hours. It was a sorry start for the success of organised protests on the Ballarat diggings. It was reported that Swindells left the Ballarat diggings a month or two after this incident and went to Forest Creek where he was also denied a licence to dig. It appears the government had set against him for his attempt to incite rebellion at Ballarat.

GOLD-WASHING AT BALLARAT.

By this time thousands of gold-seekers were soon to be found on the roads heading for Ballarat, and for all of the neighbouring diggings that seemed to open almost daily for the rest of 1851. In his book *The History of Australia*, published in 1879, David Blair offers the following report taken from a publication from the period. He begins by describing the hive of activity on the road from Melbourne to Ballarat:

> Having cleared the city we overtook the golden army of bullock-drays moving northward, surrounded by companies of men and lads; occasionally a female is seen. Four bulldogs pull one carriage, a great dog in the shafts of another, and a man pushing behind at a load of near five hundredweight.
>
> Presently the splendid panorama opened to view an extensive sweep of plains, encircled by mountain ranges in the remote distance. Far as the eye can reach, the pilgrimage, its line moving along the undulations, now hid, now rising into view — English and Germans, Irish and Scotch, Tasmanians.
>
> Sixteen days at Yuille's Ford, and nearly two hundred people. It is nearly impassable, from the fresh current of yesterday's rain …

The writer continues as he describes his first sight of the Ballarat diggings:

> Our next point is Warrenheep, where we refresh with a draught from the delicious mineral spring. Two miles from Warrenheep the hills begin gradually to slope toward Ballarat. The forest trees are loftier and denser, but the surface soil is not so richly grassed. The road emerges on to a rich bottom of considerable extent, and the hill to the left extends upwards in such a gentle slope as to diminish the appearance of its height. Within a mile and a half of Golden Point the tents begin to peer through the trees. The Black Hill rises precipitously on the right from a creek that washes its base, and through the thick forest covering the road is visible down which the carriers are conveying their earth. The bank of the creek is

---

ABOVE:

Ballaarat Flat from the Black Hill
Drawn by S.T. Gill
Lithograph published by James Blundell & Co., Melbourne 1855

The view from the Black Hill looked down across the flat and across the Eureka lead. This apparently peaceful scene belies the trouble that was brewing on these diggings.

(REX NAN KIVELL COLLECTION, NK9843/2
BY PERMISSION, NATIONAL LIBRARY OF AUSTRALIA)

lined with cradles, and the washers are in full operation. Round the base of the mountain, on the farther side, at right angles with this creek, the river Lee flows; and for half-a-mile along its bank the cradles are at work. We descend, leave the road, cross the bottom, spring over a dam, and are among the workmen. Rock, rock, rock! swish, swash, swish! — such is the universal sound …

The enormous ant-hive swarms like a railway cutting, where the crown of a hill is carried down to fill a valley. Higher up on the hill's crest, along its sides, and stretching down to the swamp far away to the right and left, are the tents, thickly clustered and pitched, and, far beyond, the lofty white-barked trees form a background.

This is Ballarat![5]

La Trobe visits the diggings

It was not long after the first commissioners had arrived at Ballarat, in the middle of September, that Lieutenant-Governor La Trobe made his first tour of the diggings. What he saw in Ballarat coloured his view of the opportunities that abounded there forever. He watched a party of five men dig 136 ounces of gold from their claim one day and another 120 ounces the next. He wrote to London and advised that the gold discoveries were to exercise 'a far wider influence upon our excitable population than did the discoveries in New South Wales upon that colony'.[6] He made the observation that the towns of Geelong and Melbourne were almost empty of men, and that all of the ships in the harbour had lost their crews to the diggings. He noted that the gold-seekers were 'not only the idlers in the community, but responsible workers and family men and not a few of the superior classes'.[7] Such was the lure of gold.

While La Trobe had first considered that the government should not issue any licences to dig until the shearing and harvest was over, he was concerned that it would have been impossible to hold back the tide of men intent on digging. He noted 'there is but one way, and that is to let the current spend itself, and meanwhile see as far as possible it is kept within proper bounds'.[8] La Trobe was absolutely unaware of the propensity for excitement that such easy riches would bring, and had no idea at all of what those proper bounds would be. He was confident of the rule of 'his' law, the power invested in him by the Crown; but the goldfields would soon bring together hundreds of men from all the world over, who had little reason to wish to abide by these laws, and who would soon openly rebel against the tightening of the military arm of that Crown.

Antoine Fauchery was one such foreigner who arrived at the Ballarat diggings at the beginning of the rush. He described his impression of the scene as he first caught sight of the goldfield:

No doubt the place I am passing through was not considered rich enough to be worth working; but a hundred paces further on still, the holes are closer together, and about ten minutes after finding the first traces of gold-seeking, at the top of a plateau at the extremity of which the road ends, the horizon widens and I am overlooking 'The Ballarat Goldfields'.[9]

Fauchery and his companions had arrived at the diggings just as the day was coming to an end and he wisely decided not to wander about in the dark, but to rest and become a digger the next day:

The sun is declining. At my feet I can just manage to see the diggers' tents scattered about. Workers, with pick and shovel on their shoulder, fan out in all directions. Fires lit at different points, and my heart grows heavy at the thought that here I am, alone once more, about to enter a new sphere. The barking of dogs warns me that it would be imprudent to venture here at this hour, and, rolled up in my blanket, and stretched out

FOLLOWING PAGES, 38–39:
Golden Point, Ballaarat
Watercolour, sketched on the spot by William Strutt, 1851

It was only a matter of a few weeks after the announcement of Hiscock's discovery that the peaceful rural landscape that had previously only heard the gentle bleat of Yuille's flocks rang with the incessant rumble of the diggers' cradles, and to the excited cry of 'gold!'

(STATE PARLIAMENTARY LIBRARY COLLECTION, VICTORIA)

Sketched on the spot by William Strutt.   *Golden Point.*

Ballaarat. 1851. Taken from the West

BELOW:
Gold Panning, Ballaarat Diggings, Victoria
Watercolour by William Strutt, 1851
(STATE PARLIAMENTARY LIBRARY, VICTORIA)

at the foot of a tree, I put off until tomorrow my first appearance on this stage.[10]

Fauchery's impression of the diggings the following morning were not quite so romantic; he allowed that in imagination one 'liked to spread out immense pictures which, sooner or later, prosaic reality encloses in wretched little frames'. He described the scene on Ballarat as 'disagreeable'.[11]

> These much vaunted Elderados are far below the idea one has formed about them in countries where gold does not normally grow, and their general appearance can hardly be compared to anything more than a common or garden collection of earthworks. These earthworks spread for a distance of two or three miles, on the back of a hill or in the hollow of a ravine, and where it has been worked over, the ground, with as many holes as a sieve, seems to have been turned upside down by cyclopean ants.

> As for that gold-fever, the epidemic that contracts the brows, makes the hair stand on end, hollows the cheeks, makes the eyes bloodshot, corrodes the heartstrings, that veritable yellow fever in short ... takes hold of all the miners and impels them to devour each other.

Fauchery described the dangers of life on the diggings; while he felt safe from attack from bushrangers, and remarked that there was less likelihood of being robbed on Ballarat than on the dark streets of Paris, he did record the dangers from the nightly practice of discharging pistols and rifles to ensure that their powder had not gone damp during the day. Diggers loaded fresh, dry powder before they settled for the night — just in case. Fauchery described this practice:

> Everybody is armed to the teeth, and if one really does run any risk, it is not from the bushrangers. Every evening the diggers between them fire more rifle and pistol shots than were fired in July 1830. It is an infernal uproar, a veritable insurrection in which, while protesting against the insurgents, it is prudent to be careful

of the guards. There are enormous chances of being killed by one's neighbour.[12]

Another eyewitness described this view of the Ballarat diggings:

> It is like the encampment of an army. In a confined space of a few hundred yards are to be seen thousands at work, busy as bees, with the same sort of hum — the rumbling of the cradles.
>
> The sides of the creek are so thickly lined with humans, that it is impossible to cross without disturbing them in their occupations. The cradling is light work, excavating is ordinary home work. The holes near the water are dangerous, as the earth falls in: one or two men have been killed in this way, one or two have been murdered, and some robberies have taken place, but on the whole they are wonderfully well conducted.

> A great proportion are respectable tradesmen and mechanics. Many are gentlemen who have property, and have brought parties of four and five, giving them wages or a share of the profits. Consequently, the first effects of the mania have been very prejudicial to the interests of the country.[13]

This description of an orderly and industrious goldfield contrasts sharply with the account of the field at Clunes, which appeared in the same report published on 29 October 1851:

> ... a volley of rank Vandemonian slang, thickly interlarded with oaths, showing that 'old hands and Pentonvillians' abounded. Elements of vice and crime, which are so largely diffused throughout the land, were already at work in this infant community'.[14]

Above:
The Gold Diggings
Oil on canvas, artist unknown, c. 1855

One observer recalled his first sight of the diggings as being like the encampment of a large army. French digger and photographer Antoine Fauchery recalled the practice of pistol-firing at daybreak and dusk, to ensure that gun-powder did not go damp, and remarked that a digger was more in danger of being shot by his neighbour than by any criminal act.

*(REX NAN KIVELL COLLECTION, NK24
BY PERMISSION, NATIONAL LIBRARY OF AUSTRALIA)*

Following Pages, 42–43:
Golden Point, Ballarat
Watercolour by David Tulloch, 1851

*(REX NAN KIVELL COLLECTION, T2253
BY PERMISSION, NATIONAL LIBRARY OF AUSTRALIA)*

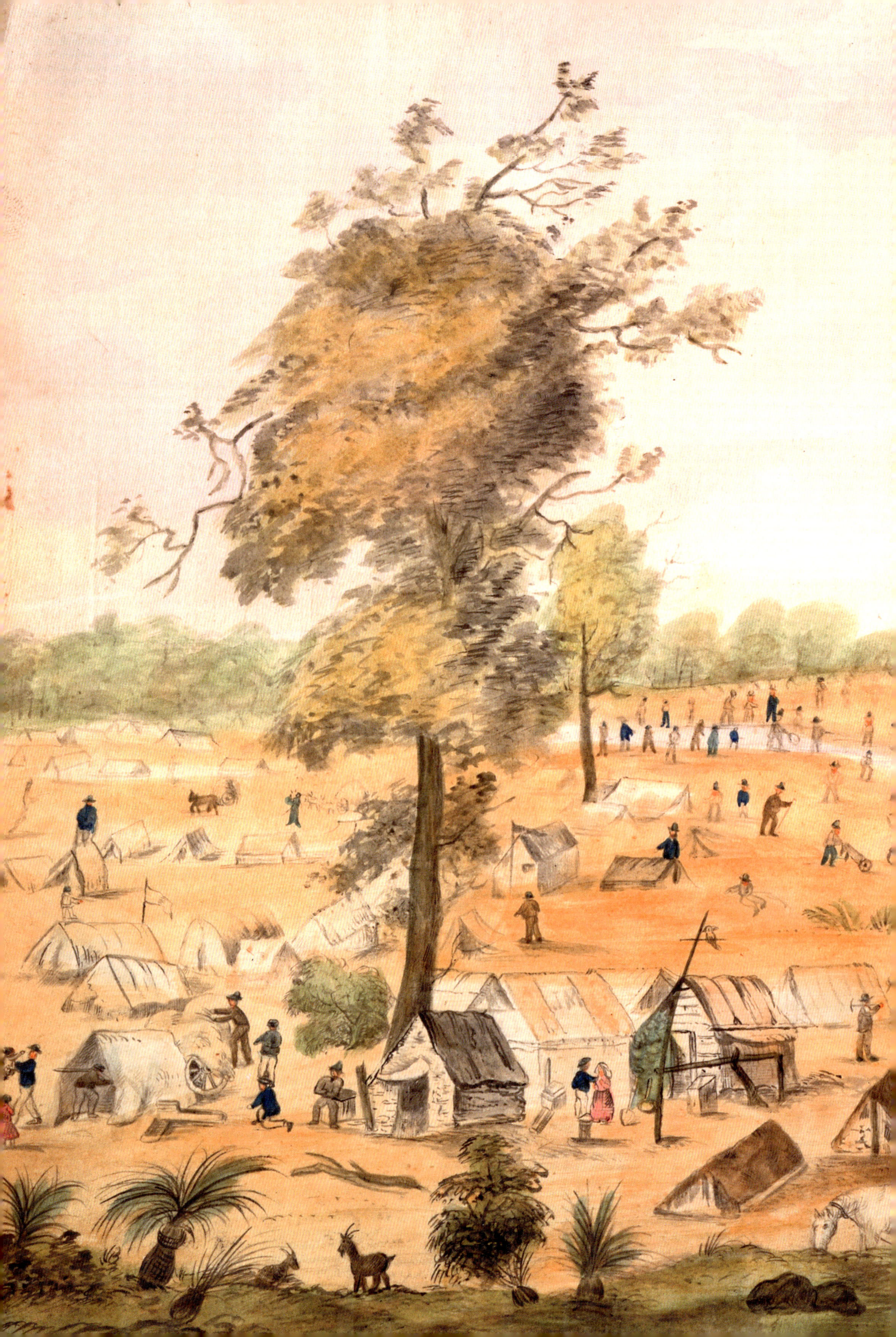

43

There were many who felt that the best way to treat this gold fever was to get in, get rich and get out — just as quickly as possible. While this was likely for those who arrived early, once the alluvial gold had gone, diggers needed to invest much more time, and their precious resources, in order to stay the distance to get rich. Usually, by that time it was too late to get out at all; however there were still those who were blessed by more good fortune than their efforts should have allowed.

When Isambard Brunel's huge, ironclad steamship *Great Britain*, arrived in Melbourne on 11 November 1852, the entire crew deserted for the diggings. One party of three sailors and two passengers headed straight for Ballarat. On their arrival, one, so keen to get into the mining business, convinced his mates to lower him into an abandoned shaft. They selected a hole at random and lowered him on a rope tied around his belly, and slung it over a tripod of sticks hastily constructed on the surface of the gaping hole — much to the amusement of all the old hands gathered around who laughed at the ridiculous sight of the 'new chums' playing at diggers.

The hole bottomed out at 15 metres; the men who had dug it out obviously had no success and abandoned it without even trying to dig any galleries out from the bottom. At 15 metres the sailor shouted to his mates that he wanted a pick and shovel sent down, and that he wasn't coming back up until he had least dug a further twelve inches (30 cm) into the earth. He simply wanted to get the feel of things, to experience the satisfaction of the labour and a job done well. His mates on the surface hauled up the dirt as he loosened it, all the time putting up with the jibes of the experienced diggers who had gathered to take some sport at the sight of the new chums at work.

Before long, the man in the shaft heard his pick strike against some metal; a flash of yellow shone through the dirt, so he dug carefully around all sides until he had revealed a mass of gold as big as a paving stone smack bang in the middle of the shaft, just a few centimetres below the level at which it had been abandoned. With some effort, the party of new chums carried to the surface a nugget weighing 132 pounds.

The five men in this most successful party were stunned; the man who had come up from the shaft was a negro and he was so shocked his face had turned grey. Once they recovered from the shock of their good fortune, they carted the nugget (which had been placed inside a bag and slung over a pole between the shoulders of two of the lucky party) to the commissioners. The five men worked all through the night and dug out a further 150 ounces by the morning. They then sold the hole for £500 and headed back to Port Phillip. Satisfied with the results of a few hours' hard labour, they left for Europe on board the same ship that had brought them out — diggers for a day, and more than £7,000 richer.

When the news of this find spread across the district, diggers rushed back to the abandoned claims. The finding of the 'Monster Nugget', as it had been named, had shown that the deep shafts on much of the Ballarat diggings had a first false bottom: below the 'rock-blockage' lay the 'jeweller's shop' where the gold lay in the ancient gravelled riverbed far below the surface. Most diggers had, understandably, given up when they hit this first layer of rock, but it was the effort to get below this false bottom that paid its own reward.

Two holes that fanned out beneath that mined by the party from the *Great Britain* saw nuggets weighing 94 and 78 pounds taken in the following week, and a quantity of fine gold recovered at the same time.

The big problem for the Ballarat miners was the time it took to get to the depths of about 50 metres and sometimes of 60 where the gold lay hidden. The work soon became long, hard, wearisome and costly. It could take several months without return to burrow down to these depths, and for all that time the licence fee had to be paid, timber cut and dressed for the shafts, and provisions paid for. Fauchery described the feeling of hopelessness that pervaded the diggers' thoughts as they struck out day after day, digging for their lives:

> What really is bitter, what breaks your heart and discourages you, what you can't disregard, though every day similar features manifest themselves, is after six or eight months of trying, sometimes a whole year of waiting and battling, to find at the bottom of a sterile shaft the ruin of all your hopes; complete, absolute, unlimited ruin...
>
> It is a craze for which there is no other antidote other than a series of fruitless attempts, and we know that each of these attempts costs, at a minimum, six months' work.
>
> As for hard cash, Ballarat has swallowed up four times as much gold as it has produced.
>
> Taking everything into account, Ballarat's flourishing richness, far from paying dividends to the miners, was costing them 1/5 per head per day.[15]

While there were many miners who were not having much success, there were plenty of others who were; it just took some time to get to it. By the middle of 1853, the deep shafts were into the old river beds; the string of shafts set out one behind the other on the Prince Regent's lead produced an average of 130–150 pounds of gold. This was in an area of about 7 x 150 metres.

ABOVE:

Australian Gold Diggings
Oil on canvas by Edwin Stocqueler, c. 1855

The constant hive of activity apparent on all the diggings has been captured by Stocqueler (pronounced Stockwell) in this painting. Stocqueler also travelled to Castlemaine and Bendigo and recorded the scenes there as well.

(REX NAN KIVELL COLLECTION NK10
BY PERMISSION, NATIONAL LIBRARY OF AUSTRALIA)

View of Gold Diggings, Victoria
Watercolour by Henry Winkles, c. 1853
(BY PERMISSION, NATIONAL LIBRARY OF AUSTRALIA)

On one part of this same lead, in an area of two and a half square metres, four Americans took out an incredible 1,300 pounds weight of gold.

On the gravel pit line, the source of so much wealth as well as so much unrest, 900 pounds-weight of gold was taken in one claim from an area of around one square metre by two and a half metres deep. Fauchery recalled seeing a man emerge from a shaft at the New Eureka diggings with his hat full of paydirt from which he washed out 17 pounds of fine gold. Such stories of these finds fired the imagination of all the diggers, infected them with gold fever, and once hooked it was almost impossible to leave; the big find was always there just waiting to be struck.

The irresistible lure of gold

The lure of the discoveries in the central Victorian region, around the foothills of Mount Alexander, which spread from Bendigo to Forest Creek, and the discoveries of gold in the west which covered Buninyong, Ballarat, Creswick to Clunes, was impossible to resist. Thousands rushed to these diggings; civil servants resigned their positions, several members of the Legislative Council resigned and took off, with Macedon in their sights, and headed for the opportunity that awaited them beyond the great dividing range. Only five constables were left in the entire colony, with just two left in Melbourne. Gaolers walked away from their posts and the warders of lunatic asylums had decamped for Mount Alexander. Fifty-nine ships were left crewless in the bay, their crews setting 'off to the diggings' (giving rise to many goldfields districts still known as 'Sailor's Gully' today). The adjacent Colony of South Australia was in danger of de-population; so many had crossed into Victoria that whole areas were known as 'Little Adelaide'.

La Trobe now had charge of a colony in turmoil. He needed to get the diggers back to proper

BELOW:
Prospecting
Lithograph by S.T. Gill
Printed by Hamel & Ferguson, Melbourne, 1865
(REX NAN KIVELL COLLECTION, NK2489/23
BY PERMISSION, NATIONAL LIBRARY OF AUSTRALIA)

employment in Melbourne and sailors back to their ships left in port. He raised the civil service wages by half — to little effect. Wages of over ten times the normal rate were being offered to anyone who would crew a ship for a return voyage to the home port — this also had little effect.

In the beginning, the licence fee of 30 shillings per month on every male adult on the goldfields (whether he was engaged in searching for gold or not) had little effect as well. The fee was no great impost on the successful digger, but it was not long before the effect of this 'tax' began to bite.

The first commissioner appointed to Bendigo was Mr. Horne. He was followed by Captain Dane who only lasted six weeks before he threw in the towel, claiming that the authorities in Melbourne lacked any system or organisation at all. He was succeeded by Mr. Cockburn, and later by Mr. Gilbert who took over early in 1852. Gilbert's wife recorded at the time that diggers had began arriving on Bendigo at the rate of 5,000–6,000 a week, with issues of licences increasing in equal proportion.

She had told observer William Howitt, (who recalled their discussion in a letter of 23 September 1852) that '… at that Digging a few months ago, the monthly licences were 6,000, then 8,000, then 10,000, and now they are 20,000.'

The population on all the diggings had grown from only a handful in 1851 to a number impossible to count only one year later. The government was unable to either control, or cope in any way, with the demands of this itinerant and increasingly independent body. The licence fee, used as one means of controlling the rush away from 'meaningful' employment, had none of the desired effect at all. Thousands continued to pour into the colony. The roads were clogged with traffic going both ways, with hopefuls heading out from Port Phillip and the lucky diggers rushing back to spend their bounty in Melbourne, while the unfortunate trailed their coat tails in the dust.

The view from abroad

The following description of the Ballarat goldfield was given in the pages of the *Illustrated Times* published in 1865, a decade and a half after the first discovery of gold. This article proves the lasting impact of the gold rushes, and their subsequent place on the world stage. The rush to the goldfields encouraged immigration and settlement and as a consequence both the agricultural and manufacturing industries developed rapidly in the colonies. In fact, the goldfields forced a change in all the colonies. The eruption of demand for social change saw the colonies emerge from a military encampment into a democratic society; from an island prison to a major player in the economy of the new world.

The *Illustrated Times* began its description of Ballarat with a report from the *Argus*. It reads:

The *Melbourne Argus*, at the time of the discovery of gold at Ballarat, said:— 'If Fortunatus had thrown the contents of his cap over the lands of Ballarat, the yield of riches would not have been increased. Here surface workings are abandoned and the substrata are delved into for riches which will repay a thousandfold the labour expended on them.

The yield is immense and seemingly inexhaustible; the gold lies in 'pockets' in the blue slaty clay, and may be picked out with a knife-point. So rich, indeed, is it that many have abandoned cradle-workings for tin dishes, which have yielded two to three ounces in one washing. Many

---

ABOVE:
The Route to the Diggings
Watercolour by William Strutt, 1851

Mr. Liardet, who was one of the more prominent of the early settlers at Hobson's Bay, joins the throng on the road to Ballarat. Liardet decided to make some money ferrying diggers to the goldfields; here they are riding in style, on board his four-in-hand coach, the *Eclipse*. The state of the roads was so bad that this coach service didn't make too many trips.

(STATE PARLIAMENTARY LIBRARY, VICTORIA)

will make fortunes, hundreds a competency, and the vast majority will do well. Nature has spread out a vast magazine of riches for the enterprise of Geelong to stretch forth her hand and take it, and strong and earnestly have her sons set about the pleasant task. I little thought that when I started to Boninyong [sic] that it would fall my lot to chronicle facts which, if embodied in romance or made the elements of a fairy tale, would have excited a smile of incredulity.

These facts were that, at Ballarat, 143 cradles and 567 men had produced in 712 days 4010 ounces, or £12,030 worth of gold. At that time the gold-fields of Ballarat were occupied by white tents, which stood on the slopes of the hills or in the green flats, and before which at night the watch-fires threw a strange lurid glare on the plain. A motley and lawless assembly soon gathered there; and the Government claims, awkwardly arranged and assorted, afterwards produced a serious riot. Soon, however, regular streets of canvas arose, and not a few 'stores', built of timber and roughly-hewn planks, were erected around the Government station. Butcher's shops, doctors' tents, refreshment-booths, sly grog-shops, gold-dealers' shanties, forges, each with its rough sign, a representative flag, made the place strangely picturesque, but yet not a little squalid and irregular in appearance.

Now this phase, too, has passed away; and Ballarat is likely to become one of the most important townships in Victoria. Its miners form companies and employ labour and patent machinery, while mining itself has become a recognised, if not an ordinary, branch of industry, yielding average profits or fair wages.

The battle of the Eureka Stockade had played a vital role in formulating this change.

ABOVE:
Life on the Diggings. Discovery of a New Reef
Engraving, published in the Illustrated Australasian Mail, March 1862

While one member of this digging party happily throws a nugget in the air, his mates inspect the digging stuff that would prove to be their own little 'jeweller's shop' — or so they hoped.
(LA TROBE PICTURE LIBRARY, STATE LIBRARY OF VICTORIA)

The Road to Sedition

'Englishmen, free from crime, were at the mercy in those days of many demoralised and ruffianly policemen, who treated the diggers like felons, and were too often abetted by their superiors in this treatment of men thus practically deprived of two centuries of political progress.'

— FRANK MCKILLOP, MOUNT ALEXANDER MAIL, *10 NOVEMBER 1908*[1]

Chronology of dissent

THERE WERE A NUMBER OF SIGNIFICANT protests against the government's licence fee that led inexorably to the emuet at the Eureka Stockade in December 1854, beginning with the 'Great Meeting of Diggers' held at Chewton near Castlemaine along Forest Creek in December 1851; it was reported that upwards of 20,000 diggers gathered there on that day, only a few months after the first gold had been found on the Mount Alexander field.

While the gold was plentiful, and men were cashed up, able to pay the licence no matter how high the fee, the diggings remained relatively trouble free; but as each ship of 'new-chums' arrived, discharging another 200–300 eager gold-seekers into the colony, pressure mounted on the limited resources available. By the end of the second year of the rush, the alluvial gold had all but disappeared and diggers were forced to become miners. By this time, most diggers joined into parties, pooling their resources in order to survive the empty months of hardwork needed as they dug down deep enough to reach the pay dirt and make their first strike.

When the diggers saw no return for their efforts, the monthly license fee began to bite. Even if they had no return at all, they still had to pay the fee simply to stay on their claim. Resentment grew apace in these days.

Commissioners were empowered to conduct daily 'digger hunts' and used police troopers to compel diggers to show their licences. Diggers were expected to carry the licence with them at all times and were stopped wherever and

Journey to the Diggin's
Engraving after a drawing by J.A. Gilfillan, c. 1853

The road to the diggings was not an easy task for most: 160 kilometres of dusty track in the scorching heat of summer, 160 kilometres of stinking mud in the bitter cold of winter — pushing all their worldly goods before them in a handcart. The irresistible lure of gold meant that the most unlikely characters attempted feats of endurance that would have seemed ridiculous back home.

The diggings sure turned everything topsie-turvey.

(LA TROBE PICTURE LIBRARY, STATE LIBRARY OF VICTORIA)

whenever it so pleased any official. It didn't matter whether the digger had just changed his trousers and was outside his tent where his licence lay — he was still in breach of the law, and suffered the consequences. The licences were only made of paper and would deteriorate quickly if kept in the trousers of a man who could spend the better part of his working day knee-deep in the creeks or doubled up in a damp shaft. Most took the risk of keeping their licences handy in a jacket, or among their kit at the top of the shaft, but that was often not good enough for the troopers; if it wasn't on the digger's person ready to be shown on demand, the poor digger was still guilty and carted away at the point of a bayonet to 'the Camp'.

Thirty shillings was a considerable sum of money and the imposition of this fee fell equally on both the unsuccessful digger and those working rich ground. The man unable to scratch out his living could ill-afford to hand the little he had over to the police. Although failure to present a licence upon demand meant instant arrest and imprisonment, many diggers avoided the gaze of the law as best they could. The diggers were particularly adept at fooling the police. They hid in their holes and invited the trooper to come in and inspect the licence; few ever did descend into the rabbit-warren like tunnels that ran beneath the ground; few were that committed to enforce the licence law if it meant putting themselves in mortal danger.

Diggers would take sport with the police and mounted troopers, and they sought ways to frustrate the officials and amuse themselves at the same time.

ABOVE:

Store Drays Camped on Road to Ballaarat
Drawn by S.T. Gill.
Lithograph published by James Blundell & Co., Melbourne 1855

All goods had to be carried up to the diggings by dray. The journey from Port Phillip could take several days in good weather; as a result, the price of all consumer goods was highly inflated.

As some measure of compensation for high prices, anything at all could be bought on the goldfields — from the finest French champagne to the most elegant silken gowns. At the height of the gold rush, and at the peak of demand, carriers would load their wagons straight from the ships that arrived daily at the wharves carrying every imaginable item from overseas.

Diggers could buy items on the goldfields that would never find their way into Melbourne's stores. The appetite to consume meant that many an improvident digger soon found that he had eaten, or drunk, his way through a small fortune.

(REX NAN KIVELL COLLECTION, NK6290/9
BY PERMISSION, NATIONAL LIBRARY OF AUSTRALIA)

At a part of the gold-field there are numbers of miners gathered together. The police appear. A miner rushes away when they are nearly upon him. There is an exciting chase for a couple of miles, the miner dodging in and out among the claims till he got a start out into the scrub, where he let himself be caught quietly, and then produced his license to the baffled police, who, on returning, found all who were left on the spot duly provided with tickets, the others having taken a holiday on some other part of the field.

Others tell of men who kept a women's apparel in their tents, ready at a moment's notice to play the part of some busy housewife, a trick not so difficult in those days when faces were shaven clean.[2]

But the troopers were ever vigilant. They marched, armed, onto the fields demanding inspection as they went, dragging men up from their pits; they invaded the sleeping quarters of the diggers, ripped through belongings in search of grog, burnt down tents and roped men together like dogs, force-marching them back to internment at 'the Camp'.

Prisoners unable to pay the mandatory £5 fine were tied to trees and fallen logs, often left outdoors for up to ten days in blazing heat, in inclement weather and the chilling cold of night.

It was also the over-zealous diligence of the troopers engaged in the search for grog on the diggings that added to the diggers' sense of injustice. It was declared illegal for any alcohol at all to be taken onto the diggings. The last watering hole on the road to the Bendigo diggings was at Sawpit Gully (Elphinstone). This notorious 'hell-hole', which marked the junction of the tracks leading into Forest Creek and to the Bendigo diggings around the base of the mount, left many an innocent migrant, fresh from a long sea-voyage, 'dragging his coat-tails along the ground' after being relieved of his 'sterling' at the bar, or by the working girls who made him more than welcome. The ban on grog only enticed the carriers whose bullock drays lined the route to the diggings to be more careful in secreting this precious cargo well away from the prying eyes and bayonets of the 'traps'.

If any grog was found on a carrier's cart, all goods were immediately impounded and taken by the police. If grog was found in a digger's tent, the tent was burnt and all goods confiscated. If any person was found in the act of 'sly-grog' selling, the same act of burning and 'looting' took place. There were many police who accumulated considerable

SLYGROG-SELLING ON THE DIGGINGS. *(From a sketch by S. T. Gill.)*

Alcohol was banned on the diggings; however, this prohibition did not stop its sale, or its consumption. Nor did it stop the 'traps' either, who profited from bribes taken from the 'coffee house' operators.

Those who wouldn't grease the palm of the trooper soon found themselves burned out of existence, and all their goods confiscated and distributed around 'the Camp'.

ABOVE:

Slygrog-selling on the Diggings
Engraved from a sketch by S.T. Gill
Published in Victoria and its Metropolis

(PRIVATE COLLECTION)

wealth from this confiscation of goods; very little was taken to be auctioned, as was the intention of the law, but made the way back to 'the Camps' for the enjoyment and profit of the 'traps'.

Troopers demanded kick-backs from grog-sellers who were then protected from loss of livelihood. Those not prepared to pay were hounded and burnt out of existence. Most honest Englishmen were unable to comprehend the rapacious delight that the traps took in the destruction and purloining of the belongings of their fellow-man.

Fines taken from the diggers often went unrecorded, making some of the troopers and police wealthy beyond their dreams. This obvious corruption further infuriated the diggers as the traps were made wealthy from their toil.

It was the capricious, often petulant and overbearing demands of the troopers in their constant inspection of the licence papers that angered the diggers most. Mr. Robert Ross Haverfield, who was one of the first in the Bendigo district, described the activities of the troopers:

… the conduct of the officials generally toward the digging population was intolerably overbearing. The chief duties of the force on the diggings were the collection of the license-tax and the suppression of sly-grog selling. These were performed in a most objectionable, insolent and outrageous manner. 'Digger hunting', as the search after men who had no license was called, was a favourite amusement of both officers and men,

---

ABOVE:

Diggers Licensing, Castlemaine Camp
Watercolour by S.T. Gill, 1869

Diggers were often forced to wait for days, corralled together like sheep, as they sought to purchase their licences. Each day spent in line was another day lost, a day wasted on red tape, and at the pleasure of the petty beaurocrats.

(LA TROBE PICTURE COLLECTION, STATE LIBRARY OF VICTORIA)

BELOW:
The New Rush at Myers Creek
Engraving published in Illustrated Australian News, *1867*
This engraving shows diggers crowding around a mobile licensing van on the diggings to the north of Bendigo.
(LA TROBE PICTURE COLLECTION, STATE LIBRARY OF VICTORIA)

and it was followed up savagely, relentlessly, and with a refinement of cold-blooded cruelty that was not only exasperating, but disgusting in the extreme.

> Men were chained to trees and logs ... whose offenses consisted simply of not being able to produce their license on demand, although they protested, and their statements were often found to be correct, that they had left these precious documents accidentally at home.
>
> But unless they had them in their pockets they were placed under arrest ... they were all subjected alike to the indignity of being treated as criminals ... Little wonder was it that disaffection was engendered to a dangerous degree.[3]

Mr. J. Bonwick wrote in his account of a visit to the Castlemaine diggings of the long line of diggers who had to waste their days queuing at the commissioners' tent waiting to purchase their licences:

> These humble suitors for liberty to dig waited their turn to pay their thirty shillings and receive the authorised protection. Some told me it was their third day of coming — their third day lost.
>
> But those were the dark days of the diggings, in which under the supremacy of the squatting lords, they were viewed as intruders in the wilds, tolerated because of their numbers, but not always treated with consideration, or benignantly regarded by the super-grand cadet, constables &c.&c. That was the glorious era when men were chained to logs for even trivial offenses.[4]

THE NEW RUSH AT MYERS CREEK.

The same stories were repeated over and over:

> Sometimes the troopers would collect as many as fifty unlicensed diggers and frequently they were roped or handcuffed together and driven like beasts before the swords and bayonets of their captors to 'the Camp', where without proper trial or right of appeal they were fined £5, in default of payment sent to work on the roads.
>
> When they were brought to 'the Camp' they were chained like dangerous animals to logs to wait the convenience of the Commissioner or Magistrate.
>
> When the troopers commenced their license hunt the prisoners had to walk with them, perhaps for the greater part of the day, over rough country, in the blazing sun in summer and slush and mud in winter until such time as a good haul was made.[5]

To break the squatter's grip

Afraid that the lawlessness that followed the discovery of gold in California would also find its way to Victoria, the *Argus* offered the following suggestions for management of the goldfields in the issue published on 28 July 1851:

1st. — The actual discoverers of gold to be liberally rewarded by Government, and even those whose claims might be disputable to be rewarded, so that every inducement to explorers might be held out.

2nd.— Land containing gold to be immediately surveyed, divided into sections, advertised for sale as gold land. Intending purchasers to be allowed to inspect, and dig for experiment, but to deliver the produce of such digging to the Government.

3rd.— Gold lands to be sold at a moderate deposit on the purchase money, and a liberal credit on the balance. The grant not to be delivered till the whole was paid.

4th.— Government to protect by a sufficient police or other force, the purchaser in his rights.

This approach sought to wrest the lands from the squatters who comprised the old residents in the Legislative Council, and held vast tracts of land — and was duly ignored by them at their eventual peril.

These were not criminals but often men simply caught without their licence. Even cooks in restaurants and others not even engaged in mining were taken prisoner if they were without papers. There were instances where men were arrested, handcuffed and driven away even as their wives brought their licences out from their tents, only to be ignored by the traps — the letter of the law was there to be enforced — and what glorious fun was to be had in doing just that.

By this time, the diggings had attracted men from all over the world. There were '49ers from California as well as refugees from all the current European wars and revolutions: Balts; Poles; Jews; the desperate Irish; Scots; Germans; French; Italians; and the ubiquitous Chinese.

They had very different notions of emancipation, freedom and suffrage to that expressed in the military camp by those who ruled the diggings with an imperial fist.

> As the population on the goldfields was a mixture of various nationalities, numerous were the doctrines of freedom and the rights of the people to which expression was given. This circumstance, however, did not militate against the success of the movement in which these different elements joined. They had a common grievance, against which they cried out in one voice.[6]

With new-found wealth from success on the goldfields, the diggers soon began to assume a power of their own: the power of common rights, of unity, equality and suffrage, and they demanded their right and equal place — under the southern skies.

Dissent grew apace, and the first real gathering of protest began near the old shepherd's hut at Chewton, on Dr. Barker's Run on the southern fringe of the slopes around Mount Alexander.

8 December 1851

On Forest Creek, the following notice was pinned to trees across that goldfield:

FELLOW DIGGERS!
The intelligence has just arrived of the resolution of the Government to double the license fee. Will you tamely submit to the imposition or assert your rights as men?

You are called upon to pay a tax originated and concocted by the heartless selfishness, a tax imposed by Legislators for the purpose of detaining you in their workshops, in their stable yards, and by their flocks and herds....

The notice continued in the same splendid style, with fine oratory, such was the hallmark of many on the diggings:

> Remember that union is strength, that though a single twig be bent or broken, a bundle of them tied together yields not nor breaks.[7]

Meetings in protest of the licence fee and the behaviour of the troops were held in Bendigo in front of Captain Harrison's tent on 8-9 December. The diggers resolved to stand by each other 'to the last', and they also carried a vote of thanks to the *Argus* and *Geelong Advertiser* for their support.

15 December 1851

The government decided to increase the fee to £3 per month from 1 January 1852. La Trobe gave as his reason for the increase the high cost of administration of the goldfields. On the Forest Creek diggings alone the expenditure on 'the Camp', escorts and the like was running at about £1,000 a month.

Frank McKillop, editor of the *Mount Alexander Mail*, wrote 'but with an honest set of officials it could have been done for very much less money.'[8]

William Howitt also wrote:

> [The] Government, in fact, has done nothing forever for the diggers but tax them! The whole amount of taxation which the squatters, who hold the whole country in possession ... pay to the Government, is £20,000 a-year. The diggers, on the contrary, pay in licences more than half a

---

ABOVE:

The Great Meeting of Diggers, 15 December 1851
Published in Ham's Fine Views of the Goldfields of Mount Alexander and Ballarat in the Colony of Victoria, *Thomas Ham, Melbourne 1852*

A crowd of around 14,000 gathered near the old shepherd's hut on Forest Creek to protest against the administration of the diggings — and this was only a few months after the goldfields had been discovered. It didn't take long at all for the Crown to alienate its subjects.

(ALLPORT LIBRARY AND MUSEUM OF FINE ARTS, HOBART)

million a-year … £542,420 in licence fees, and £50,184 in escort fees, &c. And yet the Government has actually done nothing whatever towards making roads … There are no bridges, no roads, no anything. The Colonial Government of Victoria appears to have no idea but the single one of — Taxation, and no feeling but of grasping — all they can get.'⁹

A huge gathering of diggers was held near the old shepherd's hut on the outskirts of Dr. Barker's Run at Chewton (Forest Creek) on 15 December 1851. At this meeting, which was to become known as the 'great meeting of diggers', over 14,000 men resolved to refuse to pay the licence fee. They sent Captain Harrison, Dr. Richmond and Mr. Plaistow as their delegation to Melbourne to petition the governor; he responded by sending a further 130 troops to Forest Creek.

The *Argus* warned the government that they should prepare for a serious outbreak among the diggers if they doubled the fee. The newspaper reported that the diggers were buying up arms and ammunition.

On their arrival on the goldfield, the army pensioners of the 99th Regiment were met with derision and were unable to take control of the diggings. At the time the diggers numbered over 25,000; that the governor thought he would overawe the diggers with this show of strength was 'characteristic of the petulancy, obstinacy, and incapacity of the man'.[10] He was forced to capitulate and the fee remained at 30/-.

ABOVE:
The 'Diggers' after giving 3 Cheers for The Argus &c.
Pen and ink drawing, artist unknown

Diggers' leaders stand atop an empty dray as they lead them in cheers, and groans, for the newspapers that supported their cause, or not.

(REX NAN KIVELL COLLECTION, T2249
BY PERMISSION NATIONAL LIBRARY OF AUSTRALIA)

BELOW:
Dr. John Downes Owens, diggers' leader on both the Ovens and Bendigo diggings.
(LA TROBE UNIVERSITY LIBRARY COLLECTION, BENDIGO)

September 1852

It seems that La Trobe could not get enough of the diggers' money. In September 1852, he decided to impose a duty of 2/6 per ounce on gold exported from the colony. There was such an outcry from both the diggers and the merchants in the city that he was forced to once again abandon yet another of his proposals.

The diggers, by show of strength, had again shown him to appear ineffectual. Each time La Trobe tried to add to his coffers he was forced to retreat, each time adding to his growing unpopularity. The public became so disillusioned with the governor that the *Argus* ran a banner every day with this embarrassing headline: 'Wanted! A Governor. Apply to the people of Victoria'.

La Trobe had lost control of the colony: the civil service was corrupt, the police despised, the treasury in ruins, and yet he continued to press upon the diggers who were, by-and-large, a body of stout-hearted and loyal men. They were not 'antagonistic to the Crown, but ... individuals with a deep-seated grievance against an iniquitous law',[11] and consequently, a deep-seated grievance against the enforcers of those laws!

1853 — from field to field

By 1853, the movement against the government was taking hold amongst the diggers right across the colonies. Captain Harrison, who had been one of the main agitators in the early days, took a leading role on the Bendigo 'field.

Events elsewhere thrust other men into the limelight. A digger had been shot by a trooper in the Ovens district. In January 1853, the first real action against the police was when Assistant-Commissioner Myers was dealt a bit of rough treatment by the diggers in retribution for his particularly obnoxious method of administering the law. Dr. John Downes Owens, who had been on the Bendigo diggings before he had gone to the north-east, called together one of the biggest meetings ever held in that district where he and reporter Angus Mackay then led the diggers in their protest against all the usual causes. Owens and Mackay were delegated to go to Melbourne to represent the diggers before the commission that had been established to inquire into the unrest on the goldfields.

Later on, this formidable pair were to feature prominently in the continued agitation at Bendigo. Owens was eventually elected as the first parliamentary representative for Bendigo, Mackay as reporter for the *Argus* and later as proprietor and manager of the *Bendigo Advertiser*.

Dr. Owens (above) led the first protest on the Ovens River diggings.

Owens had been in Bendigo before he joined the Ovens rush. After the troopers had shot a digger there, he presided over the biggest meeting ever held in that district. As their representative, he travelled to Melbourne several times to petition the governor, before he returned to Bendigo.

Owens was elected as the first member for the goldfields in the first parliamentary election held in 1855, as a result of the inquiry into the administration of the diggings after Eureka.

MR. HARDY, THE FIRST GOVERNMENT COMMISSIONER.

Trouble at Tambaroora

In February 1853, New South Wales saw the first armed defiance of the licence system when more than 1,000 diggers on the Turon River marched 6.5 kilometres into Sofala at the foot of the Tambaroora range. The diggers came together in protest at the squatters' champion William Charles Wentworth's Goldfields Act of 1853, which proclaimed that the licence fee should apply, for the first time, to all persons on the goldfields over the age of fourteen whether engaged in mining or not.

Wentworth's aim, just like La Trobe in Victoria, was to force the diggers back into the squatter's employ. This infuriated the diggers. They regarded the fee, and the relentless pressure of compliance, as a tax aimed simply at putting an end to their newly-found independence. Apart from the inequity of the amount levied for a licence to be on the diggings, the squatter paid a pittance by comparison for his right to sit on hundreds, nay, thousands of hectares of the best land — £10 per year — while the diggers were asked to pay 30/- a month for the right to mine a plot of the worst land measuring twelve feet square (about 1 square metre). To make matters worse, they were not even permitted to take up any land to establish themselves in any district that they may have found amenable to themselves. The diggers were not seen by the government as anything other than good labour wasted on selfish pursuits; the government would force them from their labours one way or another. Onerous taxation coupled with relentless harassment was seen as a very effective way to start. It also filled the coffers of the treasury and the pockets of many of the gentlemen in gold braid while they were at it.

When the armed band marched into Sofala to the sound of fife and drum, they marched behind a banner which proclaimed 'AUSTRALIA EXPECTS EVERY MAN THIS DAY WILL DO HIS DUTY'. If there was one thing the protestors on the Australian goldfields had learned from the Great Protest Meetings of chartists and unionists in the industrial heartlands of mother England, it was the value of a good banner to rally behind and the importance of a good slogan to chant in the face of the authorities.

When they reached the police barracks, four of their number were elected to go to the licensing commissioner and refuse to take out their licences. This act of defiance brought about the prompt arrest and incarceration of the diggers' representatives. The rest of the men were primed and ready for direct action; they demanded the release of their mates and surged forward, ready to

ABOVE:
Mr Hardy, the first goldfields commissioner on the New South Wales diggings.
Engraving from The Three Colonies of Australia: New South Wales, Victoria, South Australia; their Pastures, Copper Mines, and Gold Fields, *by Samuel Sidney, published in 1852*

(LA TROBE UNIVERSITY LIBRARY COLLECTION, BENDIGO)

pull the lock-up apart. The heat was taken out of the moment by the decisive actions of the Reverend Piddington who leapt onto a platform and reasoned with the mob. He must have been one of those old fire-and-brimstone Methodists, as the power of his oratory brought the mob to heel. He implored them not to spoil their cause by the unnecessary shedding of blood.

The mob lowered their arms and withdrew, agreeing to send another deputation to the commissioner to seek the release of the prisoners. The gaoled men were released once their fines had been paid from a collection taken up from among the rest of the protestors.

It seems incredible that such a large and angry group of men, armed and excited, should have been so easily dissuaded from their intention, but such men were not revolutionaries; they were, by and large, honest, hard-working, British subjects who were, simply, not enthusiastic about Wentworth's licence law amendments. They wanted to be heard, yet at that time there was no other way for them to represent their feelings to government, and those in the legislative council who made the regulations. They felt that they were being taxed heavily yet receiving little service back from the government in return and that they were simply paying to be harassed.

Month by month, the resentment grew across all the diggings. The government did little to ease the burden; in fact it sought new ways to increase its take. It was not just the high cost of the licence fee taxation that vexed the miners; it was the means by which it was policed that offended most, and the enforcers of the law who disgusted everybody.

Few of the goldfields officials were professional military men. Few had any experience of command, or even of military service. Most had been sent to the colonies to give them something to do. They were the indolent, intemperate, capricious

---

ABOVE:
Commissioners' Barracks at Sofala,
Gold Commissioner just starting with transport,
Diggers waiting for licenses
Watercolour by George Lacy

(BY PERMISSION, NATIONAL LIBRARY OF AUSTRALIA)

In February 1853, 1,000 angry diggers marched about 6.5 kilometres down the Turon river to petition the commissioners at the Sofala camp against the licence fee.

This was the first armed resistance to the government tax, and although the diggers were ready for it, their lust for direct action was quelled by a Methodist minister who called upon them not 'to spoil their cause by shedding blood'.

and petty-fogging sons of well-connected families who were clothed in braid, belts and buckles and allowed to play at soldiers.

There were better connected, far better educated and much more stalwart citizens with their feet in the muddied creekbeds than were to be seen parading through the government camps, their lazy bums in the saddle, their noses in the air. It is no wonder that so many otherwise loyal subjects should be prepared to no longer suffer these fools too gladly at all.

May 1853 — Castlemaine

In Castlemaine, the wanton destruction by police troopers of a tent, stores and a large boarding house on the Circular Road was the catalyst that brought the diggers together in fierce protest against "the Camp".

A much-despised trooper named Christian had been given false information that the boarding-house keeper was selling sly-grog from his tent. Although the tent was pulled down and all goods confiscated, no grog had been discovered. The troopers continued to search the boarding house and, upon discovering a keg of home-brewed beer in one of the tents in which twenty men and women were sleeping, ordered them all out into the night and destroyed this as well. Again, all goods inside were taken into police custody. Two nearby stores were destroyed and the tent-keeper, McMahon, was also taken into custody.

The troopers marched away with their swords drawn, arms laden with booty, exclaiming 'This is glorious work' ... 'What glorious fun!'[12]

The diggers were infuriated by this wanton and illegitimate display of authority. They regarded Christian and his accomplice Mangan as little more than perjurers. Most of the diggers believed that the police paid little attention to the guilty sly-grog operators but preferred to harass the respectable storekeepers on the pretext that they were selling grog. The diggers rightly felt that any one of them could have their goods confiscated and their dwellings destroyed if the troopers felt moved to accuse them of the same misdeed.

In fact, the temper of the diggers was aroused to such an extent that the military, and the police, were called out and prepared to take action.

That evening the following notice was posted all over the Forest Creek diggings:

MEN OF CASTLEMAINE!
Meet on the hill behind the Baptist Chapel to discuss relative to the proceedings of the Government on Saturday night. Chair to be taken at four o'clock this day.
N.B.— The sheriff has been invited to attend.
You are requested to come to the Police Court, on Monday next, at half-past nine o'clock, and watch the proceedings.
Police v. Mahon.
Police v. Adams.[13]

Next day, the diggers confronted the officials and demanded that McMahon be released and the troopers brought to account. One of the placards that had appeared overnight read:

> Down with trooper Christian [he had been responsible for the raid] and shoot him! Down with oppression and the tyrant Berkeley! Diggers avenge your wrongs and demand your rights or otherwise you will live and die all slaves! Down with the Camp and up with Christian! Cry no quarter, show no mercy![14]

The local magistrate, fearing a riot, took decisive action and departed from the normal regime of justice on the diggings. He heard evidence, and then considered it fairly. He then discharged the tent-keeper, and sentenced the perjurious informer Mangan to five years' imprisonment. This unusual act of fairness should have defused the situation but the spark of revolution had been smouldering for too long.

'The Camp'

The Commissioner's Camp was often referred to by the diggers as 'The Sacred Camp'. This pejorative differentiated between the digger's camps and the hallowed ground on which the despised 'gentlemen' in gold braid and white gloves strutted about. Throughout the text the tent and canvas government quarters, before the construction of brick and timber buildings, are referred to as 'the Camp'.

At another meeting held soon after in Castlemaine, on aptly-named Agitation Hill, speeches were made condemning 'the Camp', and diggers' representatives were chosen. Elected as 'People's Commissioners', these men abruptly departed for Melbourne and placed the facts before the governor. They also demanded payment of £1,900 compensation for the damage done.

While they were away, trooper Christian continued to harass the diggers and burn and destroy their property. He was eventually transferred from the district but not before he had done considerable damage to the credibility of the law.

ABOVE:
License Inspected
Watercolour by S.T. Gill

This was such a common scene. The diggers were called upon to present their licences, at any time, at any place, at the whim of the police.
(BY PERMISSION, NATIONAL LIBRARY OF AUSTRALIA)

This incident was seen as the first time on the Victorian diggings where the diggers had physically confronted the officials and pressed their demands for action. The news of the diggers' victory over the officials at Castlemaine soon spread to other diggings.

In August 1853, a huge gathering of armed diggers rose in protest about the administration of the diggings. The diggers fell in along the Bendigo Creek, and marched up the long hill to 'the Camp' and presented the commissioner there with a 30-metre long petition, signed in the preceding weeks by 23,000 diggers on the Bendigo, McIvor and Heathcote diggings. This day became known as the 'Red Ribbon Rebellion' and disaffected diggers continued to wear a red ribbon from that time on, notifying all who observed them that were in continual protest of the government.

La Trobe believed the protestors across the diggings to be 'agitators', 'people of no account', or, worse still, 'foreigners'. At the time, there were reports in American papers that the republican 'movement' in Australia was making progress and that a 'speedy declaration of Independence of the Mother Country' was imminent.

La Trobe was less concerned about American influences than he was about the 'Chartists, Socialists, and others', about whom he wrote '…we live in times of restlessness and desire for political change…'. He did, however, acknowledge that democracy postponed could not be denied, and that ' … the growing sense of importance and independence arising from unexampled prosperity, emancipation from old ties and obligations, and powers of self-support, and self-government' would eventually bring about that political change.

V. R.

Colonial Secretary's Office,
Melbourne, 1st September, 1853.

PUBLIC NOTICE.

His Excellency the Lieutenant Governor Directs it to be notified that the PROPOSED ABOLITION of the LICENSE FEE TO DIG GOLD IN NO WAY AFFECTS The obligation of any one to Pay THE CURRENT LICENSE FEES, Until a new Act may be passed by the Legislature.

In the meantime the Law must be obeyed. His Excellency relies on the good sense and loyalty of the community, and to the influence of their example in supporting order and maintaining the Law.

By His Excellency's Command,

JOHN FOSTER,
COLONIAL SECRETARY.

By Authority: JOHN FERRES, Government Printer, Melbourne.

Red Ribbon Rebellion

6 June 1853, Bendigo

A MEETING OF DIGGERS WAS HELD IN 'the Camp' reserve on a rise overlooking the Bendigo Creek where, when at their work, the diggers jostled for a foothold beside the meandering creek which ran through the flat. The diggers had gathered to vent their anger over the persistent harassment by the troopers as they pursued the licence fee. The licensing system and the tyranny of the police were denounced yet again.

As a result, the Anti-Gold Licence Association was formed in Bendigo. The leaders, G. E. Thomson, Dr. Jones and an Irish-born American 'Captain' Edward Brown, sought to represent the concerns of the thousands of diggers and their families who were on that 'field to the government. They immediately departed from Bendigo and canvassed all the neighbouring goldfields.

Newspaper reporter Angus Mackay recorded that a petition of over 23,000 signatures, plus 8,000 from McIvor, was collected to be taken to Melbourne; although the names that are to be found today on the surviving petition number only 3,000, it appears that the signatures collected on McIvor [Heathcote] went missing after the robbery on 20 July 1853, when the gold escort was attacked by a large band of thieves just outside of Kyneton; 2,230 ounces of gold, and a large sum of notes, sovereigns, bankdrafts and the signatures for the McIvor petition were stolen.

13 July 1853

A protest meeting was held a month later in Castlemaine, but was attended by only 1,000 diggers. This unusually small crowd was in stark contrast to the 'forest of hands' at a similar meeting held in Heathcote the day before. Although the

OPPOSITE:
Colonial Secretary Foster's poster, which confused the diggers. This poster, contradicted the impression given by the governor, was placarded across the diggings at the height of the troubles in Bendigo, 3 September 1853.
(LA TROBE PICTURE COLLECTION, STATE LIBRARY OF VICTORIA)

ABOVE:
Commissioner's Camp, Bendigo, 1853
Watercolour by Ludwig Becker
(MITCHELL LIBRARY COLLECTION, STATE LIBRARY OF NEW SOUTH WALES)

diggers at Castlemaine seemed more conservative, and it was well-known that those further to the east were more vocal and prone to excesses of passion, it appears that there were contradictory forces at work in Castlemaine.

It was rumoured throughout the camp that the American flag was flying in Bendigo and the army was on the move from Port Phillip to crush this so-called 'Republican insurrection'. Posters advertising the protest meeting had been removed from the trees by forces unknown, which may explain the small turnout. Others placarded the diggings with the demand:'No Chains for free Englishmen'. While the central Victorian goldfields were preparing for decisive action, it seemed that the diggers at Forest Creek were likely to absent themselves from the fray.

It is true that a good commissioner was able to defuse much of the agitation among the politically motivated diggers. Lieutenant-Colonel J. E. N. Bull, in Castlemaine, was a much respected official who actively engaged in public activities and sought to serve both the demands of government as well as the needs of the people. Panton in Bendigo was also an official keen on moderation and consultation rather than confrontation. Both were able to keep a lid on the desire amongst some of the hot-headed diggers for armed revolution.

1 August 1853

The Bendigo petition, now of some 30 metres in length and bound in green silk, was taken to Melbourne by delegates Brown, Jones and Thomson and placed before Lieutenant Governor La Trobe on 3 August 1853.

The petition read as follows:

To His Excellency Charles Joseph La Trobe Esquire Lieutenant Governor of the Colony of Victoria &c.

The Humble Petition of the Undersigned Gold Diggers and other residents on the Gold Fields of the Colony.

Sheweth —

That your petitioners are the loyal and Devoted Subjects of Her Most Gracious Majesty Queen Victoria the Sovereign Ruler of this Colony one of the dependencies of the British Crown.

That in the present impoverished conditions on the goldfields the impost of Thirty Shillings a Month is more than Your Petitioners can pay as the fruit of labor at the Mines scarcely affords to a large proportion of the Gold Miners the common necessaries of life.

That in consequence of the few Officials appointed to issues Licenses the diggers storekeepers and other residents lose much time at each Monthly issues in procuring their Licenses.

That the laborious occupation of Gold digging and the privation attendant on a residence on the Gold Fields entail much sickness and its consequent expenses on Your Petitioners.

That in consequence of the Squatter Land monopoly a large proportion of Successful Diggers who desire to invest their earnings in a portion of land are debarred from so doing.

ABOVE:

Commissioner on the Forest Creek Goldfields
Lieutenant Colonel J. E. N. Bull

Bull was one of the few camp officials who was able to bridge the gap between the community and 'the Camp'.

Trained at Sandhurst, he, like Panton, was well-fitted for command, and in 1858, four years after Eureka, he was appointed as warder and first chairman of the local court in Castlemaine.

(CASTLEMAINE ART GALLERY & HISTORICAL MUSEUM COLLECTION)

OPPOSITE, INSET:

The Bendigo Petition

When Panton accepted the petition which was handed to him in August 1853, he promised to represent the concerns of the diggers to the governor. The governor responded by sending further troops to Bendigo.

(LA TROBE PICTURE COLLECTION, STATE LIBRARY OF VICTORIA)

To His Excellency Charles Joseph La Trobe Esquire Lieutenant Governor of the Colony of Victoria &c

The Humble Petition of the Undersigned Gold Diggers and other residents on the Gold Fields of the Colony

Sheweth

That Your Petitioners are the Loyal and devoted Subjects of Her Most Gracious Majesty Queen Victoria the Sovereign Ruler of this Colony &c of _____

That in the present impoverished condition of the Gold Fields the impost of Thirty Shillings a Month is more than Your Petitioners can pay as the fruit of labor at the Mines scarcely affords to a large proportion of the Gold Miners the common necessaries of life

That in consequence of the few Officials appointed to issue Licenses the Diggers Storekeepers and other residents lose much time at each Monthly issue in procuring their Licenses

That the laborious occupation of Gold digging and the privations attendant on a residence on the Gold fields entail much sickness and disbursement expenses on Your Petitioners

That in consequence of the Squatter Land Monopoly a large proportion of successful Diggers who desire to invest their earnings in a portion of land are debarred from so doing

That newly arrived Diggers must lose much time and money before they become acquainted with the process of Gold Mining

That in consequence of Armed Men (many of whom are notoriously bad in character) being employed to enforce the impost of Thirty Shillings a Month there is much ill feeling engendered amongst the Diggers against the Government

That in consequence of the non possession by some of the Miners of a Gold Diggers License some of the Commissioners appointed to administer the Law on the Gold Fields have on various occasions chained non-possessors to Trees and Condemned them to hard labor on the Public Roads of the Colony — A proceeding Your Petitioners maintain to be contrary to the spirit of the British Law which does not recognize the principle of the Subject being a Criminal because he is indebted to the State

That the impost of Thirty Shillings a Month is unjust because the successful and unsuccessful Digger are assessed in the same ratio

For these reasons and others which could be enumerated Your Petitioners pray Your Excellency to Grant the following Petition

First — To direct that the License Fee be reduced to Ten Shillings a Month

Secondly — To direct that Monthly or Quarterly Licenses be issued at the option of the Applicants

Thirdly — To direct that new arrivals or invalids be allowed on registering their names at the Commissioners Office fifteen clear days residence on the Gold Fields before the License is enforced

Fourthly — To afford greater facility to Diggers and others resident on the Gold Fields who wish to engage in Agricultural Pursuits for investing their earnings in small allotments of land

Fifthly — To direct that the Penalty of Five Pounds for non possession of License be reduced to One Pound

Sixthly — To direct that (as the Diggers and other residents on the Gold Fields of the Colony have uniformly developed a love of law and order) the sending of an Armed Force to enforce the License Tax be discontinued

That newly arrived Diggers must lose much time and money before they become acquainted with the process of Gold Mining.

That in consequence of Armed Men (many of whom are notoriously bad in characters) being employed to enforce the impost of Thirty Shillings a Month there is much ill feeling engendered amongst the Diggers against the Government.

That in consequence of the non-possession of some of the Miners of a Gold Diggers License some of the Commissioners appointed to administer the Law of the Gold Fields have on various occasions chained non-possessors to Trees and Condemned them to hard labor on the Public Roads of the Colony – A proceeding your Petitioners maintain to be contrary to the spirit of the British law which does not recognise the principle of the Subject being a Criminal because he is indebted to the State.

That the impost of Thirty Shillings a Month is unjust because the successful and unsuccessful Digger are assessed in the same ratio.

For these reasons and others which could be enumerated Your Petitioners pray your Excellency to Grant the following Petition.

First – To direct that the License Fee be reduced to Ten Shillings a Month

Secondly – To direct that Monthly or Quarterly Licenses be issued at the option of the Applicants.

Thirdly – To direct that new arrivals or invalids be allowed on registering their names at the Commissioners Office fifteen clear days residence on the Gold Fields before the License be enforced.

Fourthly – To afford greater facility to Diggers and others resident on the Gold Fields who wish to engage in Agricultural Pursuits for investing their earnings in small allotments of land.

Fifthly – To direct that the Penalty of Five Pounds for non-possession of License be reduced to One Pound.

Sixthly – To direct that (as the Diggers and other residents on the Gold Fields of the Colony have uniformly developed a love of law and order) the sending of an Armed Force to enforce the License Tax be discontinued.

Your Petitioners would respectfully submit to Your Excellency's consideration in favour of the reduction of the License Fee that many Diggers and other residents on the Gold Fields who are debarred from taking a License under the present system would if the Tax were reduced to Ten Shillings a Month cheerfully comply with the Law so that the License Fund instead of being diminished would be increased.

Your Petitioners would also remind your Excellency that a Petition is the only mode by which they can submit their wants to your Excellency's consideration as although they

---

ABOVE:

Bendigo Goldfields Commissioner Joseph Panton
Photographic portrait by Batchelder & Co, 1867

Panton was only 24 years old when he took the posting to the Bendigo diggings. Although not military trained, he was well-educated and had the facility to judge the measure of any man. Some may have thought him unsuitable to the task, but his natural humanity, integrity and insight helped to diffuse the troubles when they arose.

(LA TROBE PICTURE COLLECTION, STATE LIBRARY OF VICTORIA)

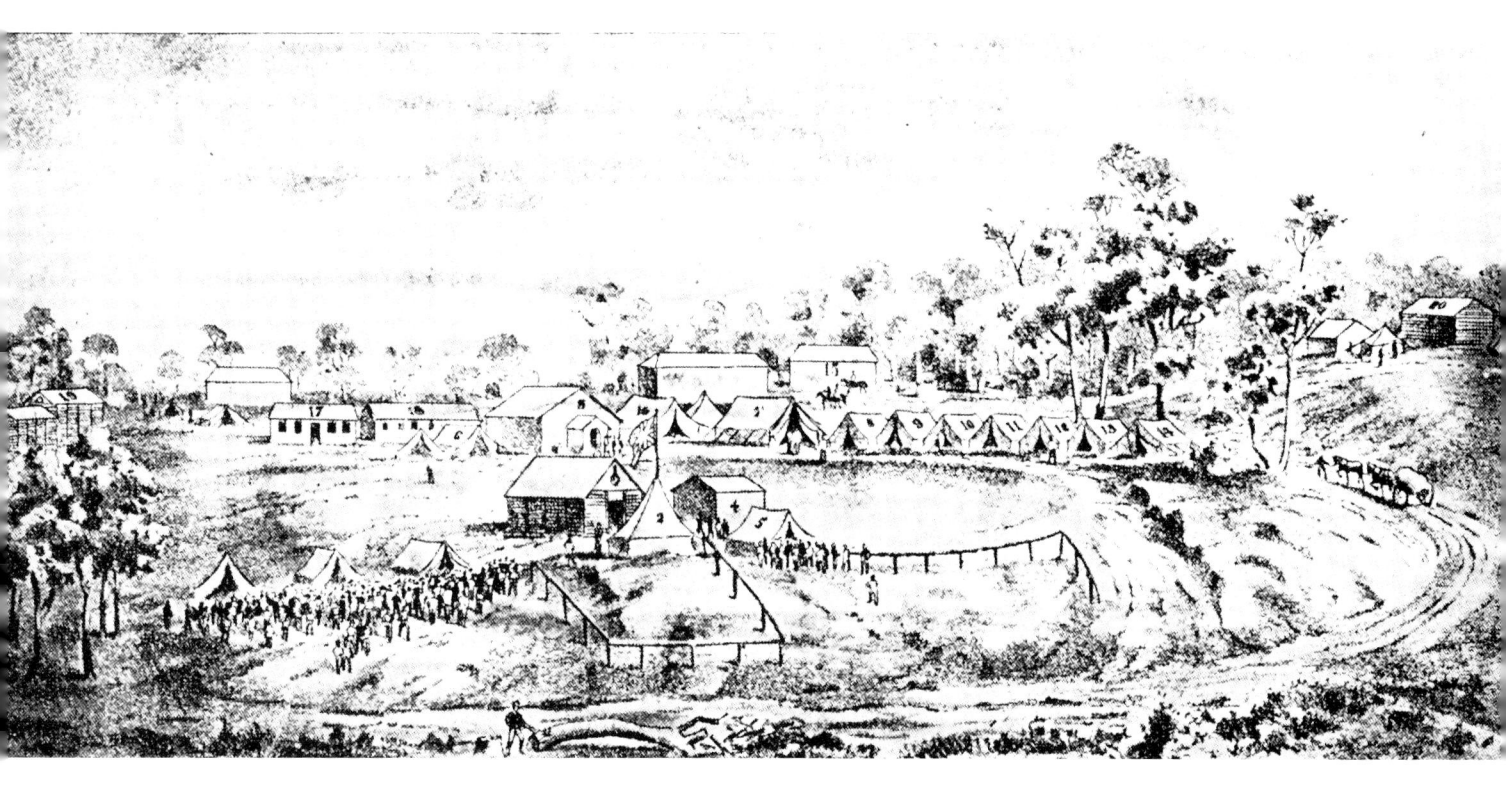

contribute more to the Exchequer than half of the Colony they are the largest class of Her Majesty's Subjects in the Colony unrepresented.

And your Petitioners as in duty bound will ever pray etc.

The diggers' banner
13 August 1853

On this day a large body of diggers gathered in Bendigo in anticipation of the return of the delegates. Over 10,000 diggers assembled on View Point, an elevated spot adjacent to 'the Camp', to greet their representatives on their return from Melbourne (some who were less inclined to hyperbole suggest the figure at around 4,000). The meeting was excited, and at times agitated with leading figures representing the great number of nations that were on the Bendigo 'field at that time.

A fife and tambourine led a parade from the White Hills. First were the Irish behind a green and gauzy banner of great length, then came the Scots, the Union Jack and the revolutionary flags of France and Germany (the Germans carried the 'schwarz-roth-und-gold' [black, red and gold] flag of the German revolution), then came the Stars and Stripes followed by other flags.

The *Herald*, which had estimated the crowd at between 10–12,000 published this report:

... gully after gully hoisted its flag ... various nationalities were well represented by different flags — the Germans in particular, seemed determined to come out strong on the occasion, having ordered some splendid new banners for that purpose. The English nation was well represented by royal standards and union jacks, and the Irish seemed not to be behindhand, and provided themselves with a very beautiful flag, with the harp in the centre, supported by the pick and shovel: but the one that attracted the greatest attention was the Diggers' Banner.[1]

William Howitt followed the procession to the rise near to 'the Camp' where a decorated tent awaited the main speakers, Captain Harrison, W. D. C. Denovan and Henry Holyoake.

In the centre of the clearing flew the diggers' flag, which had been designed by Mr. Dexter, a china painter from Devon, who had learned much from the French 'Red Republicans', and deemed it a great honour to have given his talent to the meeting.

ABOVE:
The Bendigo Government Camp in 1853
Sketched by Resident Commissioner J. A. Panton
This well-established and orderly encampment was situated on the rise overlooking the diggings stretched along the Bendigo Creek. The familiar sight of diggers massed together like cattle, waiting to purchase their licences, can be seen at left.
(LA TROBE UNIVERSITY LIBRARY COLLECTION, BENDIGO)

BELOW:
The Diggers' Banner
Drawn by Rhyll Plant for the author, 2001
This illustration is based upon William Howitt's detailed description of Dexter's flag that was carried before the diggers on their march on the Bendigo camp in August 1853.

[The flag] showed the pick, the shovel, and the cradle, — that represented labour. There were the scales, — that meant justice. There was the Roman bundle of sticks, — that meant union: 'altogether, — all up at once'. There were the kangaroo and emu, — that meant Australia…[2]

However, the delegates informed the diggers assembled that the petition had been unsuccessful. Governor La Trobe, who had been repeatedly advised by the British Secretary of State for the Colonies, Earl Grey, to be constantly on guard against 'Red Republicanism', responded by dispatching a further 154 troops to Bendigo and increased the number of police to 171.

When the diggers heard that La Trobe had in particular objected violently to the number of German names on the petition, this report was met with 'groans for old Joe'.

The petition had failed. La Trobe's reply to the diggers on Bendigo was simply that 'the government [was] not inclined' to make any change in the existing laws. He was satisfied the diggers were mere grievance mongers, and he knew his duty, and would do it at all risks. If the diggers troubled the government much more, 'he would let them hear how cannon could roar'.[3]

Although there were many who took the opportunity of this unrest to press other concerns, the anti-licence movement did not necessarily seek political change. Thomson insisted that what they demanded was 'necessary reform, not revolution'. Although La Trobe believed that the diggings were rife with 'Red Republicanism', the opposite was, in fact, the case.

When Mr. Dexter, who had painted the designs on the diggers' flag, declared himself to be the representative of 'the French Republicans' and, amongst others, began to deride the Union Jack fluttering alongside the other 'revolutionary' flags, it was the proud Englishman George Thomson, furious at the attacks on his homeland and the declaration of support for the 'foreigners' against 'British tyranny', who leapt to the fore and called for three cheers for the British ensign.

Thomson then called for 'passive resistance'. He asked that the diggers present only 10 shillings in payment of the licence fee, and when refused, to go back to their camps and paint their tents with the words 'No licence taken here'. Thomson argued that the police couldn't arrest everybody, but that the diggers should not resist arrest. They were hoping to make the situation of refusal and wholesale arrest an impossible task for the government to carry through.

The patriotic Englishmen dominated the rest of the meeting but were not themselves reticent in their protest of the Queen's representatives on the diggings.

One of the prominent diggers on Bendigo, Mr. Haverfield, opined, 'What terrible revolutionists the men composing the meeting which received the answer of Mr. La Trobe must have been when they let him hear how loyally they could roar when called upon to show their attachment to the throne'.[4]

Yet, the moderates among the diggers' leaders were alarmed at the pace of hostile dissent and called another meeting for the 21st where they would make preparations for a mass, but passive, show of strength one week later.

21 August 1853

A much larger procession than on 13 August brought the diggers back again into Bendigo where about 20,000 diggers assembled on Hospital Hill (where All Saint's Church of England now stands). Here the diggers vowed to pay no more than 10/- a month for their licence.

Thomson's proposal of 'passive resistance' which had met with enthusiastic support at the previous meeting was implemented.

Thirteen members of the Anti-Licence Agitation Committee and thirteen diggers were selected to enter the commissioners' camp and offered their 10/- apiece. They were refused, but the commissioner promised to send a messenger to La Trobe and advise him of what had taken place on Bendigo. He also agreed not to take any action against these men.

The Red Ribbon Rebellion
27 August 1853

The 'Red Ribbon Rebellion' was born soon after another meeting held on 27 August at View Point, where the diggers took to wearing a red ribbon in their hats as a symbol of their unity in defiance of the law. The ribbon was worn 'as a sign that those who wore it were pledged no longer to pay the old license-fee'.[5]

On this day, the protestors came in from all over the Bendigo field. Diggers from White Hills swirled in along the flat at the base of 'the Camp', where they met with diggers from Kangaroo Flat, Golden Square, and Eaglehawk. All had joined in rag-tag lines along the gullies leading to View Point. National flags fluttered above smaller groups gathered beneath them. It was a dank, grey, wintry day. Diggers sat at impromptu fires warming themselves, some cleaning their guns while making ready for a show of strength. If they were to be called upon they were not going to be found wanting.

La Trobe was, unwittingly, fuelling the flames of revolt. The diggers were being pushed to take direct action. They talked openly of armed resistance. It was reported that there was not a tea-chest left on the Bendigo 'field, as the diggers had

ABOVE:
George Edward Thomson
Thomson was the son of a well-connected Scottish family. He had studied law in London before he set out for the diggings in 1852. Like so many young men from the industrial north of England, Thomson was an ardent Chartist who soon found a ready audience for his ideas when he arrived in Bendigo.

stripped them of their lead linings and turned them into ammunition.

When Thomson, amidst roaring cheers, mounted a hastily erected platform at View Point, he stood alongside Dr. Jones, Captain Brown and Captain Harrison. They called for nominations to send a delegation into 'the Camp' to lay their grievances, yet again, before the commissioner.

Hundreds of men rushed to volunteer, and a delegation led by Brown, Thomson and Holyoake soon marched into 'the Camp' to again offer their 10/-. The level of continued protest had surprised La Trobe. Following a report from Wright earlier in the month, which suggested that Bendigo had little support from the other goldfields, the persistent influence of the leaders of the Anti-Gold Licence Association, who had once ranged far and wide in collecting names for the petition, had kept the spirit of agitation alive.

Nine out of ten diggers wore the 'red-ribbon' after this meeting. Red flannel, which was the raw material of the diggers' underclothing, soon became very scarce across the Victorian fields as the diggers took to its wearing, cut into ribboned strips, and displayed in eager and proud defiance. Dogs were seen with ribbons around their necks and horses with ribbons flying from their bridles. Shopkeepers painted signs proclaiming 'No Licences taken here!' across their tents and hung red ribbons from poles in order to demonstrate their support for the diggers' cause — and no doubt to ensure continued trade.

From this point on the movement was known as the 'Red Ribbon Agitation'; the 'Anti-Licence Agitation' no longer captured the imagination of the diggers:

> 'So enthusiastic was the immense audience gathered together that an hour after the meeting closed the most liberal offer of money could not purchase a bit of red ribbon, and red shirts — a common enough garment in those days — were torn to secure the coveted colour'. [6]

At the end of the day, as the diggers rolled up their banners and made their way peacefully back along the gullies to their tents, commissioners Wright and Panton watched the lines of men depart from below 'the Camp'. It was then they noticed that La Trobe's Chief Commissioner of Police, Mitchell, had disappeared. Mitchell had been sent up to Bendigo to observe the situation just prior to this meeting. He had slipped away unnoticed and was already well on his way back to Melbourne, where upon arrival he announced to La Trobe that 'Bendigo was in a state of revolution, and that if the license-fee was not reduced, or if an attempt to enforce it was made, it would end in bloodshed'. [7]

At this time, La Trobe had called for reinforcements from Van Diemen's Land and had placed the troops left in Melbourne on alert. He dispatched the remainder of the 40th Regiment to Bendigo, bringing the total number of troops there to 300. While La Trobe was preparing for bloody

ABOVE:
Captain John Harrison R.N.
Harrison was one the most persistent of the diggers' leaders. A former ship's captain turned squatter, he never lost his republican feelings, even after the battle at Eureka was lost and goldfield's reform eventually won.
(LA TROBE PICTURE COLLECTION, STATE LIBRARY OF VICTORIA)

rebellion, it seems the diggers were more intent on pursuing their protest and demanding a peaceful and democratic resolution. Only 400 diggers paid their licence fees for the next month, whereas over 14,000 had paid previously: the diggers were forcing a stand-off.

One of the diggers' leaders, Captain Brown, who had incited the men to refuse to pay for their licences, was arrested and sent to Melbourne for trial, accused by a shopkeeper of threatening to burn the man's store to the ground for not supporting the agitation.

La Trobe received the following report from his Chief Commissioner of the Goldfields, Mr. Wright, the next day: 'We are compelled to report that the reduction of the license-fee, if not its abolition altogether is inevitable ... if blood should once be shed it is impossible to foresee the consequences, but it would very possibly throw serious obstacles in the way of establishing regulations to be enforced on the goldfields.'

La Trobe panicked. He called together the Legislative Council for a special meeting where he proposed that the licence fee be abolished and replaced with a royalty on gold — and a small registration fee for police purposes. The council agreed to the suspension of the September fee and declared that a Committee of Inquiry be established to look into the diggers' grievances. The following notification was announced to the diggers, signed by Chief Commissioner Wright:

GOVERNMENT NOTICE

His Excellency the lieutenant-governor has been pleased to notify that it having been decided to propose, without delay, another mode of raising a revenue in lieu of that now derived from the goldfields, this measure will at once be presented to the Legislative Council; *but, in the meantime, no compulsory means shall be adopted for the license for the month of September.*

Several persons having applied for protection against violence, which has been threatened to

---

ABOVE:
The Commissioner's Tent, Golden Point, Ballaarat
Watercolour by William Strutt, 1852

Commissioner Armstrong can be seen in front of his tent on Golden Point, Ballarat. A pair of diggers, having just purchased their licences, walk away to their claims, safe in the knowledge that for the next month, at least, they were on the right side of the law.

(STATE PARLIAMENTARY LIBRARY COLLECTION, VICTORIA)

them, all orderly persons are assured that ample means are at the disposal of the authorities for that purpose, and that prompt aid may be relied on whenever necessary.

(Signed) W. R. Wright.

Commissioner's Camp, Sandhurst.[8]

Unfortunately the colonial secretary's department had not been notified of the September suspension, and although troopers from Melbourne worked their way out from the seat of government nailing posters to trees, advising the diggers of the change, a contradictory poster issued from the Secretary's Department went up across the diggings demanding that the fee be paid as usual:

PUBLIC NOTICE

Colonial Secretary's Office, Melbourne,

1st September 1853.

His Excellency the lieutenant-governor directs it to be notified that the abolition of the license-fee to gold diggers in no way affects the obligation of any one to pay the current license fee until a new Act may be passed by the legislature. In the meantime the law must be observed. His Excellency relies on the good sense and loyalty of the community, and the influence of their example, in supporting order and maintaining the law.

By his Excellency's command,

(Signed) John Foster.[9]

Commissioner Panton told the Bendigo diggers to ignore this second, inflammatory and contradictory, notice. In Bendigo the diggers' representatives felt convinced that they had won, and they began to relax. An old licence was posted outside the Anti-Licence Association's office with a black border drawn around it and the words — 'Old License U Dead' inscribed beneath.

The diggers' so-called 'victory' caused embarrassment for the members of the government in Melbourne, and anger and disgust from the British press. The *London Times* ran the story that the 'Government [was] humbled in the dust before a lawless mob'. There were several squatters in the Legislative Council who wanted 'to arm the young men of Melbourne and send them on horseback to make the diggers pay!'[10]

The governor was so concerned at the anger expressed by the diggers over this unfortunate mismanagement of affairs that he hastily sent requests for troops out to all of the other colonies. Only the 99th Regiment, which was stationed in Van Diemen's Land with little to do, rallied to the aid of Victoria. When the 99th arrived in Melbourne there was hardly a soldier left in the capital. The rest were already on the diggings.

The embarrassed government declared that it was not backing down but simply taking a fresh position from where the law could be put on a sound basis. There were others who suggested that to shed blood in defence of a system that must inevitably be changed would be criminal.

A new Act for the Management of the Goldfields was passed by the Legislative Council in November 1853. Whilst the aim of the Act was to quell the agitation of the diggers on a whole raft of expectations — enfranchisement, property rights, the corruption of officials and the removal of the licence fee — in the end the squatters on the council, who may well have intended to allow franchise for established 'permanent' settlers through lower licence fees, in fact contributed to the exclusion of almost all those who sought change.

The government decided not to abolish the fee altogether, but replace it with a sliding scale of new fees instead. A one-month licence was set at £1, three months at £2, six months at £4 and 12 months at £8. Only those diggers who took out the new annual licence were granted franchise. A unilateral annual fee of £50 for storekeepers on the diggings was imposed. This heavy impost hurt many smaller operators and was the cause of its own protest only a few months later. Police were no longer able to make arrests for non-compliance;

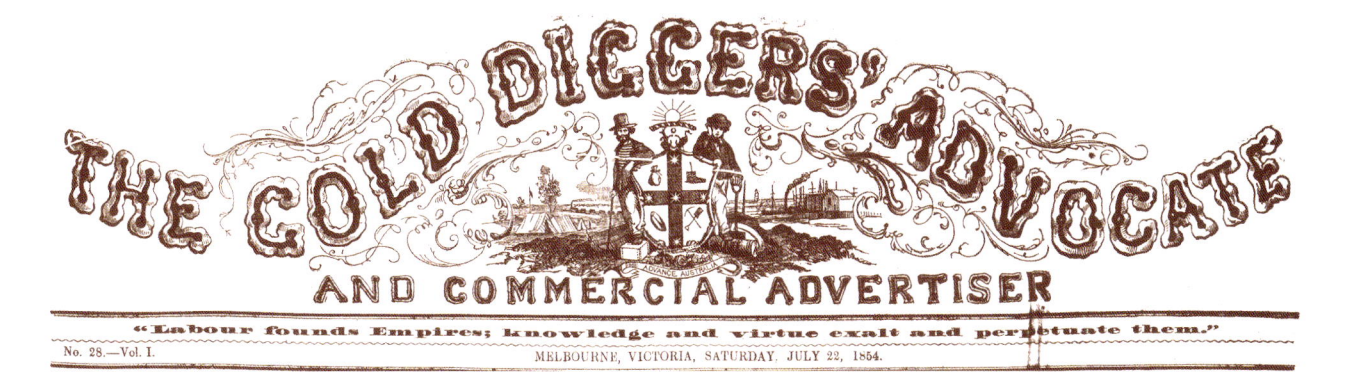

that duty resided only with the commissioner and their agents.

Although the diggers had won another great victory over La Trobe, the 'traps' retained the power to arrest those they suspected of being without a licence. The way remained open for continuance of the old 'sport' of digger-hunting.

December 1853

The diggers continued to agitate for the vote but once the licence fee proved less onerous, the support for a wider and continuing protest fell away. The diggers' leaders, however, were not so readily dissuaded from their goals. Thomson and Black established the *Diggers' Advocate* under the banner 'Liberty, Equality, Fraternity'. Considering Thomson's earlier distaste at flag-painter Dexter's 'French republicanism', this appropriation may seem contradictory — but these were passionate times.

In December, in response to La Trobe's less-than-convincing franchise proposals, the Diggers' Congress movement was forged into being. Once again, meetings were held across the diggings, and delegates sent to Melbourne to protest to the government, this time in condemnation of the new constitution. La Trobe refused to meet with them.

February 1854

The new sliding-scale licence fee began to hurt a different group working on the goldfields. In early 1854, the storekeepers protested against the £50 annual fee which was beginning to force smaller operators out of business.

By the middle of the year only half of the diggers across all the diggings bothered to take out licences. The government was in no mind to continue to press the diggers any longer. It appears that both sides had almost run out of steam. The diggers were unable to achieve their goal of universal franchise by any other means than continued refusal to pay the licence fee. The government seemed disinclined to continue with a system in which it no longer had any faith. The burden of taxation fell only on those who obeyed the law, and once again inequity and dissatisfaction ruled.

Earl Grey had long advised La Trobe that he should take measures to prevent Victoria from becoming 'another California'. He continued to warn the colonial governor that if an unbridled spirit of independence was allowed to arise within the labouring classes, it would be impossible for the squatters to sustain their unchallenged dominance of opportunity in the colonies.

The itinerant diggers were effectively disbarred from enfranchisement. The law only allowed a vote to those with freehold property valued at £100 or more. Franchise allowed only for those who had taken out the annual licence (which was also only allowed for one district and not transferable). This tied the digger to land he couldn't possibly purchase, as most of the land, once available for lease, was held by squatters who got it at the beginning of the rush and locked it up for at least a decade. The diggers were tied to goldfields that had lost their shine and able only to cultivate plots deemed by the government to be 'waste land'.

The issue of land purchase rankled the diggers almost as much as the hated licence fee. While many wished to make a new life in the region that had so rewarded them, the government and the squatters did their best to keep them from realising their aspirations. Again the only avenue for representation was through mass protest and petition. The diggers continued to press their claims on the government.

ABOVE:
Masthead of the *Gold Diggers' Advocate*, 22 July 1854.
The motto expressed on this masthead states: 'Labour founds Empires, knowledge and virtue exalt and perpetuate them' – he could have added 'only as long as the labourer is prepared to allow the Empire to stand'.
(LA TROBE PICTURE COLLECTION, STATE LIBRARY OF VICTORIA)

A New Governor

> WANTED! A new Governor.
> Apply to the people of Victoria
> — Daily Headline, the *Argus, c. 1850*

Arrival of 'old quarter-deck'

IN JUNE 1853, THE INEFFECTUAL and openly disregarded Lieutenant-Governor Charles Joseph La Trobe was at last recalled to England. The population of Victoria had long lost any affection they may have once had for Governor La Trobe. In the face of constant protest, a dissolute public service and a Treasury with mounting debt, La Trobe resigned his post in April, signed his last despatch on 1 June and sailed for England, to the delight of almost the entire population of the colony.

The new governor was Sir Charles Hotham, a naval officer ambitious enough to have set his sights on a posting to the Crimea. This glory was to be denied him; he was instead destined to win ignominy in Ballarat. As a career officer, he was well aware of the rewards proffered on those who were victorious in battle. The management of a troublesome colony, its Treasury in ruins, was not a posting that he sought at all eagerly. For years the *Argus* had advertised daily for a new governor for Victoria, and it seemed that, at last, its wish was about to be fulfilled.

The colony eagerly awaited the arrival of Hotham, and the miners on all the diggings were anxious to see what reforms he would make to the governance of the diggings districts.

Almost 12 months earlier, Governor FitzRoy in New South Wales had reduced the licence fee there to 10/- per month. In Victoria, however, at the height of the protest against the licence when armed diggers at Bendigo marched upon 'the Camp' and took to wearing the red ribbon in protest at the fee, every attempt to set the same fee as New South Wales was thwarted.

The Colony of Victoria had high hopes for the new governor. The diggers expected that he would abandon the licence fee system altogether and replace it with a system that reflected appropriate and fair taxation; however, the British government had insisted that he was to balance the disastrous colonial budget. Hotham had inherited an almost bankrupt bureaucracy with a deficit to the coffers of around £1,000,000.

Hotham spent his first few months in office grappling with the debt-ridden colonial economy and negotiating his way around the peculiarities of the legislature. He was a military man of the old school who was used to giving orders, and to being obeyed. He needed to learn an entirely new repertoire of skills if he was to make a success of a colony in turmoil, with limited franchise, an itinerant and free-willed workforce and an entrenched and ineffective bureaucracy.

June 1854, Bendigo

In Bendigo, William D.C. Denovan, an inspiring orator steeped in the beliefs of the Scottish Chartists, called together another mass meeting of diggers.

This time the concerns were not primarily the issue of the licence fee, although that remained a bone of contention on all the fields. There was now also the issue of Chinese immigration, and it was this issue that Denovan was to use to invoke the wrath of the diggers. It was also the one issue

---

OPPOSITE:
Lieutenant-Governor Sir Charles Hotham
Watercolour

District Commissioner Hotham was simply a case of the wrong man in the wrong place at the wrong time.

He really wanted to establish a kind of colonial aristocracy based on land grants to the right kind of people, similar to that proposed by squatter John Macarthur in New South Wales — his 'right kind of people' were mainly well-connected free Englishmen, or even Scottish sheep-herders who followed Mitchell's wheel tracks for a decade to establish their flocks right across Victoria.

The last thing he wanted was a rabble of Irish fenians and pistol-packing Californians who had no love at all for his Queen or for English law.

(LA TROBE LIBRARY PICTURE COLLECTION, STATE LIBRARY OF VICTORIA)

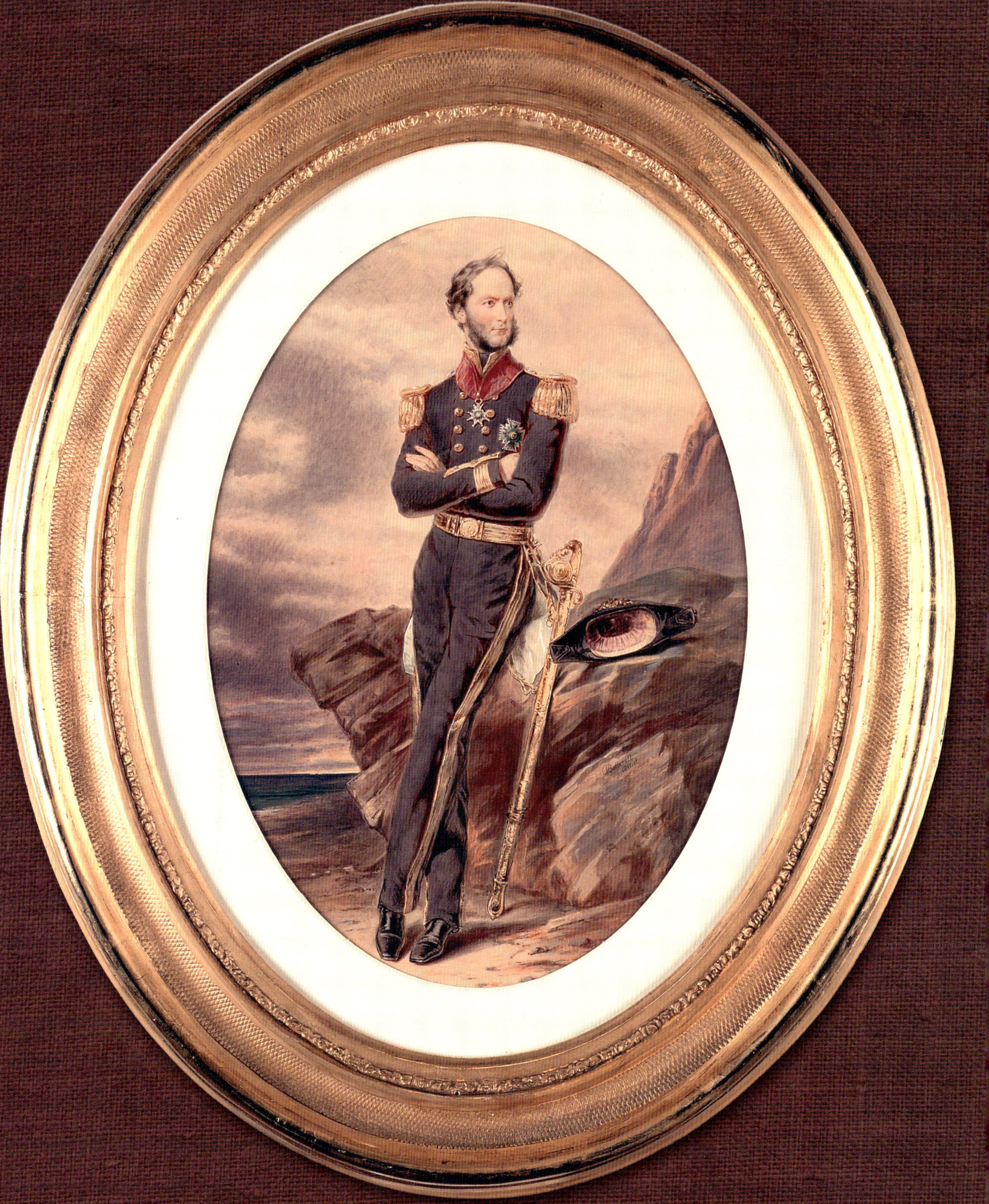

ABOLITION
OF THE
LICENSE TAX!

GREAT OPEN AIR MEETING
TO THE PUBLIC OF BENDIGO.

GENTLEMEN, a great PUBLIC

MEETING

Will be held

ON SATURDAY NEXT, AUG. 26
IN FRONT OF THE CRITERION HOTEL, AT TWO O'CLOCK P.M.,

For the purpose of adopting proper means to effect the entire Abolition of the License Tax; and also to Elect an Anti-License Central Committee. Every Man who believes that the time has come to Abolish the License Tax is respectfully invited to attend the Meeting, and to take a part in the proceedings.

The present Anti-Gold License Movement, so far as its originators are concerned, will be conducted strictly within the limits of Law and order; but every legal means will be made use of to sweep from the Statute Book of the Nation a law which is degrading to a free people, and impolitic and oppressive in its practical operations. The great majority of the Digging Community are at present unable to pay the License tax, and therefore ought not to be compelled by the Executive Officers of the law to advance fines, or otherwise submit to an unjust and tyrannical bondage. We therefore call upon the entire Digging Community to attend the Meeting on Saturday, and show, by their presence and their unanimity, that they are determined to demand, constitutionally, from the Legislature, the immediate Repeal of the obnoxious License Tax; and that, while they are willing to pay their proper share of taxation, they are fully determined to be placed on an equal footing with the other Classes of Her Majesty's subjects in the Colony.

Abolition of the License Tax and no compromise; Abolition of the Gold Commission, and Reduction in the Public Expenditure of the Nation; Representation to all Classes, and equal Division of the State Taxes; the Orders in Council revoked, and the Public Lands of the Colony thrown open to the People; Repair of Roads and Bridges, and the immediate establishment all over the Diggings of an efficient and liberal system of National Education.

All who want the above desirable objects carried out without delay, let them one and all attend the Great Anti-License Public Meeting.

At Break of Day on Saturday let there be a universal discharge of fire-arms, to spread the news of the Meeting all over Bendigo.

DIGGERS! DO YOUR DUTY!
By Order of the Anti-License Provisional Committee,

WILLIAM D. C. DENOVAN,

BENDIGO, 21st Aug., 1854.   HON. SEC. PRO TEM.

COOK & SHERBON, PRINTERS, BENDIGO TIMES OFFICE, SANDHURST.

A New Governor

BELOW:
William Dixon Campbell Denovan
A prominent Chartist, Denovan was on his way to Ballarat when he heard the Stockade had fallen. Turning back, he was shadowed all the way by a trooper. As he entered the Bendigo valley, black mourning crepe about his neck, red shirt and red ribbon worn proudly on his breast, he was greeted to a hero's welcome.

where the diggers and the government were often in agreement. Hotham disliked the 'Celestials', yet was bound to protect them. The diggers, however, resented their presence and Denovan attempted to consolidate his position as a powerful leader by railing against the Chinese.

At the June meeting, he vowed to lead the diggers and forcibly remove the Chinese from the diggings. An ultimatum was declared and the expulsion of the Chinese from Bendigo was set for 4 July.

There was also considerable agitation amongst the Chinese themselves at this time. They had even posted notices offering rewards for the killing of some of their own 'headmen'. Their own leaders were accused of skimming the licence fees that the Chinese diggers had entrusted to them, to be paid into 'the Camp' on their behalf. Denovan believed that implicit in the 'reward' offered was a threat to his own safety.

Commissioner Panton called Denovan to 'the Camp' where he was hauled before the Bendigo District Police Magistrate, Lachlan McLachlan, a man few would dare deny. 'Bendigo Mac' didn't want any further unrest amongst the Chinese, and he certainly didn't want the Europeans to confront the 'Celestials', who were already in a murderous mood. 'Bendigo Mac' was only too aware of the consequences of any armed revolt on the diggings; even one against the Chinese could soon spread to other objects of dissatisfaction and eventually overrun the colony. Denovan promptly called off the march — as much for fear for his own life as for fear of the magistrate.

26 August 1854

Hotham decided to visit the goldfields. Accompanied by his good lady wife, he planned to make the first visit to the scene of so much unrest on the Bendigo and Ballarat diggings in the latter half of 1854. Hotham was convinced that he could not make any decisions regarding the goldfields without seeing first for himself the conditions and administration there.

Only a few days before Hotham was to make a triumphant visit to Bendigo, Denovan advertised another meeting where once again there was a call for the abolition of the licence fee. At this meeting, the diggers also called for an extension of franchise to the mining population.

Fair and equitable taxation, representation and franchise were now the issues that occupied the minds of the diggers. The diggers were also interested in land reform, as many wished to establish permanent dwellings, and to invest in a future not reliant on gold. Although some land sales were held in 1853, most of the good farming land was held by the squatters. The government, made up of

MR. W. D. C. DENOVAN.

OPPOSITE:
Denovan attempted to call the diggers to protest for a second time when he placarded the Bendigo diggings with this poster. This time he left the 'Chinese Question' off the agenda.

squatters and merchants, was unlikely to readily give over the source of its fortune to the diggers.

Denovan's poster calling the diggers to the meeting of 26 August demanded:

> Abolition of the License Tax and no compromise; Abolition of the Gold Committee, and Reduction in the Public Expense of the Nation; Representation of all Classes, and equal Division of the State Taxes; the Orders in Council revoked, and the Public lands of the Colony thrown open to the People; Repair of Roads and Bridges, and the immediate establishment all over the Diggings of an efficient and liberal system of National Education.

If nothing else, Denovan was a dramatic and entrepreneurial showman at heart. His poster had also asked that the diggers spread the news across the diggings with 'a universal discharge of firearms' at 'Break of Day'.

Again the *Advertiser* commented in support of the diggers against the licence fee, and the push for fair and equitable representation in the Legislative Council:

> ... the main population forming a class of men as intelligent, and orderly as any in the colony, have been unjustly treated, by their almost total exclusion from the rights of free men, under the proposed new constitution ... claim their right to a voice in the framing and passing of laws which may vitally affect their interests.
>
> It is a matter that has long required alteration, and we trust that the diggers, while they are respectful will also be firm, in their remonstrances with the Government on the subject. We think that they must, ere this, have discovered the evils of the system. At all events, they will in all probability now be convinced of them in a very short time.

The Chartists' philosophy had spread far and wide, gaining influence as the diggers sensed their power to change the mind of the government and consequently the way they lived their lives. The diggers sensed the rare opportunity offered them to create a new kind of society with freedom and equal opportunity for all. They pressed hard to make the dream a reality. But there was still much ahead. It seemed that before they would be satisfied there were set roles to be played out, old enmities to be aired and class hatreds to be resolved. The stage was setting for the end-game.

29 August 1854

On this fine and pleasantly warm Saturday afternoon, around 3,000 diggers gathered outside the Criterion Hotel in Bendigo in response to Denovan again calling a public meeting. In a style that seems typical of Denovan's entrepreneurial showmanship, bonfires were lit to announce the meeting and a band played on the balcony of the Criterion Hotel, entertaining the crowd before the speakers assumed their positions.

The Provisional Anti-Licence Committee was established with Denovan as its pro-term Honorary Secretary, and the meeting on 29 August elected Dr. Wall as its chairman. He rose to address the crowd and amid continuous applause he began:

> Diggers of Bendigo ... we are here today to discuss the License question, to express our opinion on what we all consider an odious and unjust tax [cheers]. It is now twelve months since, you will remember, we recommended 10s. as the amount of the license we were prepared to pay, and we were then made to pay more, although the old 30s. license was reduced. There was no serious objection to the fee then demanded, as we were doing better then, and if we could not afford the money at the time, we could most of us get it from a friend, but now we are not able to do this. One-half of us are unable to pay the fee, and many of us never do so.
>
> What we want is to have the license-fee entirely obliterated, totally removed from the books ... While we have no voice in the framing of our

laws, it is unjust to demand us to pay so hard a tax as the license fee.

We have got a new Governor, and under him it rests with you to gain your just demands; for I believe that any just claim urged on him by the people will be attended to; with him we need no fear of class legislation, no reckless expenditure of our hard-earned money.

Sir Charles Hotham has already stated in public, that the government would be based upon the principle that all power proceeds from the people.[1]

The *Bendigo Advertiser* carried the following editorial comment on 25 August:

Once more our otherwise quiet population are becoming clamorous on the subject of the license-tax. It is not its reduction, but its total abolition that is now sought. A tax that can only be collected by armed bodies of men, will never be tolerated by a civilised people.

The *Advertiser* also commented on the indiscriminate manner of taxation which fell heavily on the unsuccessful diggers: '... the license law makes poverty a crime, and punishes it accordingly'.

The governor's visit

Preparations were in hand to receive the governor's party in Bendigo — with real style. Although there was considerable ill feeling towards the government over the licence tax and disappointment at the inequities written into the new constitution, the diggers expected much from Sir Charles and were not about to disgrace themselves in front of the governor.

All kinds of correspondents had pressed upon the governor that the diggers were a loyal and patriotic body. The diggers were determined to impress him with an effusive display of goodwill, while at the same time they were readying themselves for their next move.

Even Denovan, who had rattled the Chinese can only days earlier, suggested that the Chinese not 'be made a feature of in the procession as it would lead to bad feelings'.[2]

They all wanted things to go as smoothly as possible, to impress the governor and his good lady with their bona-fides, to show them a united, dedicated, loyal face, and to press their cause and win favour. They expected to succeed.

Sir Charles and Lady Hotham first travelled to Ballarat, where they arrived unannounced, and walked, unnoticed, for some time among the rows of tents until they stopped to watch some diggers at work in a deep claim. Before long, the identity of the curious onlookers was discovered and the word quickly spread across the diggings. Thousands of diggers thronged to cheer and show their loyalty to the new governor, of whom they expected so much.

I proceeded in the first instance to Ballarat, where I spent three days including the Sabbath. I found an orderly well conducted people, particularly in their observance of the Sunday, living generally in tents, having amongst them a large proportion of women and children; schools of every denomination, and people of every nation are on the diggings, and there was an appearance of tranquillity and confidence which would reflect honour on any community.

For some time I was enabled to walk undiscovered amongst them, and thus discovered their real feelings towards the government, and obtained an insight into some minor causes on which they desired redress.[3]

But Hotham was about to make his first mistake. Having seen the Ballarat miners at work he considered them to be men of capital and therefore of much the same 'class' as himself, as any other entrepreneur:

The gold at Ballarat is obtained by deep sinking, in some cases the shaft is 180 feet deep — the digger then encounters slate in which the gold is found. The miner of Ballarat must be a man of capital, able to await the result of six months' toil before he wins his prize. For this reason he will always be a lover of order and good government and, provided he is kindly treated, will be found in the path of loyalty and duty.[4]

The roads on which the regal couple were travelling were muddy and holed, so the diggers brought forward some slabs laid aside for timbering claims, and made a path for Sir Charles and Lady Hotham. Unfortunately the diggers couldn't keep up the pace and the couple reached a 'crabhole' in the newly timbered track before another slab could be laid. A well-known giant of a man, 'Big Larry', stepped forward, lifted her ladyship under the arms and carried her across the hole to safety on the other side. The crowd went wild with delight. For the next couple of kilometres all the way into Ballarat, the couple were met with cheers, and even after they were deposited in their quarters at 'the Camp' a 'great crowd gathered in respectful silence, save for an occasional cheer for the "Digger's Charlie".'[5]

What went wrong? Everywhere that Hotham and his good lady went they were treated with great respect. As they entered Castlemaine to tour the Forest Creek diggings, the shouts of loyalty deafened them as the diggers made a procession that began 4.8 kilometres out from the town. Entertained at an open-air breakfast, Hotham recalled that 'there seemed to be but one feeling towards the Queen's representative'. They had been so enthusiastically received by the diggers that Hotham made one of his many fundamental errors of judgement. He mistakenly perceived the excessive display of patriotic welcome shown to himself and Lady Hotham, wherever they went, to mean that all was well on the goldfields.

4 September 1854

Lieutenant-Governor Sir Charles and Lady Hotham arrived in Bendigo where they were greeted with great enthusiasm. Commissioner Panton had ridden out to Big Hill to greet them on their entrance into the Bendigo valley. As they came down into the flat they were met by a number of diggers who removed the horses from their carriage and pulled them all the way into Bendigo.

Hotham was no doubt shocked and somewhat relieved to have been so ceremoniously transported into the belly of the hot-bed of 'Red Republicanism'. He naturally concluded that the diggers on Bendigo were 'true and loyal'. Bendigo showed that they also expected much from him. A banner hung across the road at View Point, the scene of so much dissent, declared 'He's A Right 'un'.

The couple were feted at dinners accompanied by all the notables of the Bendigo field. A special performance of Sheridan's play *The Hunchback* entertained the honoured guests who sat in a hastily erected box amongst a packed house at the Princess Theatre. The township was illuminated and an inscription over the Criterion Hotel displayed the words: 'Welcome Sir Charles and Lady Hotham to Sandhurst', while the Hibernian in Golden Square offered the gaelic welcome: 'Cead mille failthe' — 'a hundred thousand welcomes'.

The party attended an exhibition of goods that Bendigo was sending to Paris, such was the importance that the citizens of 'Bold Bendigo' placed upon themselves.

The Bendigo diggers, however, were not about to let this overwhelming spirit of goodwill dampen their fervour for change. On that afternoon, over 8,000 diggers gathered again where a memorial was prepared and presented to the governor.

The memorial carried the usual 'distaste of the license-fee', but the issues of franchise and land ownership were now assuming equal import.

Hotham received the memorial, and having read it promised to consider all that was put before him. He expressed the view that the government was trying to open up the land as fast as they could, and that he would endeavour to keep taxation 'as light as possible'.[6]

He did add, however, that he 'Gave them to understand that they must pay for liberty and order', at which he was loudly cheered. The fact that almost half of the funds collected by the licence fee was spent on the expenses of the commissioners and police, with very little in the way of liberty or order provided, should have been evidence enough to Hotham that goldfields reform was not simply desired — but imperative.

The diggers both at Ballarat and Bendigo must have felt reassured that this 'Charlie' was finally going to do something to help them, that in Sir Charles Hotham was a man who seemed genuinely interested in their needs, and that he was seeking a way to attend to their grievances.

The diggers were most pleased with the outcome of their representation to the governor and applauded him: '… a tremendous burst of cheering from the assembled thousands greeted His Excellency at the conclusion of these remarks'.[7]

Hotham himself had agreed earlier 'that the goldfields are evidently the resort of young officers, who have no particular qualifications for a very delicate duty, and that are too often imperious in manner and tone, so they provoke the resentment of men particularly quick to vindicate their self-respect'.[8]

In what today seems typical of political behaviour, Hotham failed to mention the diggers' concerns in his speech at the opening of the Legislature soon after his return from Bendigo.

As Hotham left the diggings, he offered his opinion that the 'masses of diggers are true-hearted and loyal, and if well-treated may be thoroughly depended upon'. Why then, within the next few months, were they treated so poorly, so brutally and with such little regard for humanity?

Hotham soon betrayed the diggers' faith in his new government by stepping up the collection of fees. He introduced twice-weekly digger hunts, and he required that the troopers pursue the collection of licence fees 'at all costs'. William Howitt remarked on the attitude of Hotham's diligent troopers in the collection of his licence fees 'at all costs':

> The system of 'man-hunting' to find out the unlicensed diggers has been carried out more in the style of English fox-hunting than in that which should distinguish officers of the law apprehending law-breakers; and were it not that their necks might pay the penalty, some of these 'hunters' would as readily indulge in a day's 'man-shooting' as in a snipe-hunting excursion.
>
> The majesty of the law has been entrusted to the care of a most incompetent set of men; and the plunder of the Government, which pays and feeds them, seems in too many cases to be their sole object.[9]

Hotham set about to collect more taxes, and set himself on a collision course with the diggers. He seemed determined to force them to a showdown.

ABOVE:
Lieutenant-Governor Sir Charles Hotham
Hotham arrived in the colony to a welcoming population eager to see reforming change to its administration.
  Steeped in the ways of the military, he simply failed to understand the needs of a people desperate to see an end to governance by decree and eager to welcome in democratic franchise.
(LA TROBE UNIVERSITY LIBRARY COLLECTION, BENDIGO)

Pensioners
Forrest Creek

Joe! Joe! Joe!

WHEN MR. WALL, AS CHAIRMAN OF THE Provisional Anti-Licence Committee (formed in Bendigo in August 1854) assured the diggers there that Sir Charles Hotham's government 'would be based upon the principle that all power proceeds from the people', he seemed to have overlooked the power that was exercised by the league of gentlemen who presided over the commissioner's camps.

The young men who had arrived in the colony with letters of introduction to the military men who ruled the diggings, when kitted out in gold braid and scarlet and given a post up country, soon became lords and masters of all they surveyed — or so they thought.

The mass of diggers resented the manner in which these 'popinjays' ruled their own little kingdoms on the goldfields.

It was the actions of these military officers that drove the diggers to seek retribution through a change in the licensing laws, as much as the cost of the fee itself. It was the ongoing harassment of the diggers, culminating in the treatment of the disabled servant of the Catholic priest, Father Smyth, on 10 October 1854, that tipped the scales in favour of direct action against the Ballarat camp.

Very few of the 'gentlemen' in 'the Camp' had any training at all to deal with the likes of the digger; few even had the aptitude to make something of themselves in the colony if it were not for the power vested in their uniform.

The arbitrary and illegal acts of those petty officials aroused hostile feelings in the breasts of the diggers, who generally were quiet and well-affected to the authorities. It was no uncommon thing for men to be seized upon at a mere direction of some boy-commissioners, and chained to trees during the intense mid-day heats, the offense charged against them being simply that of digging for gold without a license.[1]

David Blair, writing in 1879, also observed that those law abiding fellows who had paid their licence were nevertheless outraged to see 'those personal privileges which are considered sacred throughout the British dominions infringed upon'.[2]

Traps! Traps! Joe! Joe!

The cry of 'Joe! Joe!' was the most well-known signal heard on the diggings. It was used first to describe the goldfields police in the time of Governor Charles Joseph La Trobe. They were

OPPOSITE:
Pensioners, Forrest Creek
From a watercolour by S.T. Gill
Lithograph by Macartney & Galbraith, Melbourne 1852
(REX NAN KIVELL COLLECTION NK1836
BY PERMISSION, NATIONAL LIBRARY OF AUSTRALIA)

ABOVE:
Where's 'yer license?'
Engraving from 'From Tent to Parliament. The Life of Peter Lalor' by James Vallens, produced by Mr James Oddie on the occasion the 50th Anniversary of the Eureka Stockade in 1903.
(BALLARAT CITY LIBRARY COLLECTION)

MOUNTED POLICE, GOLD ESCORT GUARD.

nick-named 'Joe's traps', a shortening of trooper, but which also referred to the most obvious part of their duty, the entrapment of the diggers. Even after La Trobe had departed and Hotham took charge of the colony, the police were still known as Joes. When the cry of 'Joe!' went up across the diggings, it announced to all that the police were on a raid, and another digger-hunt was on. This was soon to become an almost daily occurrence.

The diggers soon began the practice of placing a 'cockatoo' up a high tree, who kept sentinel over the field; as soon as the police were seen in the distance the cry went up. On hearing the cry of 'Joe! Joe! Joe!', the diggings sprang into life: shepherds (men who had been lounging about their shallow holes just keeping title to their claims) soon disappeared down deeper ones, as others abandoned their tubs and cradles and bolted for the safety of the trees. The police had become used to the tricks of the diggers and soon began to place spies among them.

A couple of dirty constables, in diggers' guise, jumping a claim, gentle shepherd approaches with dilapidated shovel on shoulder and proceeds to dispossess intruders in summary manner. A great barney ensues: Constable talks big a crowd gathers around, and 'a ring! a ring!!' is the cry. The combatants have just commenced to shape, when the signal rings through the flat. On come the traps in skirmishing order, driving in the stragglers as they advance, and supported by mounted troopers in the rear, who occupy commanding positions on the ranges. A great haul is made, and some sixty prisoners are marched off in triumph to the Camp, handcuffed together like a gang of felons, there to be dealt with according to the caprice or cupidity of their oppressors.[3]

The accounts of such an oppressive regime of licence-hunting seems to be most apparent on the Ballarat diggings. While the same laws persisted at other places, there are not the same reports as

ABOVE:
Mounted Police, Gold Escort Guard
Lithograph, from a drawing sketched on the spot by S.T. Gill, 1853
(BY PERMISSION, NATIONAL LIBRARY OF AUSTRALIA)

those that came consistently from Ballarat. It may be that the Ballarat mines took longer to pay any return; as a consequence, the monthly licence fee was a particular impost on the Ballarat miners, and fewer could afford to pay than on other diggings. While it is true that on all the diggings there was the same resentment of the tax, it also appears that 'the Camp' officials on Ballarat were also of a particular kind. In Bendigo, Panton was a reasonable young gentleman. Although not trained in the military, he was still suited for command and enjoyed the respect of his subordinates and the diggers alike. In Castlemaine, Captain Bull was well-liked. The others who resided in the Castlemaine camp may have been just like those on Ballarat, but Bull also led by his example and Castlemaine was relatively free of any ongoing dissent.

The art of shepherding

It was a common practice for parties on the diggings to stake out several claims on various parts of the goldfield. On Ballarat the digging was slow and few parties wished to commit to only one hole, which may see them dig for months, only to bottom out a shicer.

Parties took out as many as they had numbers, to lay claim to these little patches of earth. Each patch had to be worked regularly or they would be considered abandoned and revert back to the Crown. These claims could then be taken up by 'new chums' just arrived on those diggings.

To keep the claim alive, a 'shepherd' was needed to be seen working the ground, so they spent their days idling as best they could, smoking their pipes and chatting to mates, maybe slowly working a piece of timber to be later used as shoring within the shaft, if they could ever be bothered to actually dig one. Most shepherds would have been lucky to remove a bucket of dirt a day, if they had tried at all. But that was not the purpose of the exercise.

The <u>*Ballarat Star,* 31 June 1884</u>
One of the insurgents present at the storming of the Stockade recalled the practice in his reminiscences, published in the *Star* on the 30th anniversary of Eureka.

> The claims in those days were very small, 34 feet square for eight men. So it became customary —

'The Camp' at Ballarat was believed to be corrupt: officials were in the pay of the sly-grog operators, others colluded with ex-convicts and distorted the liquor-licensing laws to suit their own ends. Informers were recruited by the police and sent among the diggers, disguised, to set traps for them.

'When commissioners, magistrates and troopers had got used to treat the diggers as people to be

Shepherding

> owing to the great expense of sinking a shaft — for one or two in a party to 'shepherd' a couple of claims until the lead was proved near enough to warrant a shaft being sunk.
>
> A large number of claims had been taken up on the flat at the foot of the Red Streak. As the lead had not yet been proved nearby, the 'shepherds' had a jolly time of it, some sinking an inch a day in their shafts; dressing a part of a log or a slab; playing cards with brother 'shepherds', telling long winded yarns, or any other amusement to while away the time.[4]

Such idleness was the perfect breeding ground for thoughts of sedition...

ABOVE:
Shepherding
Digging life twenty-five years ago
Wood engraving published in the Australasian Sketcher,
20 December 1879

(AUTHOR'S COLLECTION)

taxed and harried at pleasure', the only possible solution for the diggers was to protest, and the only possible conclusion would come from direct action.

> The outbreak [that followed] was not that of a stupid, stolid, ignorant peasantry in arms against haystacks and threshing machines, but of a free-spirited, intelligent people, goaded to resistance by intolerable wrongs and guided — at all events during a portion of the period — by men of education and character among themselves, aided by a provincial press created and sustained for the most part by men also from among their own ranks.[5]

Withers said that 'the goldfields inhabitants being outside the mystic circle of governing power were placed in an attitude of hostility to the constituted authorities. An unnatural separation was created by the law between the majority of the people and the Crown; and to give intensity to the danger, the people here were for the most part superior in mental and bodily capacities to the countrymen they had left behind...' Their time on the diggings, as new migrants in a young colony with their backs in the sun, had given them qualities that: 'made them valuable as freemen, but dangerous as slaves'.[6]

The hated campsites

William Howitt said the the whole of the government of the goldfields 'is a pseudo-military system, and most repulsive to an English eye'. As a patriotic Englishman, his following observation was a most disagreeable one for him to make:

> The Commissioners sport a semi-military uniform. They have each a regular trooper riding after them on all occasions. The mounted police are in reality regular armed troopers. The magistrates are the judges, and decide everything without a jury, in the style of a court-martial. Numbers of horse police and foot police are constantly scouring the goldfields and the roads, man-hunting, and are constantly marching poor wretches up to the camp for lack of licenses ... While they keep one eye shut to grog-shops, for which they are notoriously paid, they have the other always open to catch any poor devil without a license. You may undermine the roads in quest of gold, sell grog, or break the laws in any sort of way, but you must furnish revenue; and you hear every day of atrocities perpetrated in enforcement of it, which were they done in Hungary or Russia, would rouse the indignation of all Europe.[7]

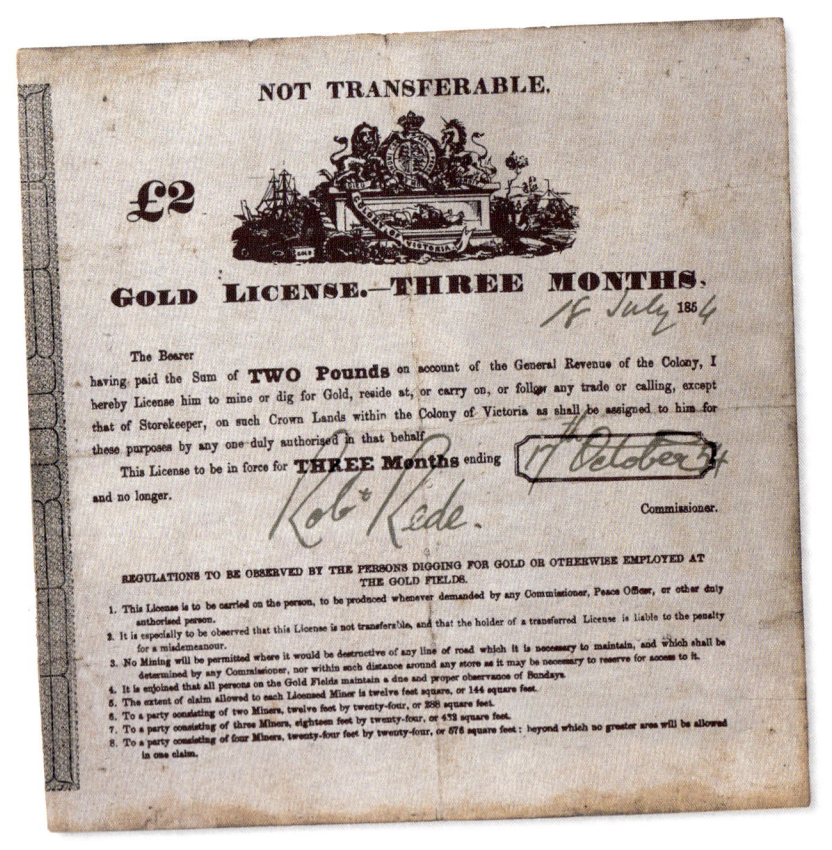

As evidenced by the diggers on the Bendigo field in 1853, when George Thomson led the loyal diggers there in three cheers for the flag, the British among the diggers had a high opinion of the 'rightness' of their system of government by common law and the rights of the individual. Although the British Crown was in abhorrence at the notion of democracy, the people believed wholeheartedly in

ABOVE:
A three-month gold licence issued by Resident Commissioner on the Ballarat Goldfields Robert Rede, dated 18 July 1854.

Joe! Joe! Joe!

their style of government as superior to all others, especially over all European systems with whom they had battled for centuries to prove the case. While the uniformed sons of the well-connected classes behaved on the diggings towards the common working man much as they were accustomed to behaving at home, their superior attitude simply fed the resentment that most of the diggers felt against the licence system. The scores of refugees from European conflicts on the diggings were also afraid that an antipodean version of the 'Hanoverian' style of government was being established on the Ballarat field. While they no doubt lived by the laws as much as any other digger, they had no affection for the Crown and felt no reason at all to bow to the demands of British military rule.

The behaviour of 'the Camp' towards this widely disparate group of men bonded them together in one cause, to resist 'the Camp', and to frustrate the commissioners at every turn.

The commissioners and the troopers didn't seem to be able help themselves. They paraded the diggings on horseback, swords jangling at their sides, their snooty noses in the air. Some even rode about wearing white gloves, so precious were their delicate hands that they could not allow them to be soiled by contact with the digger or with the earth; however, it didn't seem to stop them handling the diggers' cash, or collecting the bribes they took from the keepers of the sly grog tents whom they permitted, albeit illegally, to operate without prosecution, as long as the illicit fee was proffered.

Frank McKillop, editor of the *Mount Alexander Mail*, wrote:

> The constables as a body were a drunken lot, and frequently they were brought before the Magistrate or Commissioner for fighting among themselves. they insulted men and women, and behaved generally like the blackguards they

---

ABOVE:

Coffee Tent, from Bush Inn Diggers Breakfast
Lithograph by S.T. Gill, published by Macartney & Galbraith, Melbourne 1852

Coffee tents were the disguise of the sly-grog sellers. Here diggers are seen at breakfast with a 'nobbler' not too far away.

(REX NAN KIVELL COLLECTION, U990
BY PERMISSION, NATIONAL LIBRARY OF AUSTRALIA)

BELOW:
Dodging the Commissioner
Engraving from The Three Colonies of Australia: New South Wales, Victoria, South Australia; their Pastures, Copper Mines, and Gold Fields, *by Samuel Sidney, published in 1852*
(LA TROBE UNIVERSITY LIBRARY COLLECTION, BENDIGO)

were. Bribery, of course, was rampant, and one instance occurred in 1854, that one constable who joined the force in a penniless condition in Castlemaine retired in less than twelve months with over £1,000 to his credit in the bank; and this connection is somewhat significant to note that a number of camp officials here and on other fields who retired with a competence, and sailed for England prior to 1855.[8]

He went on to note the relatively good behaviour of the diggers in the face of such impropriety by 'the Camp' officials:

> The diggers persecuted by the officials and by robbers were surprisingly moderate, and one's blood boils to read of the indignities heaped upon them by a fatuous Government and rapacious officials.[9]

In Castlemaine, the diggers formed a Diggers' Protection Society, as the police did so little to prosecute the real law-breakers. This coming together of the digging fraternity laid the foundations for other groups who banded together in a common cause.

The gold commissioners

When one young fellow arrived at the diggings to take up his post as a gold commissioner, he found that there were several others already there commissioned for the same task. He wrote:

> There are a large staff of police; and a staff of soldiers of the line (old pensioners), whose chief duty was to act as sentries over the tent of the gold office, and whose chief difficulty was to keep themselves sober. Everything was upon the grandest scale: commissioners, inspectors, captains, sub-inspectors, lieutenants, cadets in silver-lace and embroidery, capering about on splendid horses, and new diggings continually being discovered in the vicinity.

"DODGING THE COMMISSIONER."

Not to make all reasonable allowances for the excitement of this period [1853] and the lawless feeling of the masses around, would be simply unjust and absurd; nevertheless, I am bound to say that things were done here by commissioners, magistrates, inspectors, and other officers of police, down to the youngest cadet, which were quite worthy of feudal times, being often as thoughtless and unfeeling as they were unnecessary. No doubt it frequently happened that there was no time, during the confusion, to discriminate between the respectable working miner and the escaped felon; but no pains were taken on this head, or very seldom.[10]

It appears that to 'the Camp' the digger may as well be the felon, for as much respect was given to both classes. This attitude riled the honest working man who had as much reason to resent the behaviour of the 'old lag' or Van Demonian, the cause of much of the crime on the goldfields, as did the gentlemen of the law.

There are countless reports of the treatment of individual diggers by the traps. Howitt repeated a story that had appeared in the newspapers concerning a digger who had been arrested on suspicion of robbery and chained to a staple driven into a post in the floor of a police station. The digger was kept chained this way, unable to stand erect, forced to lie on the floor for five days until he was discharged, there being no proof that could be made against him.

Howitt had formed such a poor impression of the administration of the goldfields that he wrote that he did not believe that even if La Trobe 'put the whole official body into an hydraulic press, he would be able to squeeze one tolerable soul out of

---

ABOVE:
I'm Blessed if they haven't Grabbed Henry
Watercolour by George Lacy, c. 1852

The licence-hunt. The gold commissioner inspects a licence — while some diggers hide, others bolt for the safety of the bush.
(BY PERMISSION, NATIONAL LIBRARY OF AUSTRALIA)

them — a soul having that serious moral feeling in which duty could take root':

> The machinery of the diggings in these colonies, the more I am convinced that it is altogether raised on a false basis. It is a military despotism — and a military despotism of the very worst description, because administered for the most part by men who know nothing of military affairs. The mounted police are, to all intents and purposes, a body of cavalry. They are armed, dressed, and disciplined as soldiers; and are equivalent to our yeoman cavalry at home, except that they are on permanent duty.
>
> The whole thing is a mistake and a very mischievous one. The executive system of the goldfields ought to have been a civil one — civil in two senses … Instead of a swarm of young popinjays in military costume, with gold-laced caps and coats, and galloping about with troopers at their heels — young ignorant fellows, who are much too fine and delicate to do anything; who dare not go where they ought to go, and that daily, lest they should dirty their coats, their gloves, or their fingers.[11]

Picking the diggers' pockets

William Howitt also wrote of an incident that occurred to him when he had taken out the licence in Bendigo:

> Taking out four licenses, I wanted the clerk 10s. [change] out of the sovereigns I laid before him. He took the whole, and said it was right. It was useless endeavouring to extract the change from him. I went therefore, directly to Mr. Barnard, the Commissioner of that department, and stated the case. He saw it at once, and said he was busy,

---

ABOVE:
The Digger Hunt
Few diggers liked to be hauled out of their shafts at the point of a bayonet. The military manner of the goldfields police endeared them to no man.
Engraving from 'From Tent to Parliament. The Life of Peter Lalor' by James Vallens, produced by Mr James Oddie on the occasion of the 50th Anniversary of the Eureka Stockade in 1903.
(BALLARAT CITY LIBRARY COLLECTION)

but would take care and get it rectified for me against I came next to the camp.

Mentioning the fact of the clerk's barefaced dishonesty to several people on the diggings, they laughed, and said 'You will never get that half-sovereign.' I replied, 'Oh yes; Mr. Barnard has promised to pay it me the next time I go up.' 'That may be,' said they, 'but nevertheless, you will never see the money: they never do at that camp disgorge any such imbalances'.[12]

Howitt couldn't quite believe that the commissioner would not live up to his word, but the proof was there the next time he presented himself. Barnard told him that he had 'sent that young man adrift — he was a great rogue and a drunkard'. Howitt asked for his money and Barnard replied that he didn't have it at that time but would pay him back next time he saw him.

Howitt never saw his 10/- again, and said that the only compensation he felt was that it was only 10/- and not £10.

The stories told against 'the Camp' by almost every man who put his reminiscences to paper would seem to provide justification for open resistance by any group of reasonable citizens, but in Britain's colonies reasonable behaviour had been thrown out the window — military might overrode almost all other considerations — and the shadow of the Crown was cast long and low over the diggings. There were few who openly sought to defy the laws, although they had enough reason to resent being treated as they were.

> The mess-room was the rallying, plotting and jolly chamber for only the birds of a feather who flocked together; the *a la militaire* costume and *hauteur*, the studied distinctiveness of the gold-laced strutters from the cordial associations and the gatherings of the citizens; the mode of prosecutions, the dismal and horridly thronged gaol; the batches of prisoners arriving, viz., hand-cuffed unlicensed diggers; the chosen police, with officers to match, whose daily and nightly duties were burning tents and all property within … without inquiry or trial …[13]

It was also quite common for a digger to be placed under arrest for a minor misdemeanour, usually drunkenness, and have his pockets emptied before he was released from the logs. Howitt again:

> A man would be brought in drunk, who had been taken up for making a disturbance; the next day he would say, 'I had so much money in my pocket when I was seized' — 50l. or 100l., or several hundreds; for it is amazing what sums these diggers will carelessly carry about them for days or weeks. The turnkey knows nothing of it, but suggests no doubt, he had his pockets cleared out while he was drunk, before he was taken up. But whether before or after, it is all one to the sufferer — he never hears any more of it.[14]

Digger hunting

William Benson, once an escort trooper from South Australia and later a reporter for the *Ballarat Times*, recalled this experience when he was accosted by a large party of troopers brandishing swords, while on his way to Bakery Hill to seek employment as a stock-rider in 1853:

> Being dressed in somewhat digger costume, and walking near where the Yarrowee bridge now is, I heard behind me a stentorian voice — 'Hallo! you fellow.' I turned around, Speechless horror! There, at full gallop, at the head of fifteen or twenty mounted troopers, with scabbards clattering and stirrups jingling, rode a stalwart black-looking chief of the digger hunters. 'Hallo! I say, you, Sir,' thundered forth he, with a mighty flourish of his sword glittering in the beautiful sunlight, 'have you got a license.' Worse luck to me I never was a digger, even when gold could be got by pounds weight. Well, there flourished the sword of the mighty hunter, and there

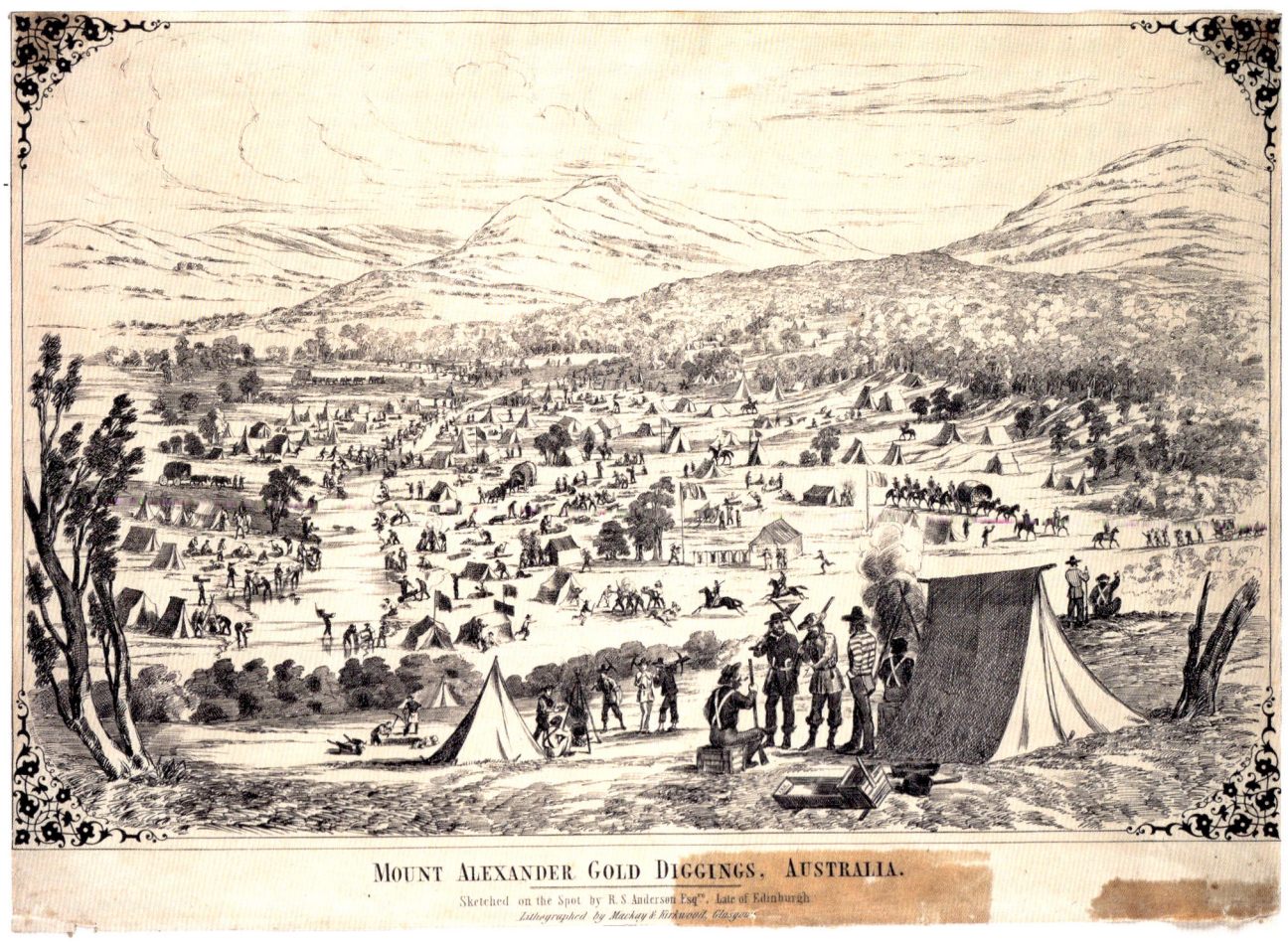

MOUNT ALEXANDER GOLD DIGGINGS, AUSTRALIA.
Sketched on the Spot by R.S. Anderson Esq'r, Late of Edinburgh
Lithographed by Mackay & Kirkwood, Glasgow

stammered I forth 'No.' At that moment up came the mounted and foot police. 'Take this man into custody,' shouts the leader of the group and off he gallops.[15]

Benson was told that he was to be taken to 'the Camp' lock-up, or the logs, as it was more commonly known. As he set off under guard he knew that they were not heading in the direction of 'the Camp'. He soon discovered that the traps were marching off, making a day of it, scouring the diggings for more unlicensed 'diggers'. Benson was assured of a long day's tramp until the traps had arrested enough to make their day worthwhile.

Another report from about the same time by Mr. R.M. Serjeant recalls an incident when he was accosted by the traps as he strode towards his hut on Specimen Gully, licence in his hand, in the middle of a raid.

He was surprised to see the traps step back from his hut rather hurriedly. When he got close he heard a young woman politely enquire of the troopers the nature of their business. She suggested that the troopers should ask her brother (Mr. Serjeant) any questions they may have. The troopers apologised for their intrusion, turned on their heels and set off in search of easier prey. Mr. Serjeant felt that he should discover the true identity of his new 'sister' when he saw her behave in a most unladylike manner, dancing around the table inside the hut. His cooking mate Joe had decided that he would never take out a licence and was going to continue to wear his new attire, if his mates had no objections — and his new name was to be Josephine. This was quite a common occurrence, before the days when luxuriant beards became the vogue, and probably saved digging parties a considerable amount of money.

Fifty years after the storming of the Stockade, John Bird, who was just a lad at the time of the battle, recalled, for a collection of reminiscences

---

ABOVE:
Mount Alexander, Gold Diggings, Australia
Sketched on the spot by Robert Shortreid Anderson

This drawing of the Forest Creek diggings shows a typical ants' nest of activity — diggers cradling in the creek, fighting over disputed claims, and brawling. The troopers are ever-present, charging in to take command of a vicious melee, as the escort departs for the Treasury, guarded by an armed troop.

(BY PERMISSION, NATIONAL LIBRARY OF AUSTRALIA)

published in the *Ballarat Courier*, seeing troopers every day out hunting for diggers:

> Being a lad at the time of the events that led up to that memorable stockade, I witnessed every day diggers hunted by troopers, and because their miners' rights had expired a few hours, they were marched off to the 'logs', as the lock-up was then called, brought before the commissioner and heavily fined. Being fleet of foot, it was my good fortune to get inside a pile of slabs and hide till the troopers had gone with their prey to the camp. My feelings were nevertheless as keen to the injustice as if I had been in the logs myself. It was a sight never once seen, as I saw it, to be forgotten — manly men of noble mein, in their diggers' clothes, their shirts rolled up with bare and brawny arms, and with sashes round their waists, marched like bushrangers between troopers with loaded carbines, bearing the insult as only Britons could bear it.[16]

Bird described himself as a loyal subject of the Crown, proud of England, the empire and the flag, but he could not have been more proud than he was of the men who 'laid down their lives for what they considered to be an injustice', when they stood against the troops on the barricade. In his reminiscences in the *Courier*, he repeated the oft-quoted epithet that Britons will 'never be base as slaves', and remembered the days when they were treated as such by their own countrymen.

Andrew Hermiston, a digger who was camped just outside the Stockade on the night of 3 December 1854, also recalled the licence hunts on the Ballarat field in this article published in the *Argus* on 3 December 1904:

> I arrived on Ballarat with several mates in 1853 ... we pitched on Pennyweight flat, and soon afterwards had a couple of claims on the Eureka lead ... most of us were young fellows, and, whether we liked it or not, we were drawn into the agitation over the licenses. It was not so much the tax that diggers objected as the high-handed way in which it was collected. When a hunt was on for the licenses the watchword was passed along the lead, 'Joe, Joe' and the men would scurry down the windlass rope, or hide, many for pure mischief, others because they had no license. All who could not show the license were handcuffed and taken along until the raid was completed, and them marched in a gang to 'the logs'.[17]

Every one of these men well remembered the reasons why they eventually stood together against oppression.

Coming Down the Flat

If a body meet a body
Coming down the flat,
Should a body 'Joe' a body
For having on a hat?
Some wear caps, some wide-awakes,
But I prefer a hat —
Yet everybody cries out 'Joe',
Coming down the flat.

The squatter loves his cabbage-tree,
With streamers hanging down —
He wears it always in the bush,
And even when in town:
The cabbage-tree may be his choice,
But I prefer a hat —
Yet everybody cries out 'Joe',
Coming down the flat.

The digger wears a wide-awake,
Wherever he may go —
At the windlass, when washing up,
And also down below.
The wide-awake may suit him well,
But I prefer a hat —
Yet everybody cries out 'Joe',
Coming down the flat.

The peeler has a leather cap,
About two pounds in weight;
In pelting rain or boiling sun,
To wear it is his fate.
The leather cap won't do for me,
For I prefer a hat —
Yet everybody cries out 'Joe',
Coming down the flat.

— CHARLES THATCHER

Old Ballarat, as it was in the Summer of 1853–54
Oil painting by Eugene von Guérard, 1884

Von Guérard's magnificent panorama of the Ballarat diggings, originally sketched 12 months ahead of the Eureka uprising, shows the ebb and flow of daily life in the encampment that stretched along the creek.

This view looks across the busy Eureka diggings towards Mt Warrenheip. Von Guérard has included St Alpius on the left, and Row[e]'s circular circus tent is prominent. It is hard to imagine that on this pleasant, green and gentle field the bloody gore of battle would stain the earth just one summer away.

(BALLARAT FINE ART GALLERY COLLECTION)

The Troubles Begin

'The Australian flag shall triumphantly wave in the sunshine of its own blue and peerless sky over thousands of Australia's adopted sons ... Go forth indomitable people! gain your rights, and may the God of creation smile down propitiously upon your glorious cause' — HENRY SEEKAMP, THE BALLARAT STAR

Countdown to bloodshed

THERE WERE A NUMBER OF SIGNIFICANT events on the Ballarat diggings in 1854 that led to the eventual battle at the Eureka Stockade, and it seems the new governor was inexorably drawn towards this bloody conclusion. With each event, the resentment felt by the diggers towards 'the Camp' was more and more palpable; with each event the governor seemed to advance closer and closer to this inevitable showdown.

Many of the contemporary commentators who wrote of the events of December 1854, and the eventual collapse of official resistance to political reform, made the same observation: that the British Crown had never given in to its subjects without first shedding their blood. Once the gutters were clotted with their gore, the Crown was satisfied and able to hand over that which was sought. It seemed that blood was the price to be paid, so that honour and dignity could first be served.

Following the disastrous events of 3 December, one witness, who was not willing to be identified, had communicated to the *Ballarat Star* that:

> Sir Charles Hotham had made up his mind before he left England what course he would pursue [on the matter of protest on the diggings] and that he even in sight of the English coast, said that the unruly gold-finders wanted 'blood-letting'.
>
> The expression may not literally be correct, but at all events it signified that he would adopt repressive measures on his arrival ...[1]

It is difficult to comprehend the events that led to Hotham making a move against the diggers at Ballarat, after he had been received so warmly on all of the goldfields, and the diggers had so much faith in his ability to bring about change in the colony.

While he seemed aware of the difficulties the diggers had with the 'young police', his own faith in British justice and the imperial system led him to make the biggest mistake of his career.

Hotham's growing fear of revolution led him to make the first strike; all he needed was the appropriate catalyst for direct action, and it was not long before the players moved into position on a hot and dusty stage.

The goldfields police were charged with the responsibility of keeping order on the diggings; they were also instructed to enforce the licence laws, to enforce the laws concerning the sale of alcohol and to settle claims arising from disputes among the diggers (usually for the practice of claim-jumping). Unfortunately, the troopers were over-zealous in the carrying-out of the first two of these duties. They treated the diggers as criminals first, not as freemen who may not be compliant with the law but as criminals with intent to deny the Crown its due.

It was the destruction of the Eureka Hotel on 17 October that would set the goldfields on the path that would determine who was to be the victor in the whole affair. Hotham had long made known his views on subordination. 'It may be readily imagined that he was furious at this open revolt

ABOVE:
Sir Charles Hotham
Hotham had arrived in the colony in June 1854, from service in South America. With his heart set on glory, he had hoped for a posting to the Crimea, but fortune did not shine favourably upon him. He was instead destined for disgrace in Victoria.
(LA TROBE PICTURE COLLECTION, STATE LIBRARY OF VICTORIA)

The Troubles Begin

against the law and fully bent on avenging the outrage.'²

The government had already begun to consider political reforms. The Legislative Council had set in place plans to unlock the lands and allow settlement by the diggers. They were prepared to discuss all of the concerns of the diggers, but like any bureaucracy they were never in any hurry, and they certainly did not like to be pushed too far, too quickly. The events and continued agitation on the Ballarat diggings were as thorns in their side, and Hotham refused to bend to the will of an 'unruly mob'. Even after three years of constant protest and petition against the licence fee, the wearing of the red-ribbon and representation to the government, the recall of one despised governor and replacement by another; and the removal and replacement of the licence fees in FitzRoy's Colony of New South Wales, Hotham still insisted that the law must be obeyed in Victoria, and the instruction went out to vigorously pursue those in its breach.

Hotham insisted that the hated licence hunts be increased and pursued with all diligence. On 13 September 1854, twice-weekly licence hunts were introduced onto the Ballarat diggings.

The death of James Scobie
7 October 1854

Late at night on 7 October, two miners who had spent quite some time celebrating their reunion on the diggings called at the door of the Eureka Hotel and enquired rather too loudly of the possibility of a drink to see them on their way.

The reply from within the hotel was not at all accommodating. Scotsman James Scobie had just welcomed his old friend and fellow countryman Peter Martin to the Ballarat diggings; by the time they reached the door of the Eureka they were already well inebriated, but they were determined to continue with their merry-making as they picked their way back to Scobie's tent on the Eureka diggings. Refused entry to the hotel, Scobie

---

ABOVE:
The Claim Disputed
Watercolour by S.T Gill, c. 1853

As well as the enforcement of the licence fee, troopers were also charged with the responsibility of adjudicating over disputed claims. Any decision made over such an dispute could only bring satisfaction to one half of the argument; the other would no doubt resent the troopers even more than they already did.
(BY PERMISSION, NATIONAL LIBRARY OF AUSTRALIA)

began to attempt to kick the door in, breaking a pane of glass in the process.

Now this kind of provocation would have annoyed any normally pleasant and hospitable landlord, but the landlord of the Eureka was James Bentley, an ex-transportee from Van Diemen's Land, who having served his time had joined the rush to Ballarat where he soon made comfortable arrangements with Mr. John D'Ewes, Senior Magistrate and Chairman of the Licensing Bench. Bentley's house, the Eureka Hotel, was a popular watering hole for the troopers and goldfields police, and for the large contingent of Californians who also populated the Eureka lead. To the diggers it was known as a 'slaughterhouse': the biggest hotel on the diggings. The strong-arm men who worked there were not afraid to use their muscle when it come to chucking out. All of the diggers knew that it was rough-house, that robberies and beatings were common, and that a digger could easily lose his purse as he travelled from one room to another — but it did offer many distractions for the digger weary of the pit and dry from their toil.

After the window had been smashed a brief altercation followed and, unfortunately for Scobie, he made some rather disparaging remarks concerning the hotel-keeper's wife (at Bentley's trial it was recorded that Scobie called Mrs. Bentley a whore). As Scobie and Martin hastily beat a retreat into the darkness, Bentley decided to teach them a lesson for the insult to his wife.

By most accounts, James Bentley, his strong-arm men, ex-convict John Farrell, roustabout Tom Mooney and till-keeper Hervey Hance, followed the drunken Scotsmen into the night. About fifty metres from the hotel, a scuffle broke out when Scobie and Martin were attacked from behind. Although beaten to the ground, Martin was able to get away but Scobie was bashed over the head with a shovel, knocked to the ground and kicked until he fought no more.

It was probably not their intention to bring about Scobie's death. When Martin had recovered from this attack, he returned to find his friend lying still on the ground. He sought help from the nearby tents. At around 2.00 o'clock, Peter Martin and Dr. Carr knocked on the door of the hotel and asked if they could carry Scobie's body inside. It was then that Bentley and his cronies first recognised the result of their cowardly attack. Scobie was dead. The following morning the news spread around all the surrounding diggings like wildfire.

The arrest of Bentley

Bentley was arrested and brought before the magistrate's bench, presided over by his benefactor John D'Ewes who refused to allow Bentley to be tried by jury. At this initial inquiry, it soon became apparent to all who attended the courtroom that Magistrate D'Ewes was determined to see Bentley go free. Any witness who spoke against Bentley was subjected to harassing cross-examination from the bench. In fact, D'Ewes even allowed the defendant, Bentley, to cross-examine Lawrence Welch, a ten-year-old lad who was a witness to Scobie's death. The conduct of the inquiry made it almost impossible to get at the facts of the case.

James Bentley 1818–73

Born in Surrey, England, James Bentley was transported to Tasmania in 1843 convicted of the crime of forgery.

He was granted a conditional pardon in 1851 and joined the rush across Bass Strait to the diggings. On arrival in Ballarat, he first set up as a storekeeper, where he came to the attention of the law when he was convicted for selling liquor and was fined £50.

Magistrate D'Ewes dismissed the charge and recompensed Bentley for his troubles. This may have been the first instance where D'Ewes came to the assistance of James Bentley. He later assisted Bentley in gaining a licence for the Eureka Hotel, and with Robert Rede was responsible for acquitting him of the charge of Scobie's murder. It was this act of complicity with the despised Bentley that incited the riot responsible for the burning of the Hotel.

Bentley died by his own hand in Carlton on 10 April 1873.

Lawrence Welch told the court that he and his mother were both awake after midnight on the morning of the 7th and had both heard loud voices outside their tent. They were camped just thirty metres from the Eureka Hotel. Both recalled the same story: that the voices they heard that night were those of Mr. and Mrs. Bentley, and that they had seen them at the scene accompanied by three or four other men.

Peter Martin told the inquiry that he and Scobie had made their way up to one of the windows at the front of the hotel and asked if they could get in for a drink. Martin told the court: 'Deceased went up to one of the windows and asked to get in and a blow was struck at the head of the deceased through the window as if by a man's hand … I was knocked down and then quickly ran thirty to forty yards from the scene of the attack'. Martin then told the inquiry that he had come back to the scene to find Scobie unconscious, after which he rushed to Archibald Carmichael's butcher's store, nearby, for help. Archy had shared a claim with Scobie.

Bentley told the inquiry a slightly different version of the events that night. He said he and his wife had been woken after midnight by 'some drunken men wanting drink — about an hour and three-quarters after that we were aroused and told that Dr. Carr wanted to bring a person in who was supposed to be dead'.

While he and his associates, Mooney, Farrell and Hance denied having taken any part in the death of Scobie, they did admit that the two men had come knocking at their door after midnight.

Mary Anne Welch, Lawrence's mother, told the inquiry she had been woken by the sound of two or three men passing close by her tent on that night. She heard a voice warn, 'Don't throw anything', followed by a tremendous thud, then another voice she believed to be that of Mrs. Bentley crying out, 'How dare you break my window?' She heard her again saying, 'That's the way to treat these sweeps.' The party then returned to the hotel and were seen throwing a spade on the ground. Mary Anne Welch told the inquiry she had witnessed this by peeking through a hole in her tent.

Her account of the incident was not exactly confirmed by butcher George Bassar who had a shop opposite the hotel. He told the court that he remembered that Friday night very well:

> I was standing outside my own shop door at the time, when I saw two men coming at the door of the hotel and begun kicking at the door. I saw the watchman coming round and he said to them 'Don't make that noise, go home.' The two men then went away a short distance, and passed by Mrs. Welch's tent, and were wrangling as they were going away. I heard a scuffle and then a violent blow given.[3]

Bassar remembered that he had then seen two women and four men come up in the dark from the direction of the gravel pits at the same time as the alleged murder. He could not identify this party, but he also told the inquiry that he saw no one enter or leave the hotel — by the front door. Bassar said that anyone could have gone in and out of the back door, and he would not have seen them at all.

Edward Gad, who was the barman and manager of the bowling saloon attached to the hotel, told the inquiry that:

> He was awoke by a noise at the front door on the night in question. Mr. Bentley who was in his bedroom gave orders not to open the door. I can positively swear that Mr. and Mrs. Bentley did not leave this bed-room, from the time I heard the first noise, until Dr. Carr came at the front door to say that a man had been killed outside, when Mr. Bentley got upon his horse and made for the Camp, to inform the police of the circumstance.[4]

It is obvious that in the courtroom there were those who would corroborate Bentley's story, and

Where's Your Licence?

The morning was fine,
The sun did brightly shine,
The diggers were working away;
When the inspector of traps,
Said now my fine chaps,
We'll go licence hunting today.
Some went this way, some that,
Some to Bendigo Flat,
And a lot to the White Hills did tramp;
Whilst others did bear
Up toward Golden Square,
And the rest of them kept round the camp.

Each turned his eye,
To the holes close by,
Expecting on some down to drop;
But not one could they nail,
For they'd give 'em leg bail —
Diggers ain't often caught on the hop.
The little word Joe,
Which most of you know,
Is a signal the traps are quite near;
Made them all cut their sticks,
And they hooked it like bricks,
I believe you, my boys, no fear.

Now a tall, ugly trap,
He espied a young chap,
Up the gully a-cutting like fun;
So he quickly gave chase,
But 'twas a hard race,
For, mind you, the digger could run.
Down the hole he did pop,
While the bobby on top,
Says — 'Just come up,' shaking his staff —
'Young man of the crown,
If yer wants me come down,
For I'm not to be caught with such chaff.'

Of course you'd have thought,
The sly fox he'd have caught,
By lugging him out of the hole;
But this crusher no fear,
Quite scorned the idea,
Of burrowing the earth like a mole:
But wiser by half,
He put by his staff,
And as onwards he went sung he —
When a cove's down a drive,
Whether dead or alive,
He may stay there till doomsday for me.
— CHARLES THATCHER

no doubt sought some kind of official largesse as a result; and those who would see the hotel-keeper pay for his crime. However, Bentley had friends in high places. Magistrate John D'Ewes presided over the inquiry alongside resident gold commissioner for Ballarat Robert Rede and Captain Johnstone. D'Ewes badgered Johnstone until he was able to force a ruling and with the assistance of Commissioner Robert Rede, Bentley was acquitted on a vote of two to one.

When the inquest into Scobie's death returned an open verdict, the diggers were infuriated. Everyone was convinced that Bentley had been the cause of Scobie's death and they soon began to clamour for justice. Few, if any, of the diggers had any liking for Bentley, as it was well-known that he was in collusion with the police and his hotel supported by corrupt officials, the most obvious of these being his benefactor John D'Ewes. Most resented the apparent impunity for Bentley's actions that he enjoyed under this 'camp protection'. Bentley's arrest, and subsequent acquittal, was the spark that ignited the Eureka field.

The arrest of Gregorious
10 October 1854

While for most of the diggers the licence hunt was an annoying cross they had to bear — and at times they had some fun in deceiving the traps — they were incensed by the arrest in early October 1854 of Johann Gregorious, the Armenian servant of the Roman Catholic priest Reverend Father Smyth.

Thomas Arnot recalled the incident that inflamed the diggers and set them against the authorities in this report published in the *Ballarat Times* on 11 October 1854:

> On Tuesday last, the servant of Rev. Smith [sic] went to a neighbouring tent to visit a sick man; while inside, a savage trooper, foaming at the mouth like a mad dog, came galloping up to the

tent door and shouts out, as we have been informed, 'come out here you damned wretches, there's a good many like you on the diggings.' At this summons, the man with the other inmates came outside and stood before the savage and cowardly trooper: the latter asks the servant if 'he's got a license?' The servant, who is a native of Armenia, answers in imperfect English, that he is a servant to the priest: the trooper says 'damn you and the priest'.

The servant [who] is a disabled man, unable to walk over the diggings, but [says he] would go directly to the Camp if the trooper would take him there. This infuriates the monster; he strikes and knocks down the poor, disabled foreigner, drags him about, tears his shirt … Commissioner Johnson rides up. What does he do? Does he order the trooper under arrest! No, he commends him, and says to the crowd about him that he should not be interrupted in the discharge of his 'dooty!' [5]

A meeting was held in the Roman Catholic chapel on Bakery Hill following this incident, which condemned this and other actions by the troopers in their pursuit of the diggers over the possession, or not, of the licence. One digger, Irwin, confirmed Arnot's account in a letter to the *Geelong Advertiser* published on 23 October 1854. Irwin added that Gregorious had been visiting a sick man in the tent of a group of foreigners whose language that he knew. When trooper Lord ordered the 'damned wretches' to come out of the tent, his anger was fired by racist overtones, an attitude not lost on the large number of 'foreign' diggers on the Ballarat field.

The practice at the time was to secure those under arrest together and force them to follow the trooper's horse all day until the digger-hunt was complete. Sometimes those caught early in the day could face a march lasting several hours, in all weathers, across the pitted and rough country that was left of the goldfields terrain. When Gregorious offered to go straight to 'the Camp' he was not attempting to deny the trooper his arrest but was simply admitting that it was not possible for him to tramp all day behind the trooper. The disabled Gregorious offered himself up to 'the Camp' to avoid what for him would have been an impossible task.

Irwin wrote:

> As Gregory [sic] is not very strong-limbed, he requested to be allowed to go to the Camp himself, as he was not able to follow the force while visiting the various diggings looking for unlicensed miners… but on Gregory's appearing unwilling or unable to follow, the trooper ill-used him, and only let him off on Mr Smyth depositing £5 bail for his appearance. [6]

Gregorious duly appeared at the police office where he was then fined £5 for not having a licence, even though the regulations clearly stated that servants did not need one. As he left the police office he was called back in and the charge was withdrawn; however, he was then charged with assaulting the trooper instead. This was clearly a trumped-up charge as Irwin added: 'the trumpery story of a cripple assaulting an able-bodied mounted trooper is too ridiculous to warrant serious attention'. [7]

Gregorious was forced then to leave the original £5 bail in the hands of the officers. Throughout the whole affair Father Smyth received little courtesy from the police, and the diggers were once again led to the suspicion that the goldfields police were simply lining their own pockets at the diggers' expense — or that of any one else they could squeeze a pound note from.

As a large number of the diggers were Irish, and Roman Catholic, they no doubt saw the treatment meted out to Gregorious as an insult to their priest, an insult therefore to their faith, and ultimately to their Irish national heritage and aspirations. The trooper who uttered the phrase 'damn you and the priest' might as well have struck the match that set Eureka ablaze himself when he offered such an insult.

While events on the Ballarat diggings were stirring up a real hornet's nest, the 'Ballarat Reform League' was forged into being following the anger that continued unabated after Scobie's death — and Bentley's release.

In Bendigo, the diggings were much more peaceful. On 14 October another mass meeting was called where resolutions were again passed to continue to press the government for reform. The 'Goldfields Reform League' was formed at this meeting to represent the diggers in a united organisation across all the diggings.

14 October 1854

Not everyone was enamoured of the diggers' cause or their actions. There were plenty of others who supported 'the Camp' in its attempt to keep control of the diggings. The uncertainty that pervaded the diggings after Scobie's death, and the continued agitation for an investigation into the affair, prompted local businessmen to place the following notice in the *Ballarat Times* on 14 October:

> To James F. Bentley Esq. Proprietor of the Eureka Hotel.
> The Undersigned Storekeepers, Diggers, and Inhabitants of Ballarat, duly appreciating the conduct and manner you have evinced in carrying on the Eureka hotel, and feeling that you could not either directly or indirectly, in the late lamentable occurrence have been in any way accessary; hasten to express the pleasure and gratification we feel at the judicial termination of the investigation of that unfortunate affair, and we are assured that your urbanity and manly behaviour will still continue to guarantee to so well a conducted a house, its full share of public patronage.

A long list followed in the columns of the *Ballarat Times*, signed by a large number of the aforesaid storekeepers and diggers who wished to see and be seen, in their efforts to keep at arm's length from the dispute.

Just prior to the attack on the Stockade, the rebels would scour the stores commandeering food and provisions for what they considered could be a long time in the Stockade under siege, and without the opportunity to replenish. The merchants were left quite terrified of what was about to take place, and quite terrified of their future if the insurgents won the day.

The Ballarat bank robbery
14 October 1854

Just to add further fuel to the fire already smouldering on the diggings, four men dressed as diggers, wearing sou'wester hats, faces covered with crepe, walked into the Bank of Victoria on Bakery Hill (the timber-framed building was known locally as the 'Iron-Pot' as it was constructed of galvanised iron) and walked away with notes and gold to the value of £15,000.

Just as a notice was being placarded across the diggings offering:

> '£500 REWARD for the discovery, apprehension and conviction of the murderer of James Scobie'

a similar notice went up which read:

> £500 REWARD increased by Government to £1,600!! for the apprehension and conviction of the robbers of the Bank of Victoria.'

Four Van Demonians, John Bolton, Henry Garrett, Henry Marriott and Thomas Quinn, were responsible for the robbery, which they conducted with unloaded weapons as Quinn would not take part if there was to be any violence. After they had cleaned out the safe, they headed for an abandoned shaft near the gravel pits where they divvied up the loot. All were eventually caught.

Bolton was taken in mid-November, back in the same Ballarat Bank that he had robbed only four weeks earlier.

The fire at the Eureka Hotel
17 October 1854

The diggers were constantly demonstrating their ability to organise themselves along true democratic lines as they seemed to be ready to form committees at the drop of a hat.

Outside the Eureka Hotel, another committee was set up to press for the re-opening of proceedings against Bentley. This large gathering was convened by Ballarat Reform League leader Peter Lalor, who had had his claim on the Eureka Lead next to James Scobie. The meeting was held close by to Bentley's hotel, on the spot where Scobie was murdered. It had gathered to decide what to do about the acquittal of Bentley. After some spirited speeches had been made, a petition was read and adopted by the crowd.

This quite orderly meeting was about to draw to a close and the crowd ready to disperse when one digger, obviously eager for more direct action than just agreeing to petition the governor yet again, cried out, and reminded those gathered that they were standing on the very spot where the blood of one of their mates had been spilt. He went on to rail against 'the Camp', adding that 'the fountains of justice were tainted, while there was none to avenge the poor solitary gold-digger'.[8] The crowd joined in this digger's declamation of the law and soon joined together, taking up the cry 'Secure Bentley, and deliver him over to justice!'

Bentley had had a premonition of an attack on his hotel and had advised Commissioner Rede of his fears. As a precaution, he had removed all his valuables into the safe custody of 'the Camp'.

As the miners gathered at the spot where Scobie had died, the police and military formed a protective cordon around the building. Fearing an attack by the diggers Rede had stayed at 'the Camp'. Sub-Inspector Maurice Ximenes had taken the precaution of stationing a number of his policemen inside the hotel. Fearing for Bentley's safety, Ximenes offered him his horse and Bentley made his escape, galloping away from the rear of the hotel, disguised in women's clothes. Ximenes told Bentley to ride away in full view of the diggers in the hope that his departure from the scene would cool the temper of the crowd. However, Bentley foolishly headed straight for the protection of 'the Camp'.

When Bentley was noted riding flat-out for 'the Camp' the diggers were convinced of the complicity of the officials: Bentley, D'Ewes, Rede and all the others. A great roar went up from the crowd, and a cry for revenge was taken up as they surged towards the hotel. One of several young lads, who worked clearing tailings in the rich claims, who had followed their bosses to the meeting, got carried away in the excitement. He picked up a stone and threw it at a lamp hanging above the front door of the Eureka. His aim was just too good and he shattered the glass. At the sound of breaking glass, pandemonium broke out. The indignation that had been suppressed for so long spilled forth and the diggers joined in a new cry, 'Down with the house, burn it'. All of the windows of the hotel were smashed; the diggers swarmed through the doorways and leaped across the broken sashes as they prepared to pull the building apart. Grog, wine, spirits and beer bottles all smashed open as hundreds of pounds worth of the finest imported liquors were allowed to spill into the dust.

By this time Bentley had reached 'the Camp', informing the troopers that help was needed at the Eureka. Rede led reinforcements on a quick march down the Eureka lead. As they stepped out along Bakery Hill there was scarcely a man left on the gravel pits; all but those forgotten and left below, had rushed to witness the brawl. On his arrival at the hotel, Commissioner Rede leapt onto

FOLLOWING PAGES, 106-107:
Eureka Riot, 17 October 1854
Watercolour by Charles Doudiet

Canadian digger Charles Doudiet's drawing of the burning of the Eureka Hotel is the only eye-witness account of this fateful event. The destruction of the hotel put in train a sequence of events that led to the eventual storming of the Eureka Stockade just six weeks later.
(BALLARAT FINE ART GALLERY COLLECTION)

106

14

Eureka Riot
17th Oct...

one of the broken window sills in an attempt to reason with the mob; a rotten egg was hurled at him, followed by stones and bottles and bricks.

At about 2.30 or 3.00 o'clock in the afternoon, when the crowd had swollen to a number between 8–10,000, one man was seen strolling, quite coolly, to the rear of the building with an armful of paper and rags, where he set alight the bowling alley by thrusting the papers beneath the calico lining and striking a match.

All this was in full view of the troopers. Before long the buildings were ablaze.

A dark cloud passed over the scene, and just as the fire reached to the ridge-beam of the hotel, the heavens opened and rain fell just for a moment. Then the beam snapped in two and the building collapsed in on itself. There were few there on that day who were cooled by this momentary change in the weather. As the hotel burned to the ground, the commissioners and troopers who had been watching the meeting continued to be 'hooted, pelted and ridiculed'.

As the ruins of the hotel smouldered and the crowd dispersed, the police began to look for someone to blame. Affronted by this disgraceful destruction of private property, Hotham demanded that the ringleaders be brought to justice. On 21 October, Andrew MacIntyre and Thomas Fletcher were taken into custody.

On 26 October, several others were arrested: Manastra Flatow, Samuel Butler, Albert Hurd and Henry 'Yorkie' Westerby, who was inside the hotel and drunk at the time of the fire. Although Westerby was certainly not the ringleader by any stretch of the imagination, he had rather too eagerly joined in the excitement, ripping boards from the walls and smashing windows from their sills. At one stage, Westerby had staggered outside, slammed the wall of the hotel with his fist and cried out, 'I propose that this house belong to the

---

ABOVE:

Site of Bently's [sic] Hotel, Eureka, Ballaarat
Lithograph by S.T. Gill, published by James Blundell & Co., Melbourne, 1855

A comparison can be made with Doudiet's drawing on the previous pages. Here Gill shows the ruins of the Eureka Hotel surrounded by other buildings, Doudiet shows the burning Eureka Hotel standing alone. Gill drew this scene in 1855.
(LA TROBE PICTURE COLLECTION, STATE LIBRARY OF VICTORIA)

diggers.'[9] He then returned inside and fed the flames as quickly as the troopers tried to put them out.

Hurd claimed that he had helped the pregnant Mrs. Bentley to escape to a tent close by the rear of the hotel, but witnesses recall him crying out, 'Burn down the bloody murderer's house!'[10] as he ripped palings from the walls and threw burning rags into the building.

A meeting was held immediately after the arrests of those blamed for the riot, and it was resolved to head to 'the Camp' and liberate the prisoners by force if necessary. A committee was formed to co-ordinate their release, but by the time they all were brought together, bail bonds had been raised. The committee then proceeded to 'the Camp' to request that bail be granted.

The rest of the diggers had agreed to stay well clear of 'the Camp' but they gradually crept so close that an angry hum could clearly be heard from within the court. The magistrates feared that the bail application was just a ruse, and that the diggers were gathering to create a disturbance and release the prisoners by force.

Nevertheless, the men were released on bail, against Rede's furious protestation, and as they joined the throng of diggers along the main road back to their tents, revolvers were drawn and shots fired into the air. One poor fellow was seriously wounded when the digger he was walking next to failed to aim his gun above the crowd before his shot was discharged.

Andrew McIntyre's letter to his brother

The following letter was written by Andrew McIntyre, one of the three men convicted of the burning of the Eureka Hotel. His conviction was his reward for attempting to assist Rede, although Rede had assured him that he had recognised MacIntyre on the day of the riot as he attempted to assist the police in the recovery of property. At his trial, false evidence was given against him. The court was told by one of the troopers that when McIntyre had ripped the calico from the bowling alley roof, and threw it on the flames in an attempt to extinguish them, that he was actually attempting to fan the blaze. McIntyre wrote to his brother on his release from gaol, explaining the events of 17 October 1854:

29 March 1855, Bakery Hill
Dear Brother,

I have no doubt I may have got many cursings from you, and others, for not answering letter, now long past due and perhaps doubly cursed, when you learn the cause of them not being answered, to plead justification to you at the present time it is not my intention, but merely to make a statement of the facts of the case and then you may judge for yourself.

The general facts are now all over the world, and no doubt you will have learned them long ago, but still a few particulars as regards myself may not be altogether uninteresting to you. I don't think it necessary to enter into the details of the gross maladministration of the offices of the Colony generally, these are also are patent to the world, but as regards the Goldfields, and particularly Ballarat where I have had the best opportunity of judging I will say a few words.

From the construction of the Legislative Assembly of the Colony we have had the worst laws in the world palmed upon us, and from the same class still worst carried out. We had a lot of boys, half military, half school boys as magistrates, JPs (not all that inaccessible to tip) to carry out what were in themselves were; 'bad laws'. Such individuals had been Lords of Ballarat up to the time when I appear on the stage. 'Tip' was the ruling passion with the Ballarat camp officials from the highest to the lowest. The chief Magistrate of Ballarat had shares in nearly all the hotels on Ballarat, which he had for granting them licenses. But he was more particularly interested in Bentleys. In the Hotel has been committed a great many robberies and several people found dead near the place, all of which was somehow or other hushed up. Bentley himself was known to be a doubly convicted felon, although a great companion of the Commissioners in whose house they were nightly.

On the morning of 7th October last a Scotchman named James Scobie, from Arch Terarder, was murdered near the Hotel, and on the inquest it was discovered that Bentley was one of the murderers. He of course was examined at Ballarat and you can guess the result. The chief Magistrate D'Ewes presiding, with sufficient evidence to commit him for trial. He was discharged, and at the same time he left the Court without the slightest imputation on his conduct or blemish on his character.

This was considered by the people of Ballarat as a direct insult, and a meeting was called for, to be held on the 17th October, on the spot, where the man was murdered. I intended to have attended the meeting, but my mates would not go unless all the holes around about dropped work and went. They all agreed, but one or two, so it was knocked on the head. After dinner I went down the hole but found it was giving way. I came up to the top for timber to repair it. Just as I reached the top I heard a fearful noise, and went with the crowd towards Bentley's Hotel, about half a mile from my hole. It turned out that the cause of the shouting was Bentley flying off on one of the Commissioner's horses. I reached the Hotel when there was about 1,000 persons present [but] the meeting was over.

All the Military and Police were stationed around the Hotel to guard it. The Commissioners were up in one of the broken windows trying to pacify the people, telling them they had been diggers themselves, and they would see justice done to the diggers and a lot of other 'bosh'. I mounted one of the windows alongside the Commissioners, and was cried upon by the diggers to speak. I spoke for a few minutes against the conduct of the officials on Bentley's examination, but never said, nor never had any intention to advise them to take the law into their own hands.

In the confusion and noise, they may have misunderstood me, however before I got done bottles, stones, books and all sorts of missiles came flying at the commissioners heads. Resident Commissioner Rede then handed me his whip and requested me to try and get them to desist. The whip was his sceptre or Baton of Office. I did not believe at the time in destroying the property as Bentley had a good many creditors that must become sufferers. I tried to get them to desist from destroying the property, but in a minute a cry of fire was raised, and I went round with Mr. Rede. The fire had just been lighted and I drew down the lining from the Bowling Alley (paper and canvas) no water being handy, and threw it on the flames and trampled on it till I burnt myself, but failed in extinguishing the flames. I was expecting some of the Police or soldiers might say that I had been hastening on the flames, and came back and told Mr. Rede so, his answer was 'There's no danger, I can swear you have done your duty like a man', I assisted in saving property and guarding it when saved.

In half an hour the whole affair was in a heap of ashes (valued £7,000) Mr. Rede and captain carter and I had a nobbler of rum when it was all over and I was going off to my work. As I proceeded I was arrested by two sergeants of Police. They arrested me and said I would go, but wanted to see their Warrant for my Apprehension. They said they had none. Then I said 'I would be damned if I go till they got one'. The moment I said that the diggers round about rushed the police and shoved me away. I went home.

Next day I intimated to parties about the hole [discussed the events with other diggers near to his claim], my intention of proceeding to the camp, to see what they wanted with me. They volunteered to go with me in a body but I only took one, my mate, and went up and asked Mr. Rede if he remembered his words. He did not deny it. He and us went to Captain damage and he had nothing to say against me. Rede told me I might go. Saw the parties that arrested me but they said nothing. During the next two days there was reinforcements of troops arriving from Melbourne and on Friday night one of the detectives came to inform me as a friend to get out of the way as I was going to be arrested in the morning. I went home and went to bed in the expectation of being roused in the morning, in which I was not disappointed. About two in the morning we head them marching around the tent. I allowed them to remain there for two hours, then went out and asked them in to have a nobbler. There was 10 Detectives and the Sergeant Major of Police, but before we went in the diggings we were joined by three troops of Mounted Police (a fairish escort). All the Police and Soldiers had been under arms all night in case of a second rescue. I was brought up for examination at 9 o'clock and committed to take my trial in Geelong the following Thursday (this was on Saturday). As I was taken prisoner at 4 o'clock, few knew anything about it, but as the day advanced they collected, then held a meeting, where they agreed to go and demand Fletcher and I go out on bail, and if refused to have us out by force (they had previously refused bail for me).

The Committee then formed tried to prevent the crowd from approaching near the camp while the deputation was made out on bail, but they were so long that the crowd rushed up to the points of the bayonet and swords of the troops. There was about 7,000 diggers present, most of them armed. One Irish man had 6 six-barrelled revolvers in his belt, in all 36 shots. There was one man wounded, through the accidental discharge of a pistol. I was ultimately bailed out in £1,000 by parties whom I had never seen before.

When I came out the people wanted to carry me shoulder high and had a German Band there. I got them advised to desist such a demonstration. Amongst the first Committee was Frederick Vern (now Colonel Vern). You will recollect of me writing to you when he was a mate of mine of 'Lord God knows who' he was a witness to all my actions at the Hotel and as such he was subpoenaed to Geelong as well as captain Ross of whom I will speak afterwards.

We had benefits at the Theatre Assembly Rooms and in the interim and on Wednesday. Fletcher and I and 12 witnesses started for Geelong in the conveyances with silk flags (that were presented to us at starting) flying with the words on them 'Liberty and Justice for All'. On the Thursday we appeared at Geelong for trial, but they would not try us there but remanded us to appear at Melbourne on the 15th November. I had to find new securities, and I got a Jew in Geelong for one and Mr. Holyoake, a brother of George Jacobs as the other, who was also a witness in the case. We came back to Ballarat and had meetings where the diggers determined that we should not go off Ballarat and but for ourselves would have taken us prisoners and kept us themselves.

We however started for Melbourne on 13th November but were not tried till the 20th. It took from 10 in the morning till 9 at night to try us. I could have easily got out of it, but for the counsel taking too political a view of the matter, and pleading justification and not examining my principal witness. I had one of the Commissioners swear I was the most efficient man for saving the property that was there. The other would have cleared me of the matter, but the counsel just made a fool of him, so that I was brought in guilty — with a special recommendation to

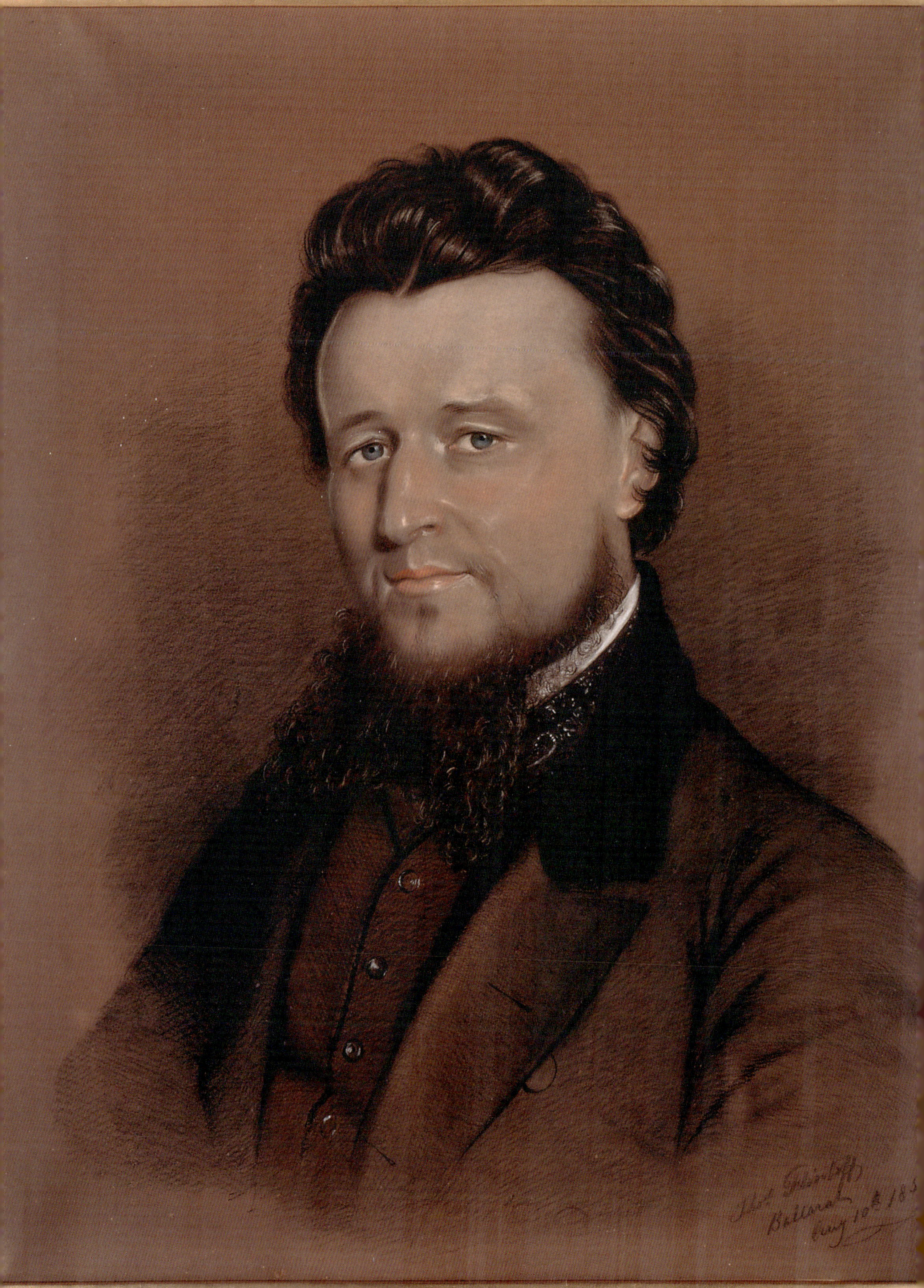

mercy on account of my praise-worthy conduct while the place was burning.

We were sentenced the following morning, me 3 months, Fletcher 4 months, Westerby 6 months imprisonment. The judge remarking that as he believed we were all men of good character he would not degrade us by giving us labour. When the news reached Ballarat that we had got sentenced they sent down a deputation to the Governor to 'demand' our release. The Governor would not accede to the word 'demand' (a very absurd word) so the deputation went back to Ballarat where a meeting was held on 29th November. Strong resolutions were put and carried and at the windup they made bonfires of their licenses and vowed they would take out no more. In the meantime the Governor sent all the policemen and soldiers in the country to Ballarat. The Marine-sailors and cannons were taken out of the men-of-war and dispatched also.

McIntyre's letter also contained the following information regarding the last licence hunt and the establishment of the Stockade:

> The day after the meeting they sent around troopers with drawn swords and soldiers with loaded muskets in skirmishing order to collect licenses. The diggers 'Joe'd' and threw bottles & stones at them when the troopers fired on them, one or two of the diggers that had firearms on them fired back on them. The diggers met again in the afternoon and agreed to arm themselves. They went around all the stores collecting firearms, etc., horses, saddles & bridles and retired to the Eureka and erected a stockade. Meanwhile they had barricaded all round the Government Camp, even the Gaol in Melbourne was all barricaded with sandbags and troopers guarding it.
>
> At first there was about 1,500 men of all arms in the insurgent mob, but by Saturday morn the most of them thinking nothing was going to be done, went home and in the evening there was not over 200 in the stockade, of course the Government spies reported how things stood at the camp so they dispatched about 500 mounted troopers & soldiers before daybreak on Sunday morning (3 decb). Few of the diggers were there, they showed the stuff they were made of.

22 October 1854

After Mass on Sunday 22 October the Catholics of Ballarat held a meeting in the chapel in protest of the treatment of their pastor and his servant. At this meeting they resolved that a grave insult had been made to Father Smyth at the hand of Commissioner Johnson in the manner of the treatment of Johann Gregorious — and the subsequent fine

OPPOSITE:
John Basson Humffray
Moral force advocate and diggers' leader.
Pastel drawing by Thomas Flintoff, 1859
(LA TROBE PICTURE COLLECTION, STATE LIBRARY OF VICTORIA)

John Basson Humffray

Humffray was born in Newton, Glamorganshire, Wales on 17 April 1824. He joined the rush to the Australian diggings, arriving in Ballarat in 1853.

Self-educated, and a gifted speaker, he was a natural leader of men. Humffray was filled with the Chartist zeal, but was not a fire-brand. He believed in 'moral force', that right would defeat might. This belief caused him to walk away from the diggers when the Stockade was proposed and he took no part in the battle. Yet, it should be acknowledged that he, as much as any 'physical force' proponent, did play his part in the insurgency.

Humffray was elected as Secretary of the Ballarat Reform League at the first big meeting on Bakery Hill on 11 November 1854, and with his guidance many of the demands of the league reflected the Chartists' manifesto.

The moral force followers had their headquarters in the Star Hotel, in Main Street, Ballarat East.

After the storming of the Stockade Humffray was elected parliamentary member in the Legislative Assembly for Grenville and served as the first Minister of Mines. He was also appointed to the Select Committee to examine the Ballarat Outbreak Petition.

Humffrays died in his home in Exeter street Ballarat on 18 March 1891, and is buried in the Ballaarat Old Cemetery near to the graves of the diggers who fell at the Stockade.

paid by Father Smyth of £5. The meeting appointed delegates to wait upon the bench for a review of the case against the poor disabled man.

On the same day another meeting was called on Bakery Hill. At around midday, groups of men began to assemble between 'the Camp' and the hill and slowly moved up towards the Bakery until more than 15,000 men had gathered.

The meeting was attended by representatives of the major newspapers. When the diggers noted the reporters among them, three cheers went up for the *Ballarat Times*, and three groans for the *Argus*, the once-popular paper that had ceased to promote the views of the common working man. Henry Holyoake, now back in Ballarat and taking a prominent role in the organization of the reform league, addressed the crowd and proposed that the meeting subscribe funds for the defence of McIntyre, Fletcher and Westerby.

Thomas Kennedy proposed the motion that the diggers protest against 'the daily violation of their personal liberty' and he condemned 'the manner in which the laws were enforced at Ballarat'.

John Basson Humffray then took the stage and proposed the resolution that:

> If the laws had been fully and impartially carried out, the burning down of Bentley's Hotel would not have occurred, and the entire responsibility rests with the Camp officials.[11]

Humffray also called a further investigation into Scobie's death, and demanded that all officials involved be removed from the Ballarat diggings.

At the end of the meeting, diggers were asked to subscribe to the defence of McIntyre, Fletcher and Westerby. Not everyone present was able to give at that time, so arrangements were made for donations to be lodged at stores across the diggings. Noting the emptiness of the coffers, Mr. Vern stepped up and withdrew £10 from his purse and offered it to the committee, as a loan, to get the ball rolling.

27 October 1854

Commissioner Rede had written to Colonial Secretary Foster, requesting that a military man be sent to Ballarat to take charge of the troops. He suggested that 'Captain Thomas, of the 40th Regiment, or some other officer of known capability' would be most suitable for the task.

Fearing an attack on his troops at 'the Camp' even before he left from Melbourne, Captain Thomas devised his plans for its defence. He proposed to stack bags of grain outside the surgeon's house and the officer's mess and hang tents between the chimneys as cover. All women and children were to be sent to the store for their safety. He also ordered that 'the utmost silence' be observed at all times, that no one was allowed to speak louder than a whisper. Eureka District Commissioner Amos had his horse stolen from its stable, leading Rede to believe that the Eureka mob were planning a cavalry attack.

28 October 1854

The *Ballarat Times* wrote this opinion on 28 October 1854:

> The corruption of every department connected with the government in Ballarat is become so notorious and so barefaced that public indignation is thoroughly aroused; and though the expression of public feeling be for a time in obeyance, on account of the numerous armed mercenaries lately sent up from town, the fire of indignation is not extinguished; it still smoulders, only to burst forth again with unabated and unbeatable vigour.
>
> The Government deceive themselves most egregiously if they suppose that the present display of armed force is sufficient to overawe the miners into passive submission to any measure they please to bring forward, to any law they please to enact, or to protect its corrupt officials from the just indignation of a suppressed people.

In the same issue of the paper, one reporter wrote of the number of diggers brought before the magistrates every day for being caught without a licence. He had covered the court proceedings for so long that he said he didn't even need to be present to estimate the number taken. He did, however, remark on the curious lack of any real criminal proceedings; there were no prosecutions for horse thieving or for burglary 'brought before the immaculate bench, although these are crimes notoriously prevalent'.

1 November 1854

At Ballarat, a meeting of 5,000 heard the Bendigo proposal of a league representing all the diggings, but the miners gathered there were more inclined to favour 'direct action'.

The diggers' leaders disagreed about the best means of bringing about reform. The 'moral force' advocates stood firm against the advocates of 'physical force'. While 'moral force' representation had prevailed for some time, the more robust, and politically motivated, diggers were getting restless. The 'physical force' men on Ballarat were itching for a fight and 'the Camp' there seemed ready to provide them with the opportunity.

11 November 1854

After a week of increasing 'digger hunts', the Ballarat Reform League had hardened its resolve. Delegates prepared to go to Melbourne and put the concerns of the Ballarat diggers before Hotham. Holyoake, again, addressed a large meeting of around 10,000 men gathered on the 11th (a seemingly fateful date in Australian history).

The following were adopted as the principles and objectives of the Ballarat Reform League:

1. That it is the inalienable right of every citizen to have a voice in making the laws he is called upon to obey — that taxation without representation is tyranny.

2. That, being as the people have been hitherto, unrepresented in the Legislative Council of the Colony of Victoria, they have been tyrannised over, and it becomes their duty as well as interest to resist, and if necessary to remove the irresponsible power which so tyrannises over them.

3. That this Colony has hitherto been governed by paid Officials, upon the false assumption that law is greater than justice because, forsooth, it was made by them and their friends, and admirably suits their selfish ends and narrow minded views. It is the object of the 'League' to place the power in the hands of responsible representatives of the people to frame wholesome laws and carry on an honest Government.

4. That it is not the wish of the 'League' to effect an immediate separation of this Colony from the parent country, if equal laws and equal rights are dealt out to the whole free community. But that if Queen Victoria continues to act upon the ill advice of the dishonest ministers and insists upon indirectly dictating obnoxious laws for the Colony.

This charter of the league set the pattern for every event that followed.

McIntyre, Fletcher and Westerby were sent to Melbourne for trial. In the meantime a commission of inquiry into the hotel fire handed in its report to the government just a day before another mass meeting was called in Ballarat. The meeting made the usual demands: abolition of the licence fee for diggers and storekeepers, dismissal of the goldfields commission, manhood suffrage, representative government, no property qualifications for parliamentary members and an entire raft of Chartist ideals. To this was added the demand that Hotham release the three prisoners.

As a sop to the diggers, Magistrate D'Ewes was dismissed by Colonial Secretary Foster. Bentley was re-arrested, sent to trial for the manslaughter of Scobie and on 20 November, along with his

THE GOVERNMENT CAMP, BALLARAT 1854.— TROOPS ARRIVING FROM MELBOURNE.

associates Farrell and Hance, was gaoled for three years — on the roads.

Even though they were defended in court by counsel briefed by Humffray, McIntyre, Fletcher and Westerby were convicted for inciting a riot resulting in the destruction of the hotel. Three days after Bentley was sentenced, McIntyre was sentenced to serve three months', Fletcher four months' and Westerby six months' imprisonment. The result of the case further inflamed the diggers on Ballarat. Judge Redmond Barry presided over all four trials, and when asked for leniency for the three rioters, with the extreme circumstances of the case to be considered in their favour, he simply answered 'No!'. However, in recognition of their previously good behaviour, he did not sentence them to hard labour.

The American, Albert Hurd, was released without any charge laid against him, even though there were plenty among the crowd that day who would attest to his part in the riot. For some odd reason, the Americans often seemed to escape the attention of the law. There were some who believed that they were in collusion with 'the campites' — after all, they did enjoy the same rough-house company of the Eureka Hotel.

The diggers met, once again, and agreed to send delegates John Humffray, Tom Kennedy and George Black to Melbourne to demand the release of the innocent men.

The troops dispatched
16 November 1854

In an attempt to bring quiet to his colony, Hotham established a Royal Commission into the troubles on the goldfields. In response to a brief report to the government that admitted that widespread

Above:
The Government Camp, Ballarat, 1854.
Troops arriving from Melbourne
Wood engraving by Alfred Clint, from a sketch drawn by S. D. S. Huyghe. Published in the Ballarat Star, 1870.
(BY PERMISSION, NATIONAL LIBRARY OF AUSTRALIA)

While Hotham was busy engaging in polite conversation with diggers' representatives Humffray, Black and Kennedy, he despatched all available troops in the colony to Ballarat. The troops arrived before the delegates could return with news of their petition.

This was not Governor Hotham's wisest move.

corruption emanated from the Ballarat camp, Hotham sent all available troops: a further 450 foot soldiers to the diggings.

Commissioner Rede (who had been humiliated by the destruction of Bentley's Hotel under his watch, and by the threat to 'the Camp' when the diggers forced bail for McIntyre, Fletcher and Westerby), was instructed 'to use force whenever legally called upon to do so, without regard to the consequences that might ensue'. This was all he needed to allow his revenge on the mass of diggers who had so insulted his honour.

On 20 November, Colonial Secretary Foster wrote to the military authorities, canvassing the possible deployment of troops:

> Recent events have pointed out to [Hotham] the uncertain temper of the vast population of the Gold Fields; no-one from day to day can tell when an outbreak may arise, and therefore it is necessary to have a sufficient force in hand to check a riot in the bud. The Lieutenant Governor is instructed to make the earliest possible arrangement to enable the Secretary of State to dispose of the 12th Regiment and it is upon these Volunteer Corps that he depends to guard the Cities if the 40th Regiment should suddenly be required elsewhere.[12]

Bakery Hill

A meeting was arranged to be held on 29 November, on Bakery Hill, to greet Humffray, Black and Kennedy on their return from Melbourne. Rumours had spread that the delegates had been arrested in Melbourne, although the exact opposite was the case. Humffray had been introduced to Hotham by John Fawkner M.L.C. when he met him on 23 November, ahead of the arrival of Black and Kennedy in Melbourne. Humffray had put his petition to Hotham and had been told that if a proper memorial were presented the release of the prisoners could be considered. Humffray

The Reform League

> There is something strange, and to the government of this country, something not quite comprehensible, in this League. For the first time in the southern hemisphere, a Reform League is to be inaugurated. There is something ominous in this; the word 'League,' in a time of such feverish excitement as the present, is big with immense purport. Indeed, it would ill become the Times to mince in matter of such weighty importance. This League is not more or less than the germ of Australian independence. The die is cast, and fate has stamped upon the movement its indelible signature. No power on earth can retrain the united might and headlong strides for freedom of the people of this country, and we are lost in amazement while contemplating the dazzling panorama of the Australian future. We salute the League and tender our hopes and prayers for its prosperity. The League has undertaken a mighty task, fit only for a great people — that of changing the dynasty of the country. The League does not exactly propose, nor adopt such a scheme, but we know what it means, the principles it would inculcate, and that eventually it will resolve itself into an Australian Congress.

Carboni reprinted this article from the *Ballarat Times* published 18 November 1854. However, Carboni added several sardonic annotations to the original: where the *Times* saluted the league, Carboni added 'but not the trio Vern, Kennedy [and] Humffray'; where they noted that the 'league had undertaken a mighty task', Carboni added 'the trio'll shirk it though'. At the end of his transcription Carboni sarcastically added: 'Great Works!! Vote for Humffray to be Auctioneer, Kennedy to be Bellman, Vern to be Runner of the "Starring League".'

It seems that Carboni had little time for these men who sought to make such changes, yet when the time came for Carboni to take his place, he stood beside Lalor against the authorities — but he always claimed that he was not in the Stockade at the time of battle. Carboni was an insurgent with pen and paper only.

thought that this would bind the whole affair in red tape and put any decision off well into the future.

After Black and Kennedy had joined Humffray, the three delegates had met with Ebenezeer Syme, proprietor of the *Argus,* and spent the best part of the Sunday discussing the state of affairs on the diggings.

Their interview with Hotham on 27 November did not go well. Colonial Secretary John Foster and Attorney General William Foster Stawell were at the meeting and were unmoved by the petition of the delegates. George Black, editor of the *Diggers' Advocate*, believed in 'moral force'— 'right would defeat might'— as did the moderate Welshman Humffray; he spoke cautiously but upset Hotham when he told him that the diggers were tired of petitions and had demanded the prisoners' release. Hotham, half-hoping that the delegates would resist, told them they would have to wait for the outcome of his Royal Commission. Thomas Kennedy, a Scottish Chartist who had little time for the polite manners of the moderates in the Ballarat Reform League, probably felt that he best represented the heated feelings of the diggers when he reminded Hotham that 'Sir Robert Peel did not think it beneath him to change his mind'. [13]

They may have had some success but for the word 'demand'. Hotham balked at the insolence of the diggers' representatives who assumed the power to make demands of him; after all, he was the duly appointed representative of Her Majesty the Queen in Victoria's colony and would not bend to any other man's orders.

Hotham felt pressed beyond his level of reasonable endurance when the delegates *demanded* the release of these 'three martyrs to British injustice'. He reacted angrily, and flatly refused to release the prisoners.

But while the representatives of the Ballarat Reform League had been discussing the niceties of English law with Hotham, he knew that he had already dispatched the forces who could bring an end to this game. A force of 247 military officers and armed men were already on their way to Ballarat.

28 November 1854

Before the delegates had returned from their meeting with Hotham, the troops of the 40th Regiment made a defiant entry onto the Ballarat diggings. At around 7.00 o'clock in the evening on Tuesday 28 November, they marched onto the Eureka diggings, their swords drawn and bayonets fixed at the ready, to be greeted with hoots and hollers, and cries of derision. The *Ballarat Times* was convinced that had the people who lined the route been armed that night, 'nothing could have saved a collision'. As it was, when those who gathered to jeer the approach of the 40th saw the detachment of the 12th arrive shortly after; with their arms, ammunition wagons and baggage-laden drays, they surged forward and demanded of the officer in charge if they had carried any heavy ordinance to Ballarat. The officer refused to talk to the mob; he only replied rather haughtily that he would have 'no communication with rebels'.

This remark angered the crowd who, taking up the well-worn cry of 'Joe! Joe!', rushed at him. He dug in his heels and galloped away as fast as he could, leaving his men to look after themselves. Two of the carts were upturned, tipped into holes by the side of the road. The soldiers were pelted with stones and bottles, shots were fired and several of the soldiers received savage beatings. Although it was widely reported that John Egan, the drummer boy of the Regiment, was killed, it appears that he had only been shot in the leg and survived the attack. The *Geelong Advertiser* carried the report on 2 December that several of the men on the upturned cart had been badly beaten, and that 'Captain Young, who was a contractor for the conveyance of supplies from town ... was cruelly used as to render his life in imminent

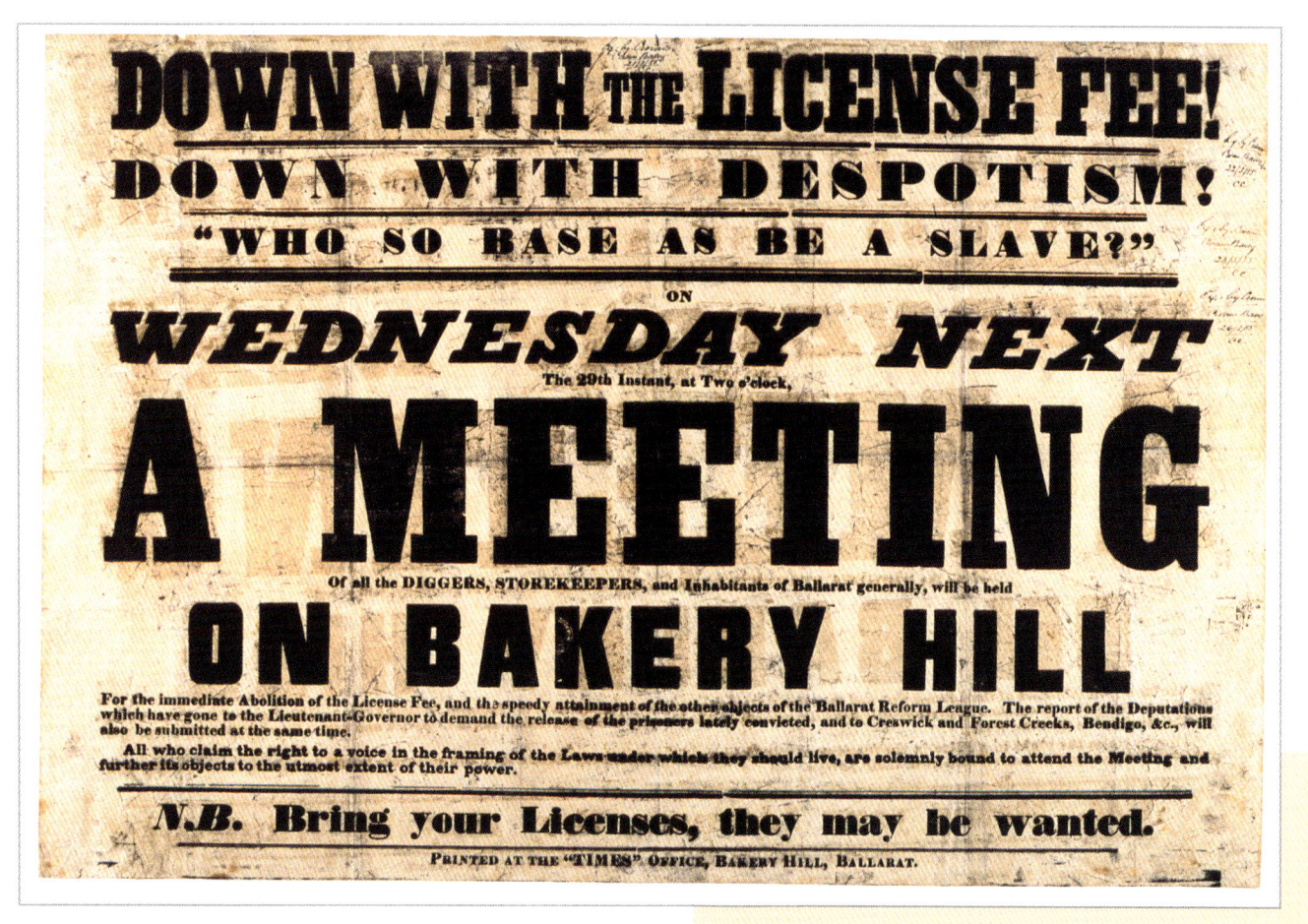

DOWN WITH THE LICENSE FEE!
DOWN WITH DESPOTISM!
"WHO SO BASE AS BE A SLAVE?"

ON

WEDNESDAY NEXT

The 29th Instant, at Two o'clock,

A MEETING

Of all the DIGGERS, STOREKEEPERS, and Inhabitants of Ballarat generally, will be held

ON BAKERY HILL

For the immediate Abolition of the License Fee, and the speedy attainment of the other objects of the Ballarat Reform League. The report of the Deputations which have gone to the Lieutenant-Governor to demand the release of the prisoners lately convicted, and to Creswick and Forest Creeks, Bendigo, &c., will also be submitted at the same time.

All who claim the right to a voice in the framing of the Laws under which they should live, are solemnly bound to attend the Meeting and further its objects to the utmost extent of their power.

N.B. Bring your Licenses, they may be wanted.

PRINTED AT THE "TIMES" OFFICE, BAKERY HILL, BALLARAT.

ABOVE:
Poster for a meeting on Bakery Hill. This poster was tendered as evidence for the prosecution of the 'digger-rebels' at the treason trials held before Judge Redmond Barry in 1855.
(PROV. 5527/P, UNIT 4. REPRODUCED WITH THE PERMISSION OF THE KEEPER OF PUBLIC RECORDS, PUBLIC RECORD OFFICE VICTORIA, AUSTRALIA © STATE OF VICTORIA)

danger … one soldier of XII … has died of a gun-shot wound.[14]

The troopers claimed that they did not fire a shot in this affray, but that when they loaded their carbines and stood their ground the mob soon dispersed. Rumours spread quickly to 'the Camp' that the drummer boy had been killed by an angry mob on the Eureka diggings. It was said that vengeance for Egan's alleged death was one of the contributing factors in the terrible retribution taken on the fallen diggers by the troops and the goldfields police after the fall of the Eureka Stockade on 3 December.

On the evening of 28 November, a banquet was given in honour of the American consul, Mr. Tarleton, who had visited Ballarat owing to the large number of his countrymen who were caught up in the affairs of the diggings. Although the banquet was to have been hosted by the Americans, there were large numbers of all nationalities present. While they were all enjoying a pleasant evening

Shot in the leg

Storekeeper Bendan Hassell was the first man to be wounded in the whole Eureka affair.

Hassell had been standing in the doorway of the London Hotel, in which he was a partner, when the 12th Regiment entered the diggings. He claimed that one of the mounted officers stopped at his door and asked him for directions to the government camp. He was caught up in the riot that followed as the diggers that had gathered to watch the troops enter the diggings began pelting them with missiles. Shots were fired, from both sides, and Hassell was hit in the shin with a stray bullet.

Although Hassell could not say positively who had fired the shot, he petitioned the government for compensation, claiming that as he was assisting the troops when he was wounded, his wound was their responsibility.

A board of enquiry would not compensate Hassell, claiming that it was not possible for him to have been struck by a government bullet as they had not fired a shot in the affray; in fact, they had marched onto the diggings with arms unloaded.

In an operation two years later, some shattered bone, and the bullet, were removed from Hassell's shin. He estimated his medical and nursing expenses to have been around £100.

BELOW:
Father Patrick Smyth (top left) is seen here with a group of brother-priests on the South Australian diggings.
(BY PERMISSION, STATE LIBRARY OF SOUTH AUSTRALIA)

together, troops had marched into Ballarat and had been attacked. Commissioner Rede, who was supposed to toast the consul Mr. Tarleton, left to attend to the affray as soon as he heard the news that lives had been lost in a riot on the road through the Eureka lead.

When it became time to toast the Queen, which was to have been Rede's pleasant and patriotic duty, not one man offered to raise his glass. An ugly silence fell across the room and for several minutes not one man responded. Eventually Dr. William Beauclerk Otway stood and offered that 'if no British subject would volunteer', he would. At length, *Geelong Advertiser* correspondent Samuel Irwin proposed the toast, stating quite pithily: 'While I and my fellow colonists claim to be and are thoroughly loyal to our sovereign lady the Queen, we do not and will not respect her men servants, her maid servants, her oxen or her *asses*.'[15]

The emphasis Irwin placed on the last word almost brought the house down.

The 'monster meeting'
29 November 1854, Ballarat

More than 10,000 attended the 'monster meeting' held at Bakery Hill to receive the delegates back to Ballarat. Humffray disappointed the crowd with his call for peaceful resistance, in which he was supported by Victoria's Catholic Bishop Goold, Father Dowling and Ballarat's Father Smyth, who had joined him in an attempt to dampen the desire for physical force among the diggers. A great many of the diggers of the league were angered that Humffray, Black and Kennedy carried

Smyth's request to Hotham

Father Patrick Smyth wrote to Hotham on 30 November 1854 requesting a temporary suspension of the licence fee, in view of the troubles brewing on the Ballarat diggings.

> To His Excellency Sir Charles Hotham HCB and Governor General of Victoria
> Sir,
> I have the honour to address your Excellency, and most respectfully beg here to state what, in the opinion of many, is best calculated to allay our present excitement. The present emergency is a pressing one, and requires all the consideration and indulgence Your Excellency can extend us. Should Your Excellency so far favour us as to suspend the operation of the License Law here for some definite period — say till the coming Commission close their enquiries — I, at least, would feel certain of our being more than partially restored to law and order. May I assure Your Excellency that my only motive for being so bold, is my concern for those who are entrusted to my care.
> I have the honour to be
> Your Excellency's Very humble and obedient servant
> Patrick Smyth
> Catholic Priest

Hotham replied in a polite letter on 1 December advising Father Smyth that the law must be upheld.

the resolutions agreed by the league, and in presenting them to the governor had failed to press their demands firmly enough.

This meeting was divided between the moderates and the activists; the vocal activists were the most successful in getting their opinions across. Humffray stepped back from the protest, knowing that he could no longer influence an angry mob, as the diggers decided that they would show their licences on request no longer. In what should have been the perfect combination of direct action and passive resistance, they agreed, by not showing their licences, to press the police to arrest them all, and then go peacefully to 'the Camp'. This would force the government to cave in through the sheer weight of numbers to be tried.

The 'red Republican' German, Frederick Vern, went one step further and proposed a motion that really set the cat among the pigeons:

> That this meeting, being convinced that the obnoxious license fee is an imposition and an unjustifiable tax on free labour, pledges itself to take immediate steps to abolish the same by at once burning all their licenses; that in the event of any party being arrested for having no license, that the united people will, under all circumstances, defend and protect them. [16]

A bonfire was set by Frederick Vern, but it is not known how many actually cast a licence worth 30/- onto the blaze.

This meeting, chaired by Timothy Hayes, was also addressed publicly for the first time by Peter Lalor, who moved that the league meet on the following Sunday to elect a committee.

The last licence hunt
30 November 1854

Rede decided to press the diggers into submission and ordered a provocative licence hunt designed to show the diggers who was in charge. The diggers, who had resolved the day before not to show their licences, turned out in their hundreds ready to bait the troops. They pelted them with stones and hooted and abused them. Fights broke out, shots were fired over the heads of the diggers, and shots were fired in return.

Just before noon, Rede rode onto the gravel pits and demanded that diggers show their licences. Lalor was in his shaft with Timothy Hayes at the windlass when he heard that the traps were firing on the diggers at the gravel pits. He rushed to the scene. When Rede saw the Eureka mob running towards him, he quickly read the Riot Act and called for reinforcements.

As Rede rode towards Humffray, he shouted out, but his voice was almost carried away by the hot northerly wind that blustered and blew about the diggings that day. 'See now the consequences of your agitation,' he called, to which Humffray replied, 'No, but see the consequences of impolitic coercion.' Dust swirled in the air as several diggers who were arrested that day (Benjamin Ewins, George Goddart, Duncan MacIntyre, Donald McLeod, William Bryan, Donald Campbell and John Chapman) were taken into custody and marched to 'the Camp'.

After the fracas at the gravel pits, a second meeting was called that day on Bakery Hill. As if by some unheard signal, diggers began to gather on the hill. Seemingly moderate Peter Lalor had never pushed himself forward, he had never assumed a prominent role in the affairs of the Ballarat Reform League, but on this day, in the absence of any other of the leaders of the league, Lalor stepped up to take control of the growing and agitated crowd who had gathered again on Bakery Hill.

With his pistol raised in his hand, Lalor leapt onto a tree stump, looked about him, and decided that his time had come. He proclaimed the diggers' oath: 'We swear by the Southern Cross to stand truly by each other, and defend our rights and our liberties.' All the men before him knelt and swore their allegiance to the brilliant azure-

FOLLOWING PAGES, 122-23:
Swearing Allegiance to the 'Southern Cross'
Watercolour by Charles Doudiet
(BALLARAT FINE ART GALLERY COLLECTION)

December 1st 1854

XIX

Swearing allegiance to the "Southern Cross"

PETER LALOR.

OPPOSITE:
Peter Lalor
Lithograph by Ludwig Becker, 1856
(REX NAN KIVELL COLLECTION NK1398, NATIONAL LIBRARY OF AUSTRALIA)

---

blue flag that fluttered in the breeze 24 metres in the air above them. The Southern Cross flew for the first time above the Eureka field on 30 November 1854.

Lalor recalled that glorious moment in his deposition to the inquiry held in the aftermath of the battle. He said:

> I looked around me; I saw brave and honest men, who had come thousands of miles to labour for independence. I knew that hundreds were in great poverty, who would possess wealth and happiness if allowed to cultivate the wilderness that surrounded us. The grievances under which we had long suffered, and the brutal attack of the day, flashed across my mind; and with the burning feelings of an injured man, I mounted the stump and proclaimed 'Liberty'.
>
> I called for volunteers to come forward and enrol themselves in companies. Hundreds responded to the call ... I then called to the volunteers to kneel down. They did so, and with their heads uncovered, and hands raised to Heaven, they solemnly swore at all hazards to defend their rights and liberties.[17]

After the troops who watched this impressive ceremony had departed for 'the Camp', a meeting of the league was held in the Star Hotel and a letter written to the delegates, Black and Kennedy, who

Peter Lalor

Peter Lalor was born on 5 February 1827 at Tenakill, Leix County (Queen's), Ireland. He joined the rush to the diggings in 1851, but on arrival in the colony began working on the construction of the Melbourne–Geelong railway. He joined the rush to the Ovens in 1853 and then Ballarat in 1854.

Although he tried to leave 'old Ireland', and old battles, behind him as he made a new life on the Ballarat diggings, this seems to contrast with the recollection of digger William Craig, who travelled to Australia on the same ship as Lalor. Craig recalled that Lalor 'never tired of descanting upon the wrongs of Ireland' and that he was a 'strong believer in the use of physical force for redressing her wrongs'. Lalor told Craig that he intended to go into politics when he got to Australia and it seems that when he decided to put himself forward he had brought all of the old enmities along with him.

Lalor simply could not shake off his political background. Like so many other Irish nationals who mourned the loss of more than 1,000,000 of their countrymen in the famine of 1846–50, their aspirations dashed by the death of Dan O'Connell in the 1847, and dismayed at the defeat of the 'Young Ireland Movement' in the failed insurrection of 1848, Lalor simply brought his history with him. His father, once a member of the Irish House of Commons, had come to prominence in the 1830s when he organised farmers, armed with pikes and pitch-forks, to show defensive resistance against evicting landlords. His brother, James Fintan, had been prominent in the disastrous rout at the battle of Wexford in 1848 and, like his father, had fought to free the Irish from 'landlordism'. James Fintan Lalor had died in 1849.

After the acquittal of the Eureka rebels, Lalor was able to come out of hiding. He subsequently stood for parliament and was elected to the Legislative Assembly where he became Speaker of the House. He was also appointed Minister of the Railways.

On 10 July 1855, Lalor married Alicia Dunne, the Irish lass who sheltered and nursed him in Geelong after he had fled the wreckage of Eureka.

Lalor maintained an interest in mining affairs and was director of the Lothair Mining Company at Clunes. It appears, however, that the times had changed for Lalor when he provoked a strike that lasted 14 weeks by refusing to accede to the request of his workers that they be allowed more than a single day off each week. Lalor responded by bringing cheap Chinese labour in from Ballarat. On 9 December 1873, the miners barricaded the Ballarat and Clunes roads and pelted the Chinese with stones and bricks in a scene reminiscent of the entry of the 40th Regiment to the Eureka lead twenty years earlier.

'Who strikes the first blow for Ireland? Who draws first blood for Ireland? Who wins a wreath that will be green for ever?' — written by Fintan Lalor

Administering the Oath, Eureka Stockade, 1854

had gone to the diggings at nearby Creswick earlier that day, advising them of the events at Bakery Hill. This letter from the league was addressed to Black and Kennedy by name, or to 'any MAN on Creswick' just in case they had already left. George Black read the letter out loud to a large gathering of Creswick miners who immediately offered their support to the cause.

The Stockade

'Moral Persuasion is all humbug. Nothing convinces like a lick in the lug'.
— THOMAS KENNEDY'S FAVOURITE SAYING.

30 November 1854

The diggers had marched from Bakery Hill behind Captain Ross and his flag and gathered together on the Eureka diggings where they began to construct a crude stockade of loosely packed logs driven into the ground, upturned carts and fallen trees. Pikes were sharpened, guns and ammunition sought and the men began drilling in 'military' fashion in preparation for military action. They had selected a piece of ground of about half a hectare, on a slight rise that was adjacent to the Melbourne Road just to the north of the Eureka lead. From there, the digger-rebels had a commanding view of the valley that stretched out between the Eureka diggings and 'the Camp', which sat on a rise less than a kilometre away to the east; however, this gave them no advantage at all at the time the troopers decided to attack.

In 'the Camp', Commissioner Rede rebuked league representatives, Black, Carboni and Father Smyth, who had been delegated to go and demand the release of their fellow-diggers taken the previous day in the licence hunt. In an outburst that surely indicated the true feelings of those decked out in gold braid, Rede snorted: 'The licence is a mere watchword of the day … a mere cloak to cover a democratic revolution.'

1 December 1854

At the Stockade, Lalor was in command. He gathered around him the most influential men from among the diggers, although only two of these men, Frederick Vern and Timothy Hayes, were prominent in the league.

There were now around 1,000 men inside the Stockade and they spent the day drilling, forming themselves into companies (some were formed on national lines to make communication among them easier) and setting about preparing their weapons and defences.

Carboni was appointed Lalor's aide-de-camp and interpreter, and was responsible for carrying orders to and bringing together the large number of foreigners in the Stockade. Captain Ross was made the standard-bearer, an appropriate task for him as he had been responsible for the design of the flag the night before and no doubt took a great pride in this work. Alfred Black, George's brother, was named 'Minister of War'. He wrote down the

ABOVE:
Diggers take the oath beneath the flag of the Southern Cross, 30 November 1854.
Wood engraving published 1 August 1888

The diggers formed a circle around the flag-pole, knelt in the dust, and with their hands on their hearts swore the diggers' oath: 'We swear by the Southern Cross to stand truly by each other, and defend our rights and our liberties'.
(LA TROBE PICTURE COLLECTION, STATE LIBRARY OF VICTORIA)

Raffaello Carboni
Italian-born, well educated and popular among the diggers, Carboni wrote his memoirs of his time on the Ballarat diggings, and published them in Italy in 1855. Although he had become a naturalised citizen of the Empire he never returned to Australia.

names of all the divisions as they formed under various captains; it is not known whether Alfred or George wrote the wordy diggers' 'Declaration of Independence'.

Carboni regarded Vern as 'vain, boasting, long-legged, [and] sky-blathering'. Lalor he admired as 'the earnest, well-meaning, no two-ways, non-John-Bullised Irishman'. He regarded Thomas Kennedy as 'the lion of the day ... [full] of the Chartist slang ... clever in spinning a yarn ... blathered with long phrases and bubbling with cant'. Carboni wrote that Kennedy took up the cause 'to hammer on the unfortunate death of his countryman Scobie, for the sake of "auld lang syne".'

Each of these men spent the next two days trying to pull the thousand or so men under their command into some sort of reasonable fighting order. There is no doubt that there was plenty of

Great Works!

Raffaello Carboni is possibly the most enigmatic of all the 'rebels' who took a stand on the Eureka digging, although his repeated rebuttal of the accusations made against him after the battle at the Stockade are a little disappointing. Carboni went to great lengths to disassociate himself from the other leaders of the insurgent force who gathered at the Stockade. Yet, it was he who stood alongside Lalor and Vern when all men were called to stand together beneath the Southern Cross for the first time, at the fateful meeting, on Bakery Hill on 30 November 1854.

Born in Urbino, Northern Italy, on 15 December 1817, this well-educated, opinionated gentleman, with fiery red-hair and a luxuriant beard to match, cut an impressive figure as he strode about the diggings. Everybody knew him and he gained the sobriquet 'Great Works' Carboni as he was so fond of that exclamation when any subject pleased, or, displeased him.

Able to speak English, German, French, Spanish and, of course, his native Italian, Carboni was invaluable to the leaders of the League in communicating with the large number of foreigners who joined them in the Stockade.

Although Carboni maintained that he was not in the Stockade at the time of the battle, and that he had witnessed the fight from a nearby vantage point, he was still arrested later that morning in the London Hotel where he was attending to the wounded. When he was taken into custody, he still had a current licence in his pocket. Carboni was one of those who didn't offer their licenses to the flames of Vern's bonfire on Bakery Hill. Carboni was insistent that he was not a 'Red Republican' but that it was the license fee that prompted his actions. He was incensed that a government could turn against its own people in their treatment and harassment of the diggers.

He soon joined the other insurgents in the 'logs' and was sent to trial in Melbourne for treason. After his acquittal he was elected to the Ballarat Local Court to adjudicate on mining matters.

Carboni was naturalised as an Australian citizen in Melbourne in July 1855 but left Australia six months later, returning to Italy where he joined with Garibaldi in the Italian Wars of Independence. He also wrote *The History of The Eureka Stockade* which was first published in Italy in 1855. Carboni never returned to Australia and died in Rome in 1875.

eagerness for a scrap among the men, but Lalor knew that they would have to be ready to take on the British Army, and he had seen what they could do in Ireland. Lalor wanted his men to be ready.

Foraging for munitions

Now elected commander-in-chief, Lalor sent parties of men out, all over the surrounding diggings, in the search for guns and ammunition. Not knowing how long they may be kept within the Stockade, they also sought provisions. Their attempts to demand supplies from storekeepers fuelled the resentment that the merchants had for the digger-rebels. While they were afraid that they may never be paid, they were even more afraid for business in the future if any prolonged period of instability upset the diggings. Lalor signed 'orders of war' to prevent the impounding of supplies being an excuse for robbery. He sent trusted men along with the parties to ensure that receipts were given to those who supplied provisions, guns and ammunition.

Withers quoted the following receipts as proof of Lalor's intentions:

Received from the Ballarat Store 1 Pistol, for the Comtee X. Hugh McCarty — Hurrah for the people.

And another:

The Reform League Comete — 4 Drenks, fouer chillings; 4 Pies for fower of thee neight watch patriots. — X. P. [18]

James Esmond, the discoverer of the goldfields at Clunes, was one of the more respected of Lalor's foragers and he kept his eye on the behaviour of his 'subordinates'. Some of the digger-rebels became high-handed as they strolled about in their new role as patriots; others may have thought how much they had quickly come to

ABOVE:

Gravelpits, Ballarat
Watercolour by Charles Doudiet

The gravel pits were on the Eureka lead. Raffaello Carboni and Peter Lalor were among those who had their claims there. In this watercolour painted by the Canadian Charles Doudiet, who had sailed to Australia on board the same vessel as diggers' leader Captain Ross in 1851, the Stars and Stripes flag of the United States can be seen flying above one of the tents.

These diggings were the most multi-cultural of them all. Just in these few men are representatives of a wide range of political inclinations and national allegiances — and even Doudiet may have shown more sympathy to the gallic, rather than the imperial, coloniser of his country.

(BALLARAT FINE ART GALLERY COLLECTION)

resemble the very class of men they were determined to defeat.

Men, some of whom were authorised and some not, went about collecting arms, ammunition and stores, with pistols in hand, and able-bodied men were forced into the stockade whether they liked it or not. As an instance of this kind of thing, one 'Flash Burke,' who was a subordinate officer, and a great blackguard, went about with a gang of other blackguards obtaining materials in the name of the stockaders. He wore a long cavalry sword, which dangled about his legs, and clanked upon the ground as he walked along. They met a couple of diggers, who by the way, were Englishmen, and demanded their presence in the Stockade. The reply was delivered with the flashing of a pistol under the marauder's nose. 'I have thrashed you before, Mr Burke, and if you are not off in double-quick time, I'll thrash you again.'[19]

Burke enquired of his defiant quarry: 'Is that you, Mr Hunter. I did not know you'. He then bid him a polite : 'Good evening.'[20]

While inside the Stockade the digger-rebels marched back and forth, others hammered yet another log into the perimeter of the Stockade, and pikeman Manning forged his scraps of steel into deadly weapons. At 'the Camp', preparations were being made for a siege. All of the main buildings were fortified. Stacks of firewood, trusses of hay, and bags of corn were stacked around the buildings, and the women and children were taken into the slab-walled store. Every man was at his post and sentinels stood watch at every vantage point. All horses remained saddled ready for action. Every trooper was armed.

Unfortunately for them, there was a violent thunderstorm that night and the mounted police spent the night soaked to the skin. By 4.00 o'clock the following morning, the entire garrison was under arms, ready.

As a precursor to the attack secretly planned for the following day, troopers swept out from 'the Camp' just after daybreak and rushed towards Bakery Hill, without encountering any resistance at all. All work had stopped on the diggings, every store was shut. A trooper coming up from Melbourne with despatches from the governor was fired at as he rode through the Eureka line. Spies among the diggers reported to 'the Camp' that the Stockade was being built and that the digger-rebels were drilling, preparing for a fight.

Rede reported to Hotham that the diggers in the Stockade were some of the 'most 'determined men and the greatest scoundrels in the Colony'. He described them, pejoratively, as one-third Swedes, French and Germans the rest Irish and Van Demonian. He later added that 'the future welfare of the Colony depends on the crushing of this movement in such a manner that it may act as a warning.'

Hotham also had the British secretary of state for the colonies, Earl Grey, constantly warning him of the possibility of revolution fired by the Californians on the diggings. While it is true that the California Brigade were influential in promoting dissent, they were not over-represented in the ensuing battle. 'The Camp' was convinced that the diggers of the Ballarat Reform League were planning to attack and overpower it. The police stayed on alert all night. In fact, the troopers stayed fully dressed in full uniform for almost a week, such was their fear that they were about to be attacked and their need to be ever-ready for action.

Arrival of the Creswick men

Marching to the strains of 'The Marseillaise' with Thomas Kennedy in the vanguard swinging his sword about his head, a large group of men headed for Ballarat taking a route straight across the hills. As they marched across the range they also were drenched by the thunderstorm; when they arrived at the Eureka Stockade the Creswick men

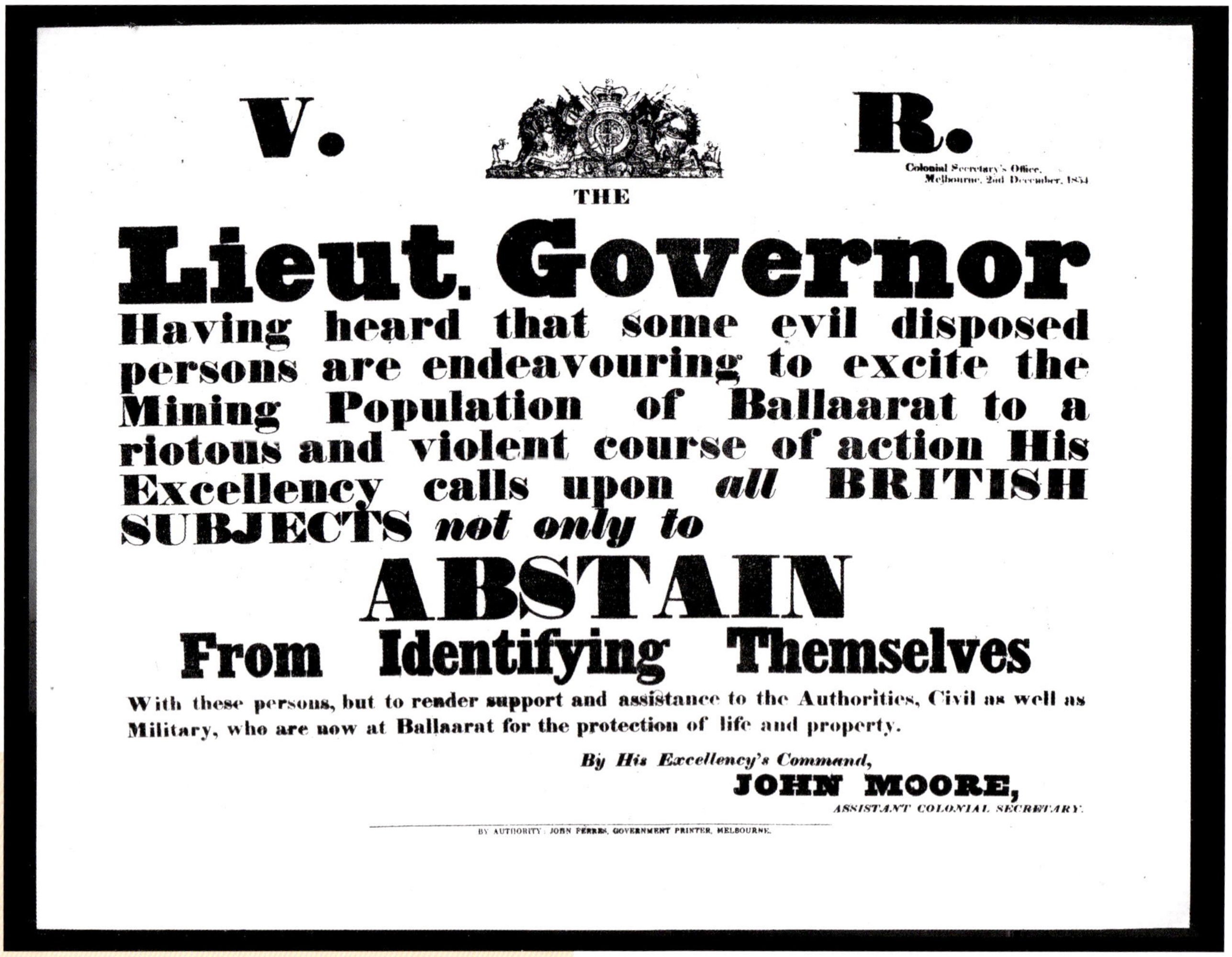

> **V. R.**
>
> Colonial Secretary's Office,
> Melbourne, 2nd December, 1854
>
> THE
> # Lieut. Governor
> Having heard that some evil disposed persons are endeavouring to excite the Mining Population of Ballaarat to a riotous and violent course of action His Excellency calls upon *all* BRITISH SUBJECTS *not only to*
> # ABSTAIN
> ## From Identifying Themselves
> With these persons, but to render support and assistance to the Authorities, Civil as well as Military, who are now at Ballaarat for the protection of life and property.
>
> By His Excellency's Command,
> **JOHN MOORE,**
> ASSISTANT COLONIAL SECRETARY.
>
> BY AUTHORITY: JOHN FERRES, GOVERNMENT PRINTER, MELBOURNE.

A profitable battle for some

The overall cost to the Treasury of the Colony of Victoria, of the Eureka affair, was in excess of £30,000.

Cobb & Co. were paid £840 to deliver 105 soldiers by wagon. G. F. Train & Co. supplied six wagons at a cost of £600. W. Smith charged £75/1/- for saddles and Mr McRae £5/19/- for whips; £60 was paid for sand-bags, and having them filled, for the defence of the Melbourne Gaol, while McEwan and Houston received £7/10/- for percussion caps.

The total amount spent on the military expedition was £19,871/-/10; on Police £230/18/-; a further £5,119/13/8 was spent conjointly and a further £1,512/6/- for contingencies.

Then there was the cost of compensation claims for damages to property by the military when they fired on the Stockade. Mrs. Diamond claimed £600 for the destruction of her store; Mrs. Bentley claimed £29,750 for the destruction of the Eureka Hotel.

There were a large number of claimants for loss of personal property and loss of livelihood due to injuries inflicted by the authorities.

were not happy at the poor accommodation and unsatisfactory repast offered to them; in fact most were disappointed at the lack of grog in the Stockade, so most of them turned around and went straight back the way they had come. Very few of the Creswick men stayed more than that Friday night.

2 December 1854

The Irish-American James McGill had ridden into the Stockade at about 4.00 o'clock in the afternoon bringing with him the support of the 200-strong 'Californian Rifle Brigade'. Due to McGill's military experience (he claimed to have trained at Westpoint), Lalor made him second-in command. When Lalor took his rest at midnight on 2 December, he handed command of the Stockade over to McGill. McGill set about and organised the sentry system at the Stockade.

ABOVE:
Poster placarded across the Ballarat diggings. Posters were about the only effective means of mass communication between the administration and the large body of itinerant diggers.

In this message, the governor is calling upon the patriotism of the British, to stand apart from the seditious 'foreigners' and firmly behind 'the Crown'.

Spies within the Stockade kept 'the Camp' abreast of all its activities. Lalor had no military experience himself and the Stockade was in a state of confusion. Everybody gave everybody else orders, nobody really responded to them. This should not be surprising. The men in the Stockade were young, fit and robust; most had spent the better part of the past few years at the hard labour of their own choosing without any need to take orders from any master. They were, for the most part, free for the first time in their lives. They were free, and just like any large group of young men thrown together, were ready for a fight — with anybody. Just as well that they had a suitable, and common enemy: 'the Camp'.

George Black, J. B. Humffray and Father Smyth came into the Stockade on Saturday to try one last time to persuade the digger-rebels to see some sense and return to their own tents. Smyth appealed to the large number of Catholics, in contrast to Hotham's belief the Stockade was by this time predominantly Irish, to lay down their arms and to join him at Mass the following morning. Humffray, Black and Smyth had heard rumours that the Stockaders were planning an assault on 'the Camp'. Lalor believed that he could rally 2,000 men and victory was likely to be his, but the moderates were successful in dissuading him from this treasonous path.

'The Camp' was, however, determined to show its force. Rede was convinced that the diggers would attack. He believed that his office represented the full power of the Crown and that 'to lose the Camp [would] be to lose the colony', so he decided to make the first move. He tried to shut the diggings down. The following notice appeared around the diggings on the day before the attack:

V.R. NOTICE.

No lights will be allowed to be kept burning in any tent within musket-shot of the line of sentries after 8 o'clock p.m. No discharge of firearms in the neighbourhood of the camp will be permitted for any person whatever.

The sentries have orders to fire upon any person offending against these rules.

By order. T, Bailey Richards, Lieut.
40th Regt., Garrison Adjutant.

The diggings shut down early for the night; even the lights of the Queen's Theatre were turned out and the performance cancelled that evening to comply with the new order. Diggers retired to their tents a little earlier than usual. At the Stockade, everything seemed peaceful; few of the digger-rebels believed that anything would happen on a Sunday, so most of them returned to their own tents outside the Stockade walls.

A lot of the men who had come into the Stockade, caught up in the excitement, eager for a bit of direct action, became disillusioned for the want of it and just slipped away into the night. Many of the Englishmen in the Stockade were not impressed that Lalor had chosen as password the name 'Vinegar Hill'. This appeared to place the Stockade clearly in sympathy with the cause of the Irish nationalism and had changed the intention of their rebellion. So, many of these men also slipped away as well.

On Saturday night 2 December 1854, there were only about 150 digger-rebels left inside the Stockade, and most of them had settled down for a Saturday evening nobbler, before retiring to bed.

Vinegar Hill

After the defeat of the English army by a body of armed peasants near Wexford, Ireland, in 1798, the military retaliated and routed the Irish insurgents at Vinegar Hill. The leaders were arrested, convicted, and transported to Van Diemen's Land.

The password 'Vinegar Hill' was first used at the aborted uprising of convicts in New South Wales in 1804. At the time Governor Hunter had complained to the authorities of the large number of 'United Irish' political prisoners, transported for seditious practices in Ireland.

The Castle Hill rioters had planned to overthrow their captors, march on to Sydney, seize ships in the harbour and make their escape. The leaders not among the fifteen killed in the riot were all hanged or flogged later.

3 December 1854

'… the stirring of the revolutionary spirit in Australia, and although the battle was lost Eureka became a symbol in the continuing battle for the people's rights.' — KARL MARX

'It was a revolution, small in size, but great politically; it was a strike for liberty, a struggle for principle, a stand against injustice and oppression.' — MARK TWAIN

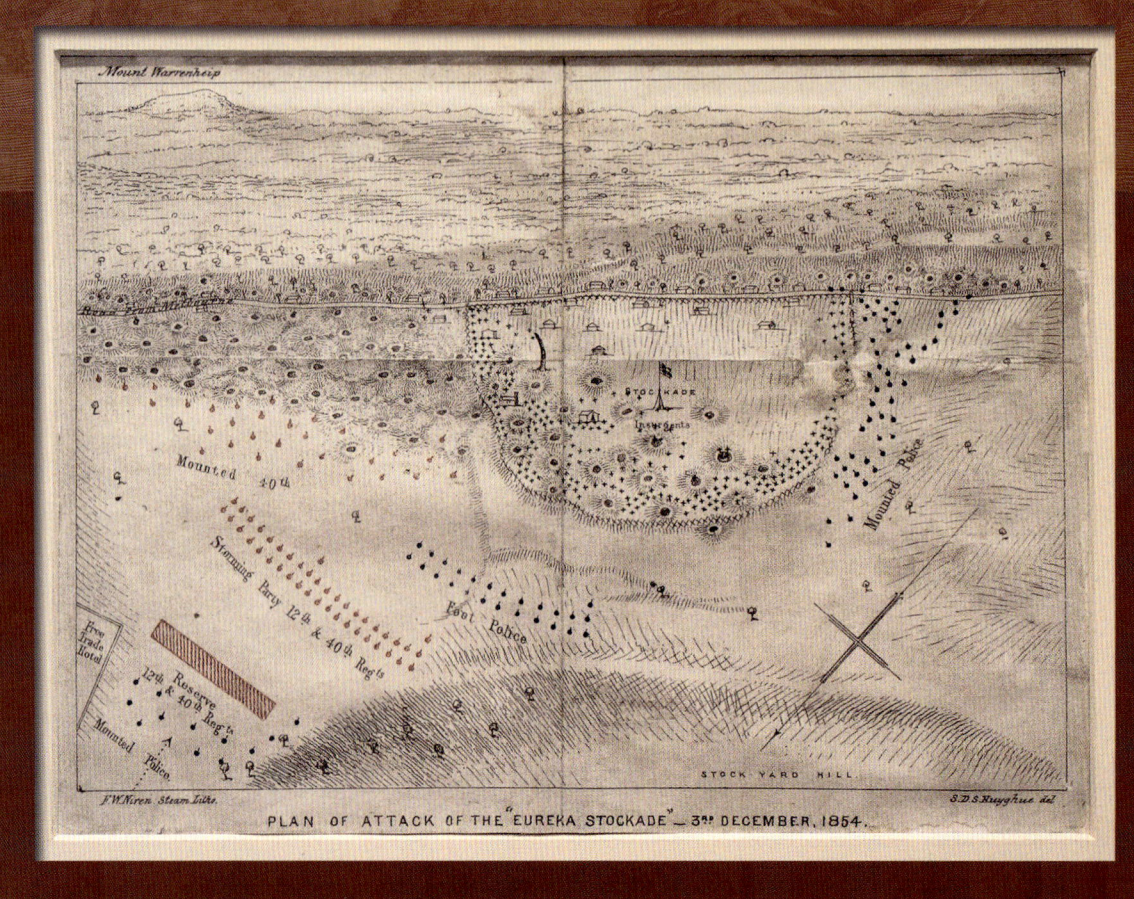

PLAN OF ATTACK OF THE "EUREKA STOCKADE" - 3RD DECEMBER, 1854.

The attack on the Stockade

'IN THIS WHOLE DISTRACTED SCENE there was one cool brain with a clear purpose in it. Captain Thomas was a capable soldier, who could form a plan, keep it hidden in the cells of his own brain till the moment for action came, and then carry it out with swift and unfaltering resolution. He had seen: an armed fort, with a strange flag, and men drilling for combat — built within cannon-shot of the spot where the Queen's flag flew'.[1]

Captain Thomas noted that an attack on the Stockade was the easiest possible solution to taking control of the diggings and re-establishing the rule of law. He knew that to try and re-establish control over thousands of diggers, and over the vast area of the scattered goldfields, was an impossible task. He believed that the Stockade had brought all of the dangerous elements together in one place. His greatest fear was that this place was within striking distance of 'the Camp'. Thomas decided to strike the Stockade first, but he waited to pick the right moment.

Captain Thomas and Commissioner Rede had placed two spies among the digger-rebels: one, Bristol-born *agent provocateur* Henry Goodenough, had been a detective in Ireland; the other, a Dane, Andrew Peters, who posed as a storekeeper. The pair mingled dressed in diggers' garb among the stockaders. They were able to convey the layout of the fortifications, its strengths and obvious weaknesses to Captain Thomas and Commissioner Rede. Most important of all, the intelligence that was relayed to Captain Thomas was that the numbers within the Stockade where unstable. Men were coming and going all the time. When they learned of a planned attack on Major Nickle, who was bringing up the remainder of the 12th and 40th from Melbourne, he decided that he must attack, and sooner rather than later.

Goodenough and Peters reported that most of the men were drifting away during the evening of 2 December, and that only a handful of the staunchest of the digger-rebels were bedded down within, never expecting any dramatic event to take place on the Sabbath. This was just the news that Captain Thomas was awaiting. He stayed his hand till night had covered the digging with its cloak of darkness. All of the lights in the town went out and, as ordered by the proclamation of the previous day, not a candle flickered in the tents on the surrounding hills. Even the glow from the great bonfires in the town and within the Stockade sank down into the night.

At 3.00 o'clock in the morning, Captain Thomas prepared his attack. He sent a whispered command to his men and, in the pre-dawn on the morning of 3 December 1854, the troops of the 12th and 40th regiments, bellies warmed by a tot of rum, marched silently from 'the Camp'.

There were several diggers camped beyond the Stockade fence who, having retired early, were

---

OPPOSITE, INSET:
A map of the Stockade drawn by Canadian artist Samuel D. Huyghe. Huyghe was chief clerk to the resident warden at the government camp. He was at 'the Camp' throughout the entire Eureka unrest and witnessed the battle. This drawing of the Stockade is believed to be the most accurate of them all.
(BALLARAT FINE ART GALLERY COLLECTION)

ABOVE:
Commissioner Robert Rede, 1815–1904
Rede trained as a doctor in London, but never practised. He took the post of resident gold commissioner on the Ballarat diggings in June 1854, stepping right into the heart of dissent. He left Ballarat in January 1855, only one month after the attack on the Stockade; a short posting with unforgettable consequences.

RIGHT:
Map of the Eureka Stockade used in the treason trials.
(PROV, 5527/P, UNIT 3. REPRODUCED WITH THE PERMISSION OF THE KEEPER OF PUBLIC RECORDS, PUBLIC RECORD OFFICE VICTORIA, AUSTRALIA © STATE OF VICTORIA)

---

woken early from their rest by the sound of troops stealing among the tents heading for the Stockade.

Captain Thomas sent the mounted police around to the east flank of the Stockade to threaten the rear. The mounted troopers of the 40th (to the west) and the foot soldiers of the 12th and the 40th were positioned in line with the front where the slope was the steepest. Thomas had figured that it was least likely to be defended at that slope, and that even if they were fired upon it was more likely that the stockaders would shoot into the dark over the heads of his men.

In the clear light of a full moon, the troops moved silently to their positions. They stopped about 300 metres short of the barricade and awaited their next command. At a whisper, they stole forward, until, within about 150 metres of the Stockade, a single shot rang out into the darkness, shattering the silence of the dawn.

Believing that it had come from within the Stockade, Captain Thomas ordered the bugler, who had stuck to his side throughout his advance, to sound the call to fire. Thomas barked his command: 'The Queen's troops have been fired upon. Fire!' There were many Stockade survivors who claimed that the first was a warning shot fired by Harry De Longville, one of their sentries, to wake them up, and was not fired at the troops at all. Others believed that it was fired by spies within the Stockade as a warning to the troops. Wherever the truth may lie, the single shot into the dark gave Captain Thomas the excuse he needed to open fire in reply.

John Dunlop, a 75-year-old soldier who had seen service in India, was woken by the bugle call and cried out to his mate, 'That [call] means extend to skirmishing order, the military are here'. They leapt from their beds and rushed to defend the

Skirmishing order

Once the bugler sounded the call to 'extend to skirmishing order', the troops were enabled to break ranks and attack at will.

At a time when military campaigns were usually well-planned in advance, and attacks, no matter how disastrous, were pursued like set play on a chess board, the skirmish attack was totally at random and men charged in any direction, firing at will, until the day was won — or the battle lost.

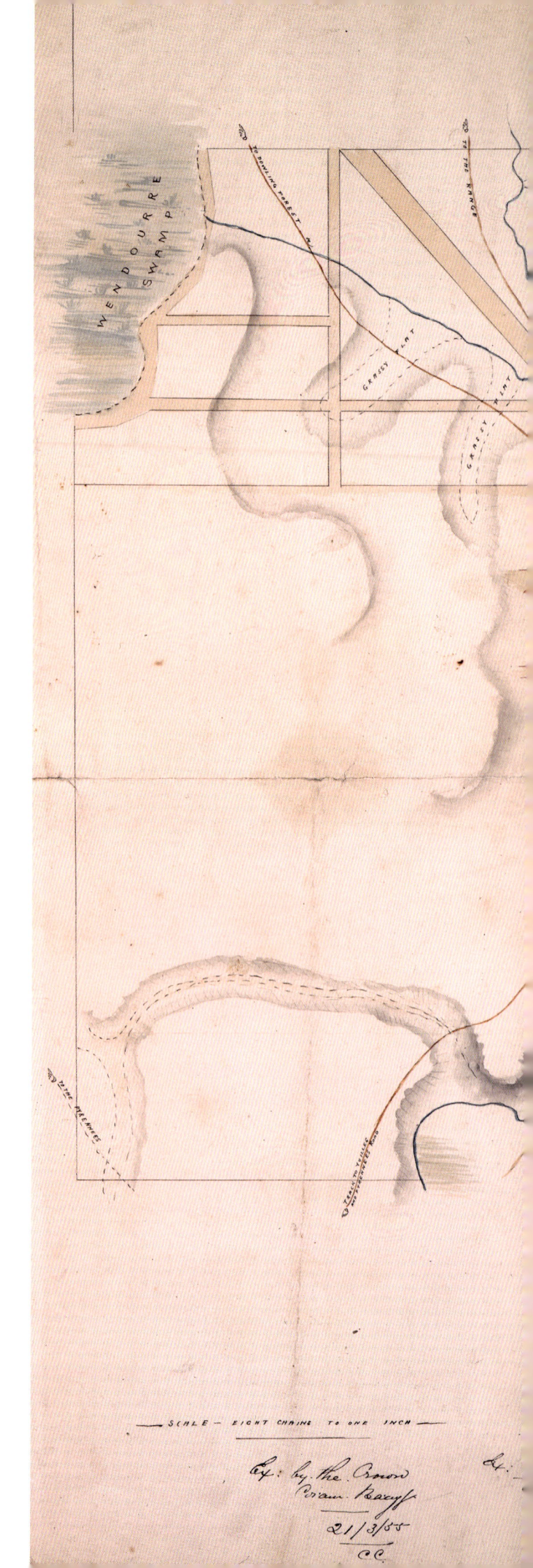

Map labels

- GRASSY PILOT
- BOOK HILL
- BLACK HILL DIGGINGS
- ROUTE OF THE TROOPS
- GRASSY FLAT
- POLICE STATION
- TENTS
- EUREKA STOCKADE
- MAIR STREET
- COMMISSIONER
- RT STREET
- ARMSTRONG ST
- LYDIARD ST
- ANA STREET
- YARROWEE RIVER
- NEW WATER CUT
- THE FLAT DIGGINGS
- WASH PIT
- THE MAIN DIGGINGS
- GREEN GULLEY
- Commissariat Tent
- LOCK-UP
- Commissariat Tent
- THE CAMP

Stockade detail (lower right)

- BROKEN GROUND DIGGERS HOLES
- FLAG
- STORES
- GUARD TENT
- POINT OF ATTACK

Annotations (lower centre)

Queen v. Beattie & Tushy
Ex by the Crown
Coram Barry J
23/3/55
CC

Ex by Crown
Coram Barry
26/3/55
CC

Crown
Barry J
18/55
CC

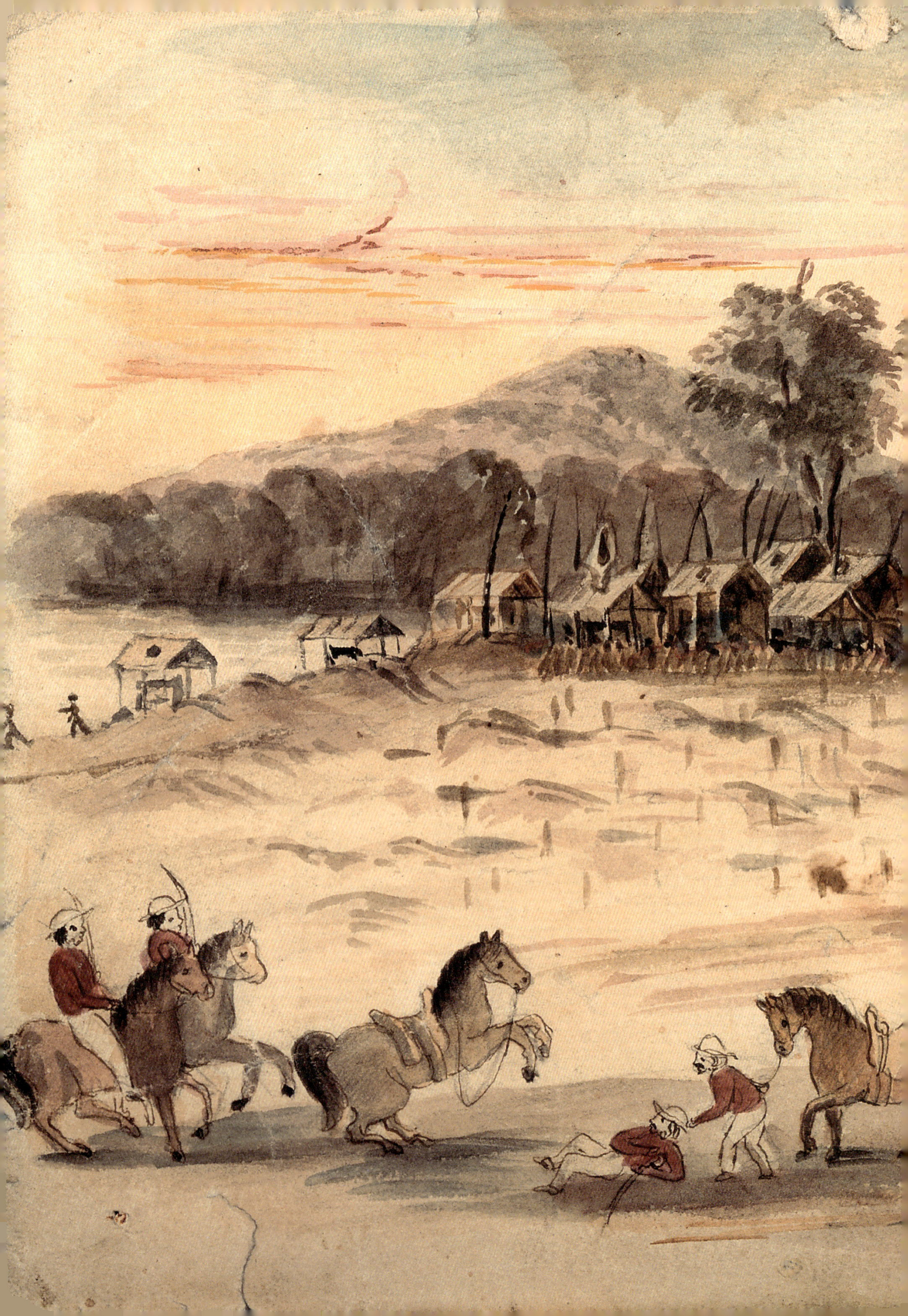

3 December 1854

Eureka Slaught[er]
3d. December

PRECEDING PAGES, 136-7:
The Eureka Slaughter, 3 December 1854
Watercolour by Charles Doudiet
(BALLARAT FINE ART GALLERY COLLECTION)

OPPOSITE:
A reward of £500 was offered for the capture of Frederick Vern, who had dashed to escape at the first sign of shooting.

The officials at 'the Camp' erroneously believed that Vern was 'commander-in-chief' of the rebels. This reward was underwritten by Colonel Edward Macarthur, the son of John and Elizabeth Macarthur, prominent New South Wales squatters.

---

barricade. On arrival, they were confronted by a line of musket fire lighting up the pre-dawn. The soldiers' fire formed an almost unbroken line of flame; their fixed bayonets glowed golden in reflection and the sporadic bursts of fire from within the Stockade suggested to the soldiers that they had the benefit of total surprise.

This may not have been the case at all. It is more likely that the 20 or so men who remained of the Independent Californian Ranger's Rifle Brigade (who had made rifle pits from the 'shepherd's' claims that littered the slope to the eastern front of the barricade) had a warning of the possible pre-dawn attack. The Canadian, Thomas Buddle, a school-mate of Captain Ross, had heard the approach of the troopers and mounted police. He rushed from his tent, which was quite near the Stockade, to warn Ross of the troops' movements. He advised his old friend to leave, suggesting to him that to resist would prove fatal. At least Buddle's intelligence meant that the men in the pits were warned; they were ready and waiting for the first sight of the troops. As they were scattered about in the pits, their fire may have seemed to the troops to be uncoordinated — as it probably was.

It was suggested that the bulk of the Californian Rangers had ridden out to intercept Major Nickle's 800-strong force as it advanced through the Warrenheip Forest; no doubt brandishing their Colt's revolvers and with their Mexican knives thrust defiantly in their belts. Whatever the reason, only about twenty of McGill's men were at their posts in the shepherd's holes when the troops attacked on the slope.

At the sound of the bugle, the troops abandoned their lines, and in skirmishing order surged forward. Several of the soldiers in the front line were hit by the fire that rained down from the Stockade. It was plain to the officer in charge of the foot soldiers that the men within the Stockade would have the best of the battle if it was to be confined to shooting, so he ordered a bayonet charge.

With a cry of '40th, follow me!' the red-coated troopers dashed for the barricade as Captain Wise led the charge forward. As Wise breached the barricade he received a vicious wound in his right thigh. He fought on bravely until he was struck again. A shot fired by Robert Burnette, Captain of the Californian Brigade, smashed into his elbow. One of Wise's men was gored by a pike thrust, straight through his gut, in the first moments of hand-to-hand fighting.

Lalor, woken by the first volley and the call of the bugle, leapt to his post and tried to rally the drowsy, half-drunken men who joined him. William Craig explained later that:

> When the alarm was first sounded Lalor made strenuous efforts to organise an effective line of defence, but it was labour in vain. Many of the miners had freely indulged in strong drink the previous night, and when they were hurriedly turned out at daylight in a semi-stupid condition, they failed to comprehend the orders that were issued, and utter confusion ensued on every side.[2]

LEFT:
Bugler of the 40th Regiment.
(COURTESY, A.K. MACDOUGALL)

FOLLOWING PAGES, 140-41:
The Storming of the Eureka Stockade, 3 December 1854
Watercolour by J.B. Henderson
(DIXSON GALLERIES, STATE LIBRARY OF NEW SOUTH WALES)

3 December 1854

V. R.

Colonial Secretary's Office,
Melbourne, 11th December, 1854.

£500
REWARD
FOR THE APPREHENSION
OF
Frederick Vern

WHEREAS

A Man known by the name of VERN, has unlawfully, rebelliously, and traitorously levied and arrayed Armed Men at Ballaarat, in the Colony of Victoria, with the view of making war against Our Sovereign Lady the QUEEN:

NOTICE IS HEREBY GIVEN

That whoever will give such information as may lead to the Apprehension of the said VERN, shall receive

A REWARD OF £500

being the Reward offered by SIR ROBERT NICKLE.

By His Excellency's Command,

JOHN FOSTER.

DESCRIPTION OF VERN.

Tall, about 5 feet 10½ inches, long light hair falling heavily on the side of his head, little whisker, a large flat face, eyes light grey or green and very wide asunder. Speaks with a strong foreign accent. A Hanoverian by birth, about 26 years of age.

BY AUTHORITY: JOHN FERRES, GOVERNMENT PRINTER, MELBOURNE

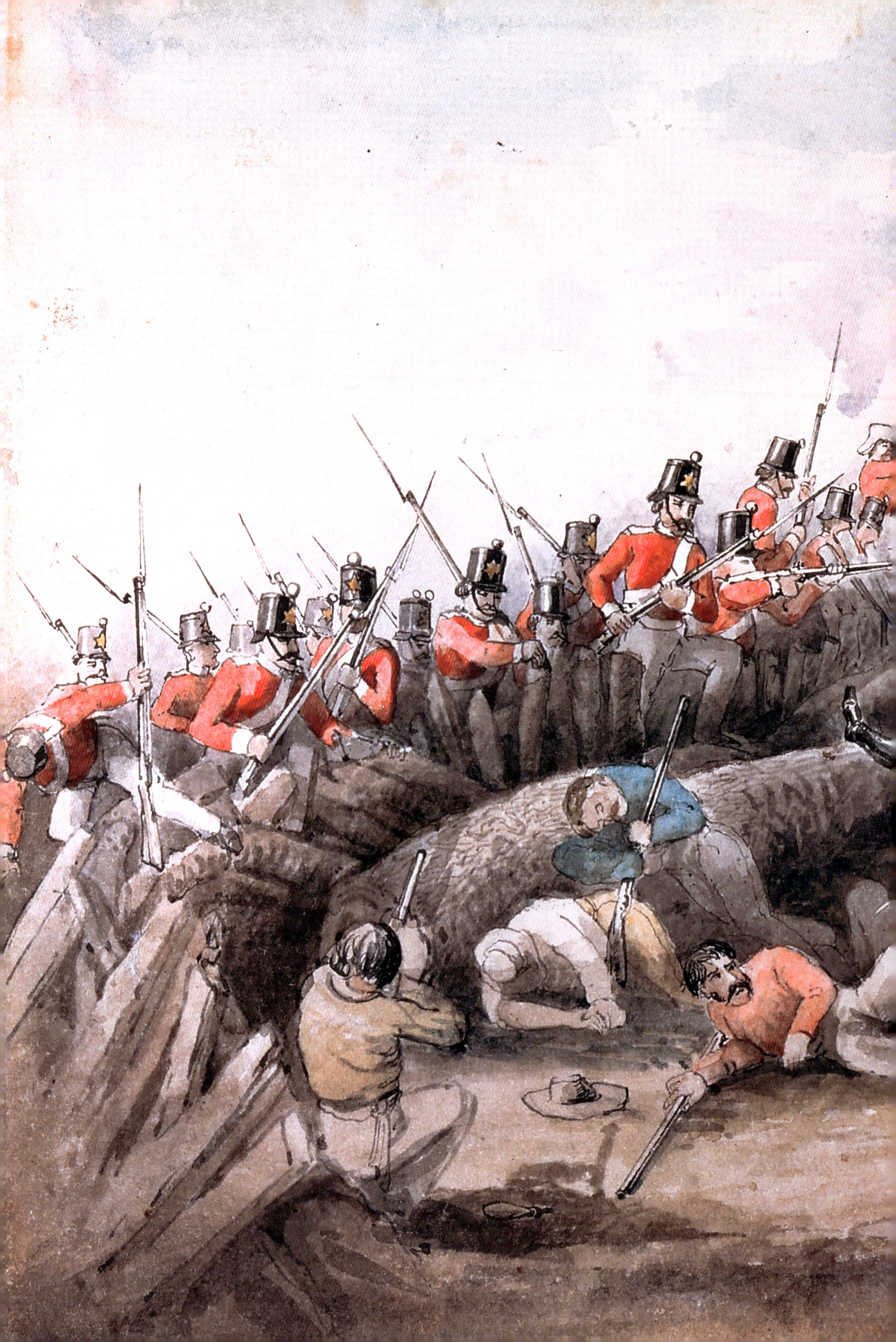

141

Carboni, who was sleeping in his own tent just beyond the Stockade, had woken sharply and rushed to watch the battle. He caught sight of the 'long-legged Vern' in the light of the still-burning Stockade fires, running as fast as his long legs could carry him to make his escape at the sound of the first volley. Where was Vern's promised German Brigade? Carboni thought he saw one of the Stockade captains urging one of his riflemen to cut him down, and to bring the Hanoverian to a halt, but then he lost sight of him.

Quite a number of the leaders, along with those men who had been perfectly at home parading through the streets the day before, levying tolls on storekeepers and foraging for supplies in the 'name of the Republic', were also nowhere to be found. Most had disappeared down shafts or up log chimneys as the first shots rang out. Carboni crawled up inside his own chimney to wait the battle out.

The only leaders of the insurgency who stood to fight were Commander-in-Chief Peter Lalor and his standard-bearer Captain Ross. Ross was soon felled by a shot to the groin as he stood his ground near the flag pole upon which still fluttered, proudly, his noble standard.

The American pikeman who never left Ross's side was himself felled as a shot ripped into his thigh.

The German blacksmith John Hafele, who had spent the previous day fashioning pikes, had the top of his skull sliced clean away when he tried to stick Lieutenant Richards of the 40th with one of the weapons he had made. His body was slashed with 16 or 17 sabre cuts.

Prussian-Jew Edward Thonen, the popular lemonade seller, blacksmith and master of the pikemen, had his jaw shot away and fell stone dead. A group of his men stood their ground until they too were cut down one by one.

ABOVE:
The Eureka Stockade
Photographic print hand-coloured by Beryl Ireland.
(LA TROBE PICTURE COLLECTION, STATE LIBRARY OF VICTORIA)

National Gallery School-trained artist Beryl Ireland painted over a photograph of this cyclorama of the battle of the Eureka Stockade which was originally exhibited in the 'Battle of Waterloo' building, in Fitzroy, around 1891. The original cyclorama, painted by Izett Watson and Thaddeus Welch, has long since disappeared.

Beryl Ireland was the niece of Richard Davies Ireland, the defendant for the Eureka rebels in 1855.

Lalor, still standing upon the barricade, taking aim with his pistol at the oncoming troops, was urging his men to stand against the ferocity of the military onslaught when he was hit by a musket-ball in the left shoulder. He dropped his gun and grasped his broken shoulder with his right hand. He then stooped to pick up his weapon and came down from the vantage point on top of a shaft. He did not fall, but ran towards his men telling them to 'get away, boys, as quickly as you can; the Stockade is taken'.[3] Lalor, weakened by the loss of blood and the shock of his wounds, slumped down upon a pile of pit-slabs. His men turned to urge him to escape, but he wouldn't leave his Stockade. Lalor would not leave his comrades lying, wounded, or worse, in the dust. Fearing for his safety at the hands of the troopers, fellow Irishman, John Dalton, Lancastrian James Ashburner and James Heffernan, helped to carry Lalor to a digger's hole outside the Stockade. They lowered him into the shallow shaft and secured some slabs over him. Lalor remained hidden until it was safe for him to escape later in the morning.

Michael Canny, a 19-year-old from County Clare, his brother Patrick and two friends, Teddy Moore and John Hynes, had positioned themselves behind a dray that had been turned over, its shafts in the air, when they saw Captain Wise fall. The lads watched in horrible fascination as two soldiers dragged him by the shoulders to safety behind a heap of mullock. Canny's mates, Moore and Hynes, were killed as they stood beside him. His brother was hit next, shot through the leg, Paddy collapsed to the ground, where he lay until the battle was over and he was taken prisoner. Michael was returning the troopers' fire with his own rifle (that he had brought with him into the Stockade) when he too was hit. A bullet went through his right arm, into his side and out again under his breastbone. Even though he had felt no pain Michael was so shocked when he saw blood spurt out from beneath his shirt that he dropped

A taste for Xenophobia

Men of all nationalities were targets for the troopers and goldfields police. The governor had often expressed his distaste of 'foreigners' in the colony and was fearful, almost to the point of paranoia, of the influence of political agitators with a republican bent. While this attitude is entirely understandable for an English military gentleman in the reign of Victoria, the young queen upon whose empire the sun never set, it was at odds with the rest of the world.

This attitude is also apparent in the opinion expressed by William Howitt, who travelled the Victorian goldfields in the early days. After the battle at the Stockade, Howitt added this footnote to his book *Land, Labour & Gold* which was printed in England in 1855:

> ... the foreigners were at the head of these disturbances. It was they who were foremost in the fray, and who were chiefly shot. This is as might be expected ... and marks the low, red-republican foreigners as a very bad element on the diggings — a class of men far below the lowest English in a knowledge of the principles of moral reform and progress, who have no ideas but of physical force, and the demolition of any existing authority. This class requires the closest attention of Government.[4]

Interestingly enough, the list of those who were killed or arrested at the Stockade show the facts do not agree with his opinion, unless the Irish were also considered to be *foreigners*.

It may have suited the authorities to believe that it was the foreigner who plotted against the Crown, but there were plenty of the Queen's loyal subjects who also saw the need to take their stand against despotism and corruption.

Hotham was to write to Grey after the battle, urging for a further grant from Britain for his secret service, for he believed that:

> ... secret societies everywhere exist, but I have to trust to myself alone for the means of counteracting them ... the French Red Republican, the German political metaphysician, the American Lone Star Member and the British Chartist here meet not to dig gold but to agitate, overturn the government and seize the Land.[5]

OPPOSITE:
A poster for the apprehension of Lawlor [sic] and Black — promising only £200 each for Lalor and Black, compared to £500 for Vern.

It says a lot for the way Vern pushed himself forward in the early days of the league, but was found wanting when the shooting started. The authorities genuinely believed that he was the ringleader.

The date of their alleged sedition coincides with the demands made on the governor, at the time of McIntyre, Fletcher and Westerby being sent to Melbourne for trial.

---

his rifle and took off as fast as he could, over the Stockade fence, flat out towards Pennyweight Flat where his tent stood.

Four other brothers from County Clare, John, Michael, Patrick and Thomas Callinan, fought together as well. Michael was hit by two bullets in his thigh, Patrick was bayonetted between the shoulder blades and cut beneath his left breast, Thomas was wounded but John remained unharmed.

Another Irishman, George Donaghey from Donegal, died of gunshot wounds.

A Londoner, Frederick Coxhead, was hit by a musket ball and dropped dead.

One pikeman, Thomas O'Neill from Kilkenny, had his two legs smashed and was sitting on his bloodied arse on the bare ground with a musket ball lodged deep in his chest, but was still wielding his pike around his head, when the troopers surged across the Stockade ground and finished him off.

Petersburg-born 20-year-old William Emmerman's short life was brought to an abrupt end when he died of gunshot wounds in the Ballarat dust.

The only Australian who died in the battle was Will Quinlan from Goulburn, New South Wales. Although he had nothing to do with the rebellion, storekeeper Martin Diamond was hit in the back as he tried to make his escape into the bush from the store he and his wife Anne kept which had been enclosed, half-in, half-out of the Stockade boundary. He stumbled and fell flat on his face. The troopers set fire to their tent then proceeded to hack at his lifeless body and stab his corpse with a bayonet. Diamond was cruelly murdered in front of his wife Anne.

William Burke, who had his tent about 250 metres from the Stockade, watched as one of the foot police, John King, in the first rush over the barricade make for the flagstaff. Under withering fire from the digger-rebels, he climbed the pole, snapping it in two when he was nearly 4.5 metres off the ground. The pole had been splintered earlier by musket fire. The Southern Cross was dragged from its hoist, and at the sight of this the soldiers let out a great 'Hurrah!' and the fight went out of the rebel heart. The flag was thrown from man to man, kicked and trampled in the dust and stabbed with bayonets, then King, an Irishman from Antrim, stooped down, picked up the flag, and tucked it beneath his tunic. The largest number of the digger-rebels had drawn back to a cluster of tents near the blacksmith's shop. As the troops began to set fire to the tents, the diggers abandoned the little safety afforded them and fought hand-to-hand in the open ground, pike against bayonet, pistol-to-pistol until they were done.

The fight had lasted less than half an hour.

When the shooting stopped, the acrid smell of gunpowder slowly dissipated into the fresh air of the Sabbath morn. Smoke wafted away to mingle, like early morning mist, in the green-grey leaves of the eucalypts. The sun then came up in a beautiful blue December sky.

RIGHT:
Storming the Eureka Stockade
From *Victoria and its Metropolis*, published 1888
(PRIVATE COLLECTION)

V. R.

Colonial Secretary's Office,
Melbourne, 18th December, 1854.

£400 REWARD

Whereas Two Persons of the Names of

Lawlor & Black,
LATE OF BALLAARAT,

Did on or about the 13th day of November last, at that place, use certain

TREASONABLE AND SEDITIOUS LANGUAGE,

And incite Men to take up Arms, with a view to make war against Our Sovereign Lady the QUEEN:

NOTICE IS HEREBY GIVEN

That a Reward of £200 will be paid to any person or persons giving such information as may lead to the Apprehension of either of the abovenamed parties.

DESCRIPTIONS.

LAWLOR.—Height 5 ft. 11 in., age 35, hair dark brown, whiskers dark brown and shaved under the chin, no moustache, long face, rather good looking, and is a well made man.

BLACK.—Height over 6 feet, straight figure, slight build, bright red hair worn in general rather long and brushed backwards, red and large whiskers, meeting under the chin, blue eyes, large thin nose, ruddy complexion, and rather small mouth.

By His Excellency's Command,

WILLIAM C. HAINES.

BY AUTHORITY: JOHN FERRES, GOVERNMENT PRINTER, MELBOURNE.

BELOW:
A portion of the flag flown by the miners at the Eureka Stockade. This snippet was given to Frank Riley by a caretaker at the Ballarat Art Gallery and sent on to Riley's father for safe-keeping in 1912.
(BY PERMISSION, NATIONAL LIBRARY OF AUSTRALIA)

Fourteen rebels lay dead from the battle. Only one trooper, Private Michael Roney of the 40th, lay among them, dead of a gun shot wound to the head. Fifteen others were seriously wounded. Eight men from the 12th and seven from the 40th Regiment, including Captain Wise, were carried from the battleground to 'the Camp'.

Nine-year-old James Campbell was one of the first to enter the Stockade after the battle had ceased. The young lad saw the dead bodies of the diggers lying about, their faces contorted in the pale grimace of death. He saw the wounded troopers as they tried to raise themselves to be carried from the scene. He saw the little pikeman's terrier dog sitting, howling, on the stilled chest of his beloved master. He saw the tents ablaze, the blood oozing from terrible wounds, running in crimson rivulets, mingling, clogging, in the dust — and he saw the flies.

Campbell watched in horror as the troops then went about their grisly business.

Taking their revenge

The troopers began to round up their prisoners.

The behaviour of the victors in this short, but bloody, battle was disgraceful. While they scoured the tents for the insurgents and roamed the nearby bush, they set to and burned any tent they wished. It is not known how many died after the battle; shot, or burnt to death, as they lay wounded inside

The Eureka Flag

The are a number of claimants to the original design of the flag, and it seems almost as many ideas about its design. Carboni described a flag (inset) that looks nothing like the one in Doudiet's watercolour (pages 122–23) — yet both were eyewitnesses to the event.

Most accounts, however, give credit to Canadian Captain Charles Ross, who was wounded in the battle and died the next day in the Star Hotel.

Ross apparently asked some diggers' wives to make the flag, based on drawings he did on a scrap of paper. There are also a number of accounts of the nature of the material used. Some say that bunting gained from a local tentmaker was used, and the most attractive suggestion was that it was made from the silken wedding dress of the woman who sewed it.

Another account suggests that at the meeting held in a tent the night before the 'monster meeting' that John Wilson, Inspector of Works for the Police Department, who was sympathetic to the diggers, stepped outside, looked up into the clear night sky and the idea struck him. He called out to Kennedy and exclaimed 'I've got it. Here's the idea … There. The Southern Cross, five white stars on a blue field.'

Wilson said that it was about 11 o'clock at night. Nevertheless, they went to the tent of a tarpaulin and flag-maker and created the flag there and then.

The flag displayed in the Ballarat Art Gallery today is, however, made of a very fine blue woollen fabric, with a high sheen, making it appear silk-like. Cotton twill was used for the cross and fine cotton lawn for the stars. The stitching is very fine and varies in style, suggesting that more than one person was involved in the sewing. This would corroborate the prevailing opinion that it was made by three women, including Anastasia Withers and Anne Duke, diggers' wives who were in the Stockade during the battle. The blue material is of a standard 'dress length', which would suggest that it was destined to be a petticoat.

It is a heartwarming thought that colonial Australia's only battle of insurrection was fought beneath a flag which, in happier times, could have been someone's underwear.

There was also the suggestion that the design was based on the old Canadian fleur-de-lys, which also had a blue ground; this idea could assist the bona-fides of the Ross design.

3 December 1854

tents fired by the troopers. While they did round up 127 prisoners to be taken under guard back to 'the Camp', there were many who suffered swift retribution and summary justice.

Benjamin Welch watched, horrified, as the mounted police set to and murdered a Welsh digger, 34-year-old Llewellyn Rowlands, near the Catholic chapel (where St. Alipius now stands). Rowlands had foolishly dashed down the slope to watch the fire-play when some prisoners broke away from their mounted escort. Rowlands chased the troopers for a short distance, but when he saw two coming up the slope towards him he turned and bolted for the cover of a nearby tent. He threw himself under the ropes just as one of the troopers called to him to surrender. 'No,' he replied, 'I'm going home. I had nothing to do with the fight. I've just come from my work'.

The trooper continued with his demands that Rowlands surrender, but he refused again. Angered by Rowland's persistent refusal, the trooper dismounted, walked up to Rowlands, levelled his pistol at his chest and shot him through the heart. The trooper then swung himself back up into his saddle and rode away.

Welch ran to where Rowland lay but the poor fellow was already dead. Welch searched Rowland's body and on opening his money pouch discovered his licence — current, and fully paid.

Dennis Dynan, from County Clare and recently arrived on the diggings, was caught as he rushed back to rescue some money left under a pillow in his brother's tent. A trooper had watched him as he entered the tent and ordered him outside. He refused. The trooper then ordered the tent to be set alight and Dennis decided that frying was not the best option. As he emerged from the tent, one trooper raised his pistol, cocked the trigger and took aim. Quick-thinking Dynan dropped to the ground as a musket-ball ripped into his shoulder.

ABOVE:
Catholic Church, Eureka, 6 August 1853
Pencil drawing on blue paper by Eugene von Guérard, 1853
Father Smyth had built this large tent-styled Catholic church on the rise between the Eureka diggings and Bakery Hill. St. Alipius stands on the same spot today.
(LA TROBE PICTURE LIBRARY, STATE LIBRARY OF VICTORIA)

RIGHT:
The Eureka Flag, 1854

This is the flag flown from the top of the 24-metre pole cut from Byle's swamp in the Bullarook forest and carried to the top of Bakery Hill ready for the monster meeting of Thursday 30 November 1854.

Inspector of Works John W. Wilson had been in the company of Lalor, Humffray, Kennedy and others the night before when the design for the flag was decided.

Wilson had command of a number of diggers who had been arrested for not having licences and he used these willing labourers to cut, carry and dress the pole which was erected for the great meeting ready to fly the flag for the first time.

The flag was then carried by Captain Ross as he led the men to the Eureka diggings to begin to build the Stockade.

There have been many attempts to discredit the claims to originality of this flag, but a snippet given to Mr. F. J. Riley by Mr. Oddie at the Ballarat Art Gallery in 1912 was matched with a scrap taken after the battle, and the pair proved to be of the same material.

In fact, when Riley requested a bit of the flag, he was shocked that the gallery keeper so readily cut a piece for him. Riley wrote to his father in 1912 saying:

> No one seems to value it [the flag] in the least, it is hung over a trestle affair — fully exposed to the public — well I got into a conversation with the caretaker of the gallery and persuaded him to give me a bit of the flag, and much to my surprise and astonishment he gave me a bit. I was with him when he tore it off.
>
> It seems wanton sacrilege, vandalism or something worse to tear it — still he did …

There could have been other flags made to the same design that could have been flown at the Stockade. John W. Wilson claimed that he had a copy of this design made by a tent-maker and had put it in his tent for safe-keeping the night before the battle.

Another digger also pulled a blue flag from beneath his shirt at the 'monster meeting' on Bakery Hill, but no one remembers it having any cross or stars on it. Most who did recall it said that it was similar to the flag that flew on the Catholic chapel.

This flag was presented for permanent loan to the Ballarat Art Gallery by Mrs. King, widow of trooper John King who climbed the pole and brought the flag to the ground.

Ownership of the flag was transferred to the gallery in 2002 by King's descendants, a fact that continues to rankle with the descendants of Peter Lalor, John Basson Humffray and Michael Canny, who have fought tooth and nail over it with the gallery for years.

(COURTESY BALLARAT FINE ART GALLERY)

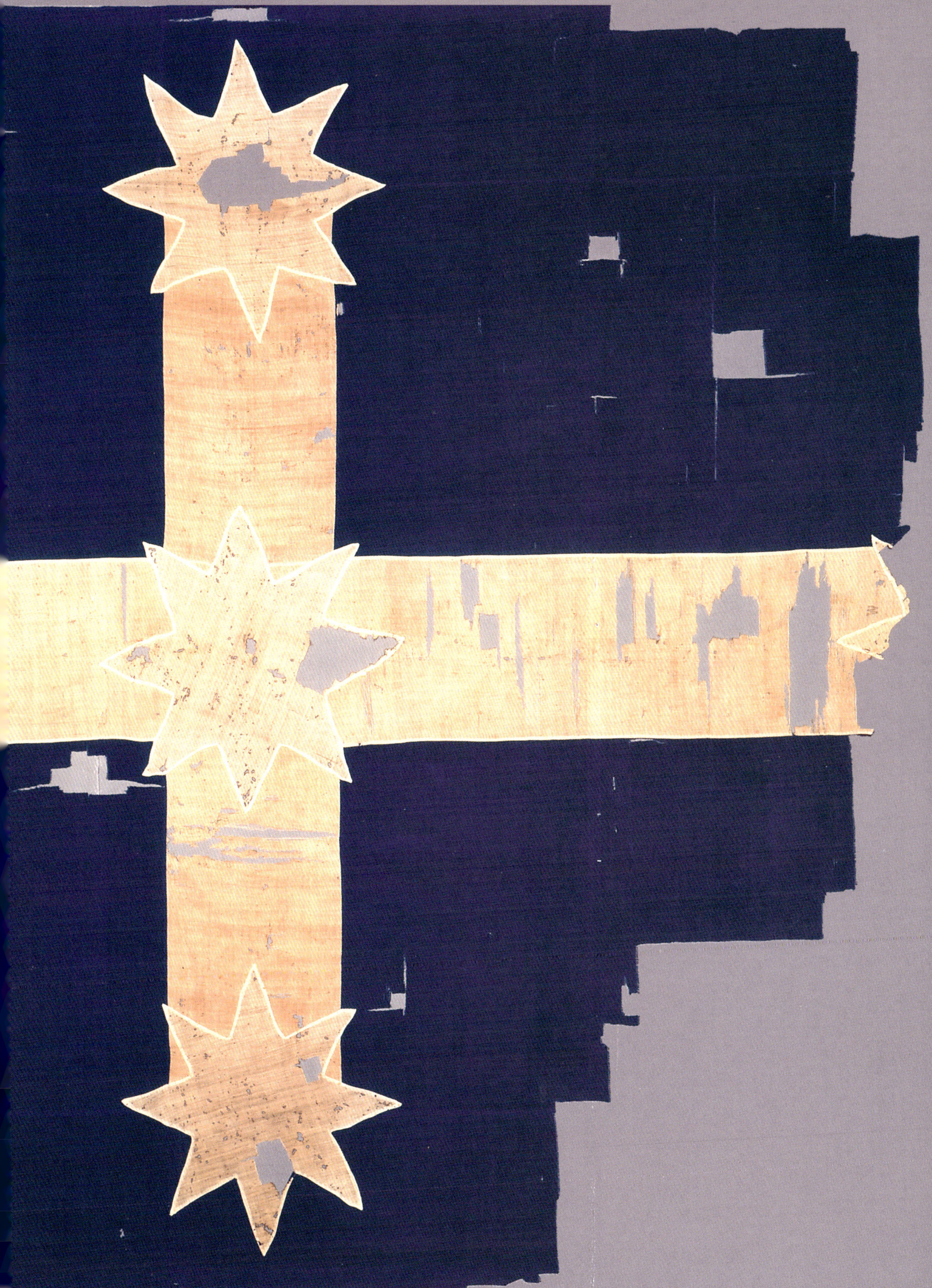

He picked himself up and dashed away, just before the troopers could manoeuvre their horses to trample him into the dust. Dynan collapsed at the foot of a tree, and was attacked where he lay. Suffering from the stroke of a sword he cried out 'Murder!' and lay still pretending to be dead. One of the troopers stood over him as another shouted, 'Stick him through, he's not dead!' Dynan was sure that he was about to be killed there and then but the troopers simply left him and rode away.

He was one of the lucky ones that morning.

Dutchman Jan Vennick nearly had his ear sliced off when he was taken prisoner. He was in his tent 300 metres outside the Stockade, with his mates, countryman Cornelius Peters and the Corsican Le Fronzis Romeo, when they were called upon to give themselves up. They only vacated their tent when the police warned them they would be shot where they stood if they didn't come out. They were handcuffed when one of the policemen took a swipe at Vennick with his sword, almost severing his ear. He then struck him two or three more times on the head. Then they were driven off at bayonet point to be locked up in 'the Camp'.

Henry Powell was a 23-year-old who had walked over from Creswick on the Saturday to visit his mate William Cox, get some money and spend the night with him. About 9.00 in the evening, they retired to their beds — Cox in his own tent, Powell in an adjoining one, both outside the Stockade. When the firing began, Cox yelled to Powell that he was going over to see what was up. When he got to within sight of the Stockade he heard a voice crying out, begging for mercy. Cox recognised his mate Powell who had already got up to watch the battle, and watched in horror as the mounted police rode their horses back and forward over him as he lay on the ground screaming for help. The police slashed at Powell with their sabres as some took pot-shots at him. One eyewitness, George Pobjoy, said later that he had seen the police shoot Powell down after a shot had been fired from one of the diggers' tents. He said that it couldn't have come from the tent where Powell had spent the night. Pobjoy said that he had heard one of the police cry out, 'Ride the bugger down', as they rounded on the wounded Powell and hacked at him with their swords.

When Powell was later taken to Dr. Wills (father of John Wills, the explorer) it was discovered that he had suffered three bullet wounds, three sabre cuts to the head and cuts to his elbow and finger. Powell died three days later, but not before he had identified Special-Constable Arthur Akehurst as his attacker. Akehurst was found guilty of the killing of Powell by a coronial jury held in Ballarat, but was acquitted by a Melbourne jury on a technicality in January 1855. The inspector who took Powell's statement, just before he died, had forgotten to swear the dying man. British justice!

O'Neil, a digger who had come from Creswick, was shot and burnt to death when the troopers fired his tent.

Arthur Arnold, an American actor playing in the theatre at Red Hill at the time, had joined McGill's revolver corps and should have been inside the Stockade. He watched the troopers as they first marched to the site of battle. He followed them, and sneaking around got himself inside the Stockade. After the battle was over he watched as the troopers rounded up their prisoners.

He saw one man lying face-down, 'wounded, kicking and throwing his arms about. A soldier was standing over him, and I saw the latter put his bayonet right through the stockader's back, he kicked no more'.

Arnold helped to pick up the dead and wounded and put them into carts to take them to 'the Camp'. He saw Captain Wise placed in a spring-cart and driven away. He was one of the men who picked up the body of the pikeman whose little terrier fought so bravely to stop his master being taken from him. Every time the dog was removed from the cart, he leapt back in to sit with his master. They had to tie the dog up before the body could be carted away.

Carboni went among the wounded men to assist Dr. Carr and see to their wounds. He was disgusted at the diggers who had come to gawk, and their wives and children who strolled about the battle scene staring, open-mouthed, at the dead and the dying, as if they were watching a Shakespearian tragedy on stage and the curtain was about to come down. No one offered any help. It was none of their business, they were innocent bystanders after all. Nothing to do with them.

The dead and the dying

Carboni helped Dr. Carr to ferry the wounded diggers back to their tents or to the nearby hotels where they could be treated for their wounds.

The sorely wounded men had little hope for their survival. In the days before drugs, before antibiotics, and even before the concept of sterilisation and nursing had been established, most doctors were of the cut and cauterise kind. Amputation was the only remedy for smashed limbs — a painful death, for those cut with deep and damaging wounds. Little could be done for them. Whereas lead can be dug out, and wounds will heal, the bayonet tears into the flesh, and worse, deep into the source of life itself, cutting irreparable, slicing punctures from which blood gushes freely. Sabres split and hack apart with violent disruption, leaving gaping wounds of flesh and gore. The cut man had little chance at all.

When Carboni first walked into the Stockade after the firing had stopped, he saw his friend, 20-year-old Thaddeus Moore from County Clare, lying, stretched out on the ground, shot in both thighs. Teddy raised himself and asked Carboni for a drink of water. He died later in the day.

The standard-bearer Captain Ross, the man who had drawn the design for the flag of the Southern Cross, and shot so cruelly in the groin, had been taken by stretcher to the Free Trade Hotel, helped

The Riot Act

Passed in Britain in 1715, at a time when there was considerable disquiet among the toiling classes, the Riot Act gave local magistrates, or other officials, the legal machinery to take direct action against troublemakers, when twelve or more had gathered together in 'riots or tumults'. Now, this could be interpreted to mean almost any gathering at all where people came together to give vent to their displeasure at the prevailing system of government, or civil management.

To quell any disturbance, officials were required, after first publicly reading the terms of the Riot Act, to allow one hour for the public to disperse. Then they could take action. The reading of the Act gave the magistrate or any person operating under his orders indemnity for any damage, particularly the maiming or killing of any aforesaid rioters, that may ensue.

Sedition: the act of organising or encouraging to subvert or overthrow the government.

Treason: this is the greatest of all crimes in British Law. Plotting to overthrow the Crown, by subverting its authority and making war on the head of state (at the time of Eureka, Queen Victoria).

At the treason trial of the Eureka insurgents, they were accused of planning to overthrow the government and to kill the Queen. That seems to have been a gross overstatement by the prosecution. Parading under arms, drilling armed forces, stockpiling arms and ammunition, and honouring another flag, however, are all acts considered to be both seditious and treasonable. And the digger rebels had certainly made a great show of all those things.

Police magistrate Charles Hackett had accompanied Captain Thomas in the stealthy march to the barricade on Sunday morn. His main task was to read the Riot Act, before any action could be taken, and to follow the letter of the law. As it turned out, the single shot in the dark started the battle before he could attend to his task. The courts made great play over whether or not the reading of the Act had been done as required, whether or not it was necessary, and consequently, whether or not the troops were indemnified of all their actions on that day.

It should have been quite clear that during the battle all was fair in love and war, but the recriminations, death and destruction that followed were not fair at all.

by another old schoolfriend, Swiss-born Canadian, Charles Doudiet, whose watercolours of the Eureka affair provide the best eye-witness account of the struggle. Ross died two days later.

Eddie McGlynn, a 36-year-old from Tipperary, died later in the day.

James Brown, a 29-year-old from County Clare, dead.

Scottish Chartist A.W. Crowe, dead.

John Crowe, a 39-year-old from Kilkenny, dead.

Fenton, dead.

Captain Wise, bold, brave Captain Wise, who had so valiantly led the 40th to breach the barricade lay close to death in 'the Camp' hospital. He lingered for two days, rallied, then infection took its toll. Wise took one long, last draught of the summer's day then expired. He was 26 years old.

The troopers roamed the diggings for days, looking for prisoners and firing tents and shooting at 'insurgents' until they had captured all those they would blame for inciting the rebellion.

Two days later, Michael Canny, who had been shot early in the fight, was lying bandaged on his cot inside his tent on Pennyweight Flat when he heard the troopers moving along the road. Canny watched in fear as Major Robert Nickle rode onto the diggings ahead of 800 men, bringing up two field guns, two howitzers, and marines from Her Majesty's warships which were laying at anchor in the bay. Canny believed the rumours that had spread among the diggers since the battle, that the British were going to kill them all, especially those who would so readily exhibit that they had been wounded — of late.

To escape the stabbing death that most men fear the worst and without even thinking to grab his hat or his shoes, Canny bolted for the bush, running towards Warrenheip. When he snuck back later in the day, his feet where so badly cut that he could hardly walk at all. The wound in his side was also sorely aggravated. It took him at least another twelve months before he was right again.

Captain McGill was seen riding away from Ballarat, for a rendezvous in the Warrenheip woods.

Bendan Hassell was troubled by his injuries for months. An operation in 1855 removed shards of broken bone and the bullet from his leg. His wound suppurated for years to come. He complained that his health had been ruined from the day he stood in the road and offered help to the troops, and was shot.

A 34-year-old, Robert Julien, died on 14 January as a result of his gunshot wounds.

Frederick Coxhead died 15 months later.

Mass meeting in Bendigo
3 December 1854

In complete ignorance of the frightful events that had transpired in Ballarat earlier that morning, another mass meeting was held in Bendigo to further protest against the treatment of the diggers by the troopers and police.

Mr Holyoake addressed the Bendigo meeting. He informed the men assembled of the stand being taken on the Ballarat diggings, the raising of the Southern Cross flag, the declaration of the diggers' oath and the construction of the Eureka Stockade. Denovan was appointed as the representative of the Bendigo diggers and left, with Holyoake, for Ballarat to pledge the support of Bendigo in their cause.

While Holyoake had the benefit of a horse, Denovan made the journey on foot. They reached the Guildford Arms Hotel that night.

4 December 1854

The following morning, just as Denovan and Holyoake were to set off for Ballarat, the news that the Stockade at the Eureka diggings had been overrun by troopers had carried as far as the Guildford Arms. The news of the death and destruction that was retold to Holyoake and Denovan suggested to them that the diggers' cause was lost. Despite the news of the fall of the

Stockade, Denovan and Holyoake continued as far as Creswick where they were informed that martial law had been declared within a ten-mile (16-km) radius of Ballarat.

Not seeing any point in proceeding to certain arrest, the pair parted company. Holyoake headed south for Geelong, while Denovan turned back for Bendigo, stopping first to address a meeting gathered in Castlemaine.

Lalor loses his arm – gains a bride

It was some time after the battle had ceased and the troops had marched their prisoners back to 'the Camp' that Peter Lalor was able to leave the confines of the shaft in which he had lain since his left arm was shattered by the musket ball.

Dalton, Ashburner and Heffernan had hidden him well, although Carboni had described Lalor's hours of distress rather bleakly:

> Peter Lalor, who had been concealed under a pile of slabs, was in the agony of death, a stream of blood from under the slabs heavily forcing its way down hill ... [6]

He was helped to safety and stayed in a hut among the diggers beyond the ruined Stockade where they treated his wounds.

Digger Peter Cumming helped Lalor to escape from Eureka. He said that he had seen a man dressed in a frock coat and belltopper hat walking towards him in great pain, his arm in a sling. Cumming took him to his tent and gave him food and drink. Cumming then helped Lalor to get to Father Smyth's Presbytery, shepherding him all the way. Cumming carried a loaded rifle just in case there was any attempt by the troopers, or any others, to do Lalor harm.

Dr. Doyle, another Kilkenny man who had the honour of naming the Eureka lead, amputated Lalor's arm on the night of 4 December 1854.

Lalor then made his escape from Eureka diggings, on Father Smyth's grey horse, to be cared for by well-wishers in Warrenheip.

He was eventually carried to Geelong, hidden in a carrier's wagon, where he underwent further surgery. Alice Dunne, a young woman who had a special place for Peter Lalor in her heart, had had a vision of him in the early morning of 3 December. She said that Lalor had appeared before her

ABOVE:
On behalf of 'the Crown', in this poster Ballarat Commissioner Robert Rede called upon all 'well-disposed' persons on the diggings to get back to work and to forget about the troubles. With the rebels in custody, business was supposed to return to normal. Before the game was played out, however, this affair saw the end of Rede, as it ushered in the beginning of a new era in the colony.

'wounded and bleeding'. Lalor stayed in hiding while he was recuperating in the home of his sweetheart until all of the trials were over. They married on 10 July 1855. After all of his compatriots had been acquitted, Lalor was then in a curious position. While all of his co-accused were free, he, along with Vern and Black, were still wanted men with large rewards posted for their capture.

Quite a number of the more easily recognisable of the insurgents had also found their way to Geelong. Lalor, Esmond, Kennedy and Black were all billeted among supporters and friends. Although the police generally knew of their whereabouts, as they were housed with some of the more influential citizens in Geelong, they felt it best to leave these sleeping dogs lie, for a while.

In a gesture of defiance, Lalor arrived back on the scene in Ballarat when he purchased some of the first allotments offered after the inquiry into the affairs on the diggings, which granted almost all of the matters that had caused the whole affair.

Even though there remained, for a time, a considerable sum offered for the capture of the insurgents, not one person ever sought to profit from their indiscretions in the 'battle for justice'.

It was the first Saturday after the Eureka battle when Denovan entered the market square in Castlemaine. The diggers were so excited to see him they gathered him up and carried him on their shoulders to the platform.

Wearing a black crepe armband, Denovan addressed the diggers and soon convinced them to continue in their protest. While the Castlemaine diggers were naturally fearful of any retribution by the government troops, Denovan convinced them all to bring out their red ribbons again and show solidarity and sympathy for the Eureka fallen.

While in Castlemaine, he was watched by the police at every turn. Even Sub-Inspector Barclay, who was staying in the same hotel as Denovan and had dined with him, had let him know he was prepared to arrest him 'on the spot' the moment he incited the diggers to any unconstitutional demonstration.

Denovan turned back for home. A tall man, he was an impressive figure as he strode off towards Bendigo, still wearing the black crepe band over a bright red shirt which had been given to him by one of his supporters.

With his red ribbon flying, it was impossible not to see him on his march. All along the way, he was greeted with loud cheers as the diggers encouraged him to keep up the fight. A trooper shadowed him all the way to Bendigo. As he got closer to Bendigo, his 'escort' rode ahead to inform the authorities of his imminent arrival.

A huge crowd then gathered to welcome the 'diggers' representative' back from 'battle'. Rumours had already reached Bendigo that he had been arrested in Ballarat and the diggers were delighted at his safe return.

It was also rumoured that 500 armed diggers had set out from Bendigo to avenge their 'brothers'. This was later shown to be incorrect, but no doubt the government troops were doubly alert for any sign of unrest around Bendigo.

The great Melbourne meeting

'Actual rebellion, with all its bloodiest consequences is before our eyes! It is VICTORIA'S HOUR OF TRIAL. It will require the wisdom, the energy, the co-operation of all her best citizens to bear her safely through it'. — THE AGE.

5 December 1854

When the news that the diggers at Ballarat had taken up arms and begun to parade in military style beneath a 'foreign' flag reached Melbourne, there followed a general state of alarm. The leading citizens conjured up a vision of 20,000 swashbuckling miners, adorned with red sashes and brandishing pistols, marching on Melbourne and capturing the city.

The Mayor called a public meeting to decide how Melbourne would defend herself against this alleged digger army. Yet, there was quite considerable sympathy for the diggers' cause, even among the wealthy and the professional classes.

Most of the members of the Legislative Council were in attendance at this meeting. Thousands assembled in Swanston Street to hear what was going on inside the Mechanics Institute hall. Resolutions were adopted which showed that the people of Melbourne supported the government. As the meeting was drawing to a close, the Mayor of Melbourne vacated the chair and Dr. Embling stepped forward.

The third resolution was still under discussion when Embling changed the tenor of the meeting almost immediately. Embling issued a series of resolutions that showed sympathy for the digger and called on the government to act on their behalf — sooner rather than later.

The promoters of the meeting, along with the members of the Legislative Council, were not at all happy with the turn of events. They believed that

OPPOSITE:
Poster placarded across Melbourne two days after the battle, calling the citizens to a public meeting to form a citizens' militia for the protection of Melbourne from the threatened onslaught of insurgents, who were (falsely) rumoured to be on the way down from Ballarat.
Letterpress poster printed 5 December, 1854
(LA TROBE PICTURE COLLECTION, STATE LIBRARY OF VICTORIA)

3 December 1854

To the Right Worshipful the Mayor of Melbourne.

SIR,

WE, the undersigned Inhabitants of Melbourne, considering the Unsettled State of a portion of the Diggings, and the necessity of taking measures for the better

PROTECTION OF THE CITY,

and upholding the cause of Law and Order, hereby request your Worship to convene

A PUBLIC MEETING

of the Citizens, without delay, for the above purpose.

HENRY MILLER, M.L.C.
WILLIAM NICHOLSON, M.L.C.
THOMAS FULTON, Engineer.
JOHN HODGSON, M.L.C.
AUGUSTUS F. A. GREEVES, M.L.C.

FRANCIS MURPHY, M.L.C.
JOHN STEAVENSON.
JOHN O'SHANASSY, M.L.C.
J. P. FAWKNER, M.L.C.
GEORGE ANNAND, M.L.C.

4th December, 1854.

I hereby call a PUBLIC MEETING of the Citizens, for the purpose above stated, at the

Mechanics' Institution,

At ONE O'CLOCK precisely,

On TO-MORROW, TUESDAY,

THE 5TH DECEMBER.

J. T. SMITH,
MAYOR.

BY AUTHORITY: JOHN FERRES, GOVERNMENT PRINTER, MELBOURNE.

V. R.

NOTICE!!

Recent events at the Mines at Ballaarat render it necessary for all true subjects of the Queen, and all strangers who have received hospitality and protection under Her flag, to assist in preserving

Social Order
AND
Maintaining the Supremacy of the Law.

The question now agitated by the disaffected is not whether an enactment can be amended or ought to be repealed, but whether the Law is, or is not, to be administered in the name of HER MAJESTY. Anarchy and confusion must ensue unless those who cling to the Institutions and the soil of their adopted Country step prominently forward.

His Excellency relies upon the loyalty and sound feeling of the Colonists.

All faithful subjects, and all strangers who have had equal rights extended to them, are therefore called upon to

ENROL THEMSELVES

and be prepared to assemble at such places as may be appointed by the Civic Authorities in Melbourne and Geelong, and by the Magistrates in the several Towns of the Colony.

CHAS. HOTHAM.

BY AUTHORITY: JOHN FERRES, GOVERNMENT PRINTER, MELBOURNE

3 December 1854

A GREAT PUBLIC MEETING AT MELBOURNE, VICTORIA AUSTRALIA.

the meeting had been hijacked by 'agitators [who] had burst in upon a meeting of persons mostly of opposite views, and had by mere noise carried the resolutions their own way'.[7]

Henry Frencham, 'the man with the curly-mo' and one of the discoverers of the Bendigo field, spoke in support of the Ballarat digger-rebels when he said that the people 'must go forth with their brother diggers to conquer or die'.[8]

Melbourne was not the only community wary of the outcome of a nascent insurgency. The citizens of Geelong also petitioned the governor to repeal the onerous system of licensing diggers:

> … convinced as we are that all the troubles and bloodshed that menace this colony originate in the manner in which such system is carried out.

And just to hedge their bets lest Hotham would accuse them of treason, Geelong added:

> We publicly profess our loyalty to the throne, and our intention is to support the law; but our hearts bleed for the sufferings of our fellow-colonists at the diggings.

Martial law declared

Major Sir Robert Nickle, and his 800-strong troop of reinforcements from the 12th and 40th regiments marched, unhindered, onto the Ballarat field at around 2.30 on the afternoon of 5 December. The diggings were all but deserted.

Few miners were game to be about; most families stuck to the comparative safety of their tents. How safe they were was debatable; several were wounded inside their tents by stray bullets fired by troops on the hunt for suspected insurgents.

It had been rumoured that a large band of disaffected 'Leaguers' had taken to the Warrenheip woods and were planning an attack on any further troops that were on the way from Melbourne, but Major Nickle made a safe and event-free entry on to the Ballarat field. He even passed along the road that bordered the Eureka lead without any bother. The ease of their passage caused the authorities to worry that maybe they had been allowed to enter Ballarat and that the Leaguers were planning to mount an attack on the now unguarded

---

OPPOSITE:
Poster printed 4 December 1854. The Stockade affair certainly kept the government printer busy in the days after the battle. The governor could not rely on the newspapers to carry his message to the public; few were on his side; in fact, most favoured his demise. The only course of action for Hotham was to create public declarations such as this.

ABOVE:
A Great Public Meeting at Melbourne, Victoria, Australia
Wood engraving by J. R. Clarke, 1857

(REX NAN KIVELL COLLECTION, NK2106/127,
BY PERMISSION, NATIONAL LIBRARY OF AUSTRALIA)

Melbourne. Rumours soon spread across the city and the good burghers of Melbourne called together a meeting to be held on the same day that Nickle, on behalf of the Lieutenant-Governor, declared martial law in Ballarat.

Nickle tightened control of the diggings.

As soon as martial law was declared the diggers were up in arms again. Would they be allowed to work at night? The greatest concern for the deep-shaft miners was the restrictions imposed by a military curfew; their practice was to work around the clock. The shafts filled constantly with water, and any shaft left untended was destroyed within a day or two. The water made the walls unstable, and the entire enterprise was lost. Nickle needed to understand the community of diggers before he pulled the shutters down too quickly.

On the following day, the first Wednesday after the battle at Eureka, a second 'monster' meeting was held in Melbourne alongside St. Pauls Cathedral, at which 5,000 gathered after hearing the distressing news of the fall of the Stockade that had just reached the city. Wildly exaggerated reports had been carried down from Ballarat and excited the already agitated crowd — 50-100 diggers dead, and the entire district of Buninyong under martial law. The mob turned angrily against the government. Although most would have disapproved of the miners' decision to take up arms, their true feeling was against Hotham. They were led to this degree of dissatisfaction with the government by the newspapermen, the old colonist John Pascoe Fawkner, journalist David Blair, Thomas Fulton and Dr. Embling, who were again among the main protagonists at this meeting.

Hotham was taking no chances. He was well aware of the feeling against the government. He had taken the precaution of posting fully-armed men all around the meeting place. Three hundred mounted police had volunteered for this duty. One hundred gentlemen, mounted, were also standing by ready to take decisive action if called upon. The seamen and marines from Her Majesty's ships *Electra* and *Fantome* mounted guard over the Treasury and powder magazine. Hotham had brought the entire colony to the point where one man stood face to face against his brother, and for what? The protection of the reputation and careers of a bunch of corrupted officials on the Ballarat diggings. His show of force was totally unnecessary on that day; Melbourne was denied the attendance of the type of hot-heads who had fired Ballarat.

Similar meetings were held in Geelong and Sandhurst (Bendigo). Each condemned the government for its handling of the Eureka crisis and for almost bringing the colony to a state of civil war. This did not mean, however, that all of these municipalities were in favour of the rebellion. They, like the citizens of Melbourne, also stood for good law and good order. They were condemning the government for insisting on the prosecution of bad law and irresponsible orders. As a show of support for the law, the next time Hotham called for special constables to volunteer, 1,500 Melburnians signed up. A similar number joined up in Geelong.

Just three days after the battle, a rumour spread from Creswick's Creek that armed diggers were preparing an attack on the commissioner's camp there. The Creswick camp was under-manned, and it would have been an easy target for a riot. When

---

ABOVE:

A poster calling constables to assemble for the protection of the city. It was rumoured that an army of 20,000 rebels were heading to sack Melbourne and establish a republican government.

The government took the threat to the security of the city very seriously indeed.

Proposals were put forward to divide the city into military districts, under the command of an 'officer'. He would wear a coloured arm band, and all the special constables in his section would also wear coloured bands around their wrists. These groups of men would be drilled in military fashion and set to guard their section. This arrangement was based upon the defence of London during the Chartist disturbances there.

It seems that the authorities could only ever answer to the wishes of the public with a display of military fire-power and the rule of their laws.

However, democracy would not be denied; even though there was never any attack on the city, the rebels won in the end.

volunteers were called for to help defend 'the Camp', 200 men came forward and offered their services to the government. How quickly things had changed.

Everyone had an opinion on the events of December 1854. Caroline Chisholm, Catholic convert, philanthropist and advocate of assisted emigration, wrote an open letter to the *Argus*:

> Sir — Any thoughtful person who calmly views our present position, either commercially or politically, must feel the necessity of vigorous exertions in order to place us in the position we ought to be in. When we consider the rich and beautiful country God has given to us — a country that waits only for the plough to give us wheat — the vine to give us wine — the olive to give us oil — every luxury and comfort that man can desire is within our each, only waits our biddings. Gold lies at our feet, and yet with all these advantages we are on the verge of national insolvency, and the hands of our people are stained with blood.
>
> ... Let us be wise in time, and give to our people a fair scope for their activity — a wider and more wholesome range for their energies, and we shall soon become a happy, a peaceful, and a more contented people.

Caroline Chisholm added that the colonists had spent too long on taxing, and become a nation of consumers, when it was hard work and hands to the plough that should be the saviour of the colony. She wrote, 'if Sir Charles Hotham is a wise man, he will at once call to his assistance that first minister of finance, the Plough!' Chisholm had little time for the revolutionists. When she spoke at a meeting held in the Hall of Castlemaine in November 1854, she counselled those who would take up arms to solve their grievances to resist the call to rebellion and go home 'to their wives and families', where they live 'in peace and quietness. Only then would they know what they want'.

A change in government

There was one man in the government who copped more than his fair share of criticism over the whole affair, and he was Colonial Secretary John Foster. It was to him that Hotham looked for advice when he was still new to the job. It was from Foster that good counsel should have been given. Foster had only been given the position to bridge the gap between La Trobe and Hotham, and in the end he had to bear the brunt of almost all of the criticism. He became Hotham's scapegoat.

Hotham had been pressing Foster to resign from the beginning of November, at the start of the troubles. Foster had offered his resignation three days after the battle, but it was not until 11 November that his resignation was formally accepted. When Foster left his post, he declared that it was 'the greatest mortification of my life'. Foster admitted, in what seems a classic understatement, that he was prompted to this step by 'the knowledge that many of his official acts had become unpopular with a certain class of the colonists'.

The *Bendigo Advertiser* on 29 December 1854 added the following opinion:

> We have no disposition to crow over the downfall of any man; but for the sake of the colony and especially of its 'great interest,' the gold-fields, we cannot but rejoice most sincerely at this event. There are few, if any, who will sympathise with this gentleman. His whole career has rendered him almost obnoxious to all classes, and his resignation may be hailed as the first step to reform.

Foster had resigned to save Hotham's reputation. He may have helped to do so, but Hotham ignored him when Foster pressed the governor to grant him the pension he had been promised. Foster was kept in the public eye for some time as he battled for years to gain the compensation that

---

'When peace shall lie once more regained, and there shall be time for deliberate judgement, the citizens will reckon with the Government. Meantime, they will not pledge themselves to support it; and they will not organize themselves into bodies for the purpose of filling the place of that expensive military force, which should never have been sent out of Melbourne. [We] do not sympathise with revolt; but neither do [we] sympathise with injustice and coercion. [We] will not fight for the diggers nor will [we] fight for the Government.'
— *The Age, 5 December 1855*

Hotham had offered for his loss of office. William Clark Haines took over as colonial secretary.

After three days of comparative peace and quiet on the diggings, Major Nickle revoked the proclamation of martial law. All talk of sedition seemed at an end. Even a parade of 1,000 men through Ballarat aroused little excitement and showed Nickle no ill-will. Funerals for the victims of the battle had occupied the better part of the past three days.

Shopkeepers' protest
11 December 1854

Shopkeepers held a meeting on Bakery Hill outside Mr. Thomas Williams's Auction Mart where they petitioned for compensation for goods 'appropriated' by the Ballarat Reform League and taken to supply the Stockade. About 1,500 men, mostly miners, attended this meeting, as did inspectors Foster and McCullock, who received a rousing cheer at the meeting's end. These diggers, and the storekeepers, were making sure that 'the Camp' was aware of their allegiance to the Crown and their commitment to law and order.

The following resolutions were put to the meeting by a number of proponents:

> 1. That this meeting views with regret the proceedings of the past week, rendering it necessary to assert the sovereignty of law and order by the sacrifice of so many lives, and the proclamation of martial law.
> 2. That this meeting considers the late appeal to arms as uncalled for, and pledges itself to use every constitutional means to restore tranquillity and good feeling on the Ballaarat gold-fields.
> 3. That this meeting hopes that the officer in command of Her Majesty's forces at Ballarat will act with as much forbearance and humanity as the circumstances of the case may admit of, otherwise the lives of many innocent parties may be sacrificed, as has been the case already.
> 4. That when the present excitement shall have ceased, this meeting pledges itself to endeavour, by constitutional means, to have the acknowledged grievances of the miners brought before the Legislative Council of the colony.
> 5. That a copy of the resolutions passed at this meeting, and signed by the Chairman, be forwarded to His Excellency Sir Charles Hotham immediately; and that a deputation be appointed to wait on his representative at Ballaarat, and present him with a copy of the same.
> 6. That the following gentlemen be the deputation to the Camp: Mr. Thomas Williams (chairman), Rev. P. Smith, Mr. Humffray, Mr. Edward Donald, and Mr. Mostered.

Moderate 'moral force' proponent Humffray had proposed the fifth motion.

All resolutions were carried, in what was probably the first orderly meeting on Bakery Hill for some time.

Thomas Williams, having been elected as chairman, addressed the orderly crowd. He began by reminding them all that he was:

> ... one of the oldest diggers on Ballaarat; that every one would see the utility and policy, of abstaining from any topic even bordering on politics at the present juncture; that many had erred in seeking to obtain their rights in an unconstitutional manner. That, in his opinion, they had acted unwisely; had been led away and deluded. What their punishment would be it was hard to say. That every man of right and honest feeling, every respectable man, not only on Ballaarat, but in the colony, was arrayed against them. [Hear, hear.]

Their grievances would be redressed, for all had grievances in a greater or less degree; but that an appeal to arms was not the right means of seeking such redress. Few would wish to die like so many dogs. (Cheers.) He wished some well known digger would come forward.

The meeting was for the public good. No oratory was wanted. Business was to be the order of the day. [He] was sure that the meeting present was too intelligent, and had seen too well the futility of opposing arms to the flag of England, to say nothing of the degradation of forming themselves into bands merely for the sake of plunder. That however [he] might consider the step of the Government impolitic in searching for unlicensed diggers at the time they did, nothing could justify the employment of physical force.

Appeal, brother diggers; appeal, appeal, but in a constitutional way, and you will be respected by everyone at home and abroad.

Each man spoke to his motion, each man spoke of the need to return to constitutional order, each man firmly believed the government would listen to their concerns and the change they desired would follow.

Why they believed that the government was interested in reform is hard to fathom. After all, the government had just so recently slaughtered twenty or so of their mates and taken more than one hundred prisoners in the attempt to stifle the call for change. The representatives elected from this meeting set out for 'the Camp' to present this new raft of resolutions. Only Father Smyth was allowed in, and while he was engaged within, Humffray was placed under arrest. The others were then ushered before Rede, Mr. Sturt and Captain Pasley, who regarded the opinions of the deputation as nothing more than 'a censure on the government'. They were forced to withdraw, without success.

The *Ballarat Times* showed its dissatisfaction at this petulant rebuke of the 'moderate' representative of opinion on the diggings, and the arrest of Humffray.

The arrest of Humffray considering the position he has lately taken, and the sacred character of ambassador which he at the time bore, appears an ill-advised and most ungracious proceeding. The step cannot but have a tendency to discourage the advocates of moderate measurers and weaken their influence.

The rejection of the resolutions seems still more ill-advised a step, and calculated to produce the worst effect on the minds of the population of the gold-field. The overwhelming military force now in the Camp should have warranted the adoption of a conciliatory course by the officials rather than have prompted them to act in this irritating manner.

As the dust settled

William Howitt, writing for the *Argus* in March 1855, spared no one in his assessment of the events that led up to the battle at the Eureka Stockade. Howitt was a man with a great respect for the law and he was shocked that his fellow Britons could sack another man's property without any suggestion of remorse, let alone reparation. On the other hand he was disgusted by the behaviour of the government officials within the Ballarat camp:

The Ballaarat outrage bears with it a mark of unanimity, on the part of the people, that it is almost without a precedent in the history of riots in any civilised country. The fact that such an infamous outrage as the burning down of Bentley's house could be committed in a British colony, and that not one in a hundred of the vast population of Ballaarat can be found who sympathises with the injured man, proves most unmistakably that there is something radically wrong in the government of such a people.

When the riot occurred, some of the commissioners issued notices calling upon all the well-disposed people to assist in maintaining law and order, by enrolling themselves as special constables. Two gentlemen who arrived last night assure me that up to the time of their leaving that they had not heard of one individual offering his support to the Government …

> The diggers and other people at Ballaarat have long since lost all confidence in, or respect for, the Government officers of that district ... the Government Camp at Ballaarat is a perfect hotbed of corruption; and that officers connected with other services are alike guilty of the most glaring malpractices ... Bribery of the most direct and barefaced description has been unblushingly resorted to, particularly among the higher officials, in matters connected with publicans' licenses. Magistrates are said to be bound in unholy compact with many of the publicans ... Contracts are entered into, annulled, or altered in a most suspicious manner, a system of 'commission' being established by the Government officials.

Even once the dust had settled on the Ballarat field, the diggings were not safe for several days for ordinary men, women and their children to be about. Troops and goldfields police were still on the look-out for stockaders, looking askance at any man who could be their enemy. With twitchy trigger fingers, and in fear of mortal danger, the armed police caused the demise of an unknown number in the days immediately after the battle. The sentries fired at anything that moved in the dark. Musket balls ranged far and wide on their unknowable and deadly paths. In one tent, a mother seeing to the needs of her 18-month-old baby felt a ball pass through her hair and watched in horror as another passed through the leg of her child.

Two innocent men were dropped in their tracks as they picked their way between the tents on their way home in the dark. Everybody had stories to tell of balls that whistled past their ears, and lodged in the barrel of their windlasses. The Ballarat diggings took some time to settle down.

In a dramatic turn of events the week following the battle, 623 licences were taken out, mostly by diggers who had been too afraid to do so before.

The state of martial law was lifted on 9 December, only five days after the battle. Major Nickle had moved quickly. Most of the prisoners had been released and were back at their claims, the so-called ring-leaders charged and sent for trial. Nickle had put the affairs of Ballarat in his own hands and the days of corruption, blunder and misrule were at an end. Even the editor of the *Melbourne Morning Herald* was filled with praise for Sir Robert Nickle in his comment published on 8 December 1854:

> The martial law administered by Sir R. Nickle is about as far superior to the Commissioner's law, under which we have been so long labouring, as it is possible for anything to be. Had Sir R. Nickle arrived here a few days before, the bloodshed of last Sunday would have been avoided.

A preference for Americans

African-American New Yorker John Joseph was the only American to be brought before the courts after the fall of the Stockade, and he was abandoned by those whom he had fought alongside in the shepherd's holes during the first bayonet charge by the troops. Joseph was the first man to stand in the dock charged with treason against Her Majesty, Queen Victoria. The rest of the Americans managed to get off scot free.

McGill had disappeared from the diggings soon after the battle; it was reported that he was seen galloping into the hills. McGill claimed that he had rushed away, heading for Captain Hepburn's Smeaton station to take charge of some field-guns Hepburn had on his property. But nobody seemed to accept this. In fact, he was met at the Springs by a friend, and after disguising himself in women's clothing took the coach to Melbourne. He passed Major Nickle on his way near the Moorabool River. The brave Californian was well out of it.

McGill took refuge under the aegis of the American George Train, Melbourne agent for the White Star Company shipping lines who, along with

Cobb & Co., supported the Californian Rangers Brigade. Train arranged for McGill to board one of his ships, the *Arabian*, while he and other Americans called upon the governor and pleaded for leniency for his young countryman. Hotham was quite surprised when told McGill was only 21 and, giving him the benefit of his youthful naivety, permitted him to leave without harm. Train offered to get McGill out of the colony, but he remained, pretending to be an invalid, at the health officer's quarters at Port Phillip Heads until all of the trials of his fellow stockaders were over.

This seems to follow a pattern of representation to the governor on behalf of the free Americans. The American Consul had written to Hotham on 24 October 1854, just a few days after the riot at Bentley's Hotel, in an attempt to convince the governor that his countrymen were not in any way implicated in the troubles at Ballarat. On 24 October 1854, the American Consul wrote:

> Consulate of the United States, Melbourne
> Lieut. Gov. Sir Charles Hotham, Sir, I have the honour, as well as the satisfaction, to inform your Excellency that I have just seen an intelligent American gentleman, Mr Nichols who will call on your Excellency, from Ballaarat; and he assured me that the Americans did not participate in the late riot at Ballaarat, but, on the contrary, the Bowling Saloon that was burnt belonged in part, to an American – the riot was got up – and the prime movers were Scotchmen, as the murdered man was one of their countrymen – I am happy in hearing, and believing, and thus in informing your Excellency of this …'

Why Hotham acceded to this representation by George Train and the other prominent Americans is unclear, but he may have wanted to clear the decks to allow the courts to concentrate on the seditious Irishmen, 'the French red Republican, the German political metaphysician … and the British Chartists' of whom he was so dismissive. He seemed prepared to allow the 'Lone Star Member' to get away. After all, the Americans were a little too argumentative and the British had not won many arguments with them over the years.

A fearful empire

It is difficult to imagine the external pressures brought to bear on the colonial government at the time of the Eureka rebellion. Britain had long been engaged in the war in the Crimea, and there was a real fear that the Russians would invade Port Phillip. Fortifications were constructed at the head of the bay.

So great was the sense of paranoia that Hotham had even ordered the construction of an armed steam-sloop, *Victoria*, which was the first major vessel in the Victorian navy.

When the migrant steamship *Great Britain* sailed through the heads and announced its arrival with a fireworks display, the citizens thought that the Russians had arrived and dashed home to find guns, pick axes and garden implements to use in their defence.

There was pressure put on the Victorian government from England to find the funds for the defence of this little, but exceedingly rich, corner of the realm. Combined with all the other military excursions that the empire was engaged in at the time, the affray at Eureka may have just been like scratching an itch for the British Crown — the discipline of just one other, annoying, colonial nuisance within their global empire.

In the British press the battle was reported as a local issue dealt with at a local level, and after all the Crown had won the day. Tucked between reports of murders and tavern fires and letters from the Queen to Florence Nightingale, the battle at Eureka was reported in one British publication in the following, almost disinterested, manner:

> December 3, 1854 — Affray between soldiers and the gold-diggers at Eureka, Ballarat, who were resisting payment of the customary license-fee to dig. The troops surrounded the camp of the insurgents, and fired over their heads; but the diggers at once rushed for their guns, and shot three of the military. After a sustained fight of about twenty minutes the diggers hauled down their flag and surrendered to the soldiers, when it was found that twenty-six of them were killed; 126 were made prisoners. [9]

Order was restored, the law upheld: time for tea.

Prisoners of the Crown

The names recorded here are of those men imprisoned in the Ballarat camp on 3 December 1854. This may not be complete, as a list compiled when the prisoners' possessions were removed disappeared along with most of their personal effects.

Many of the diggers claimed later that considerable sums of money, and gold, had been purloined from their possessions taken that day.

No one received any compensation for the thefts.

This list comes from the court reports of those who stood before the bench between 9 and 12 December 1854. All but 13 of these men were released by 12 December. The prisoners whose names appear in bold were committed to stand, accused of treason, and taken to Melbourne to await their day in court.

ADAMS, Charles
ALLAIRE, Nicholas
ALLEN, Richard
ANDERSON, Carl (Sweden)
ASHBURNER, James (Liverpool)
AVONDALE, William

BARCLAY, James –
BARRY, Thomas – digger
BAZLEY, Henry – digger
BEATTIE, James – digger (Cumberland), sent for trial
BISK, Thomas –
BOHEN, Edmund –
BOX, Thomas –
BROWN, Charles –
BRYANT, –
BURN, Edmund –
BUTLER, Michael –

CAHILL, John – digger (County Clare)
CAMPBELL, James MacFie – (Jamaican-born), sent for trial
CARBONI, Raffaello – digger (Italy)
CORNISH, – (4 brothers, Christian names unknown)
COX, William – digger (Powell died in Cox's tent)

DAVIDSON, George –
DEGAN, Thomas –
DELAMERE, John –
DEVELIN, John –
DIGNUM, Thomas – (Sydney), was charged with treason but acquitted without trial. Dignum was a pikeman and was cut about the head by William Revel of the 40th Regiment. When he was arrested he was carrying a licence which bore the name of Thomas Walker.
DOOLAN, Charles –
DYNAN, Michael –

EDWARDS, Nicholas – digger
ELLIS, Joseph – digger
FENWICK, John – (Vennick) (Holland)
FERGUSON, Charles D – one of McGill's Californian Rangers who witnessed the shooting of Captain Wise. He was one the few Americans taken prisoner, and was chained to Henry Seekamp in the prison. He had worked for Cobb & Co., and had built the Adelphi Theatre in Ballarat.

GALLOWAY, William – had his tent next to Cox and was arrested because he had blood on his hands.
GILHOOLY, Patrick –
GLEESON, Michael – (Kilkenny), Gleeson's two brothers, Edward and Martin, were also in Ballarat at the time of the battle.
GRAY, Joseph –

HAYES, Timothy – Chairman of the Ballarat Reform League. (Kilkenny), sent for trial.
HEPBURN, James –
HICKEY, Patrick –
HINDON, Joseph –
HINDS, Isaac –
HOGAN, Jeremiah –
HOWARD, Patrick – digger (Dublin)
HUMPHREYS, Richard –

JOSEPH, John – digger (New York) African-American, Joseph was abandoned by the other Americans after his arrest. He was among the Rangers when Wise was shot. Sent for trial.

KEDDER, Charles –
KELLY, John –

KENNEDY, Patrick – accused of treason, discharged 9 December.
KENT, Francis –
KINNEAR, Martin –

LEADOW, John –
LESLIE, Robert –
LIVINGSTON, Charles –
LYNCH, John – digger (County Clare) helped to conceal Lalor, covering him with pit-slabs after the battle.

MCKEOWN, Joseph –
McMAHON, Edward –
MACARTNEY, Daniel –
MAGENNIS, Duguld –
MANNING, John – digger, reporter (Ireland) Sent for trial. Seekamp later claimed that Manning had been responsible for several of the more seditious articles published in the *Ballarat Times* — for which he was imprisoned.
MAYHER, Thomas –
MEADE, Patrick –
MEAGHER, Michael – discharged 12 December
MOLLOY, William – sent for trial
MURPHY, Thomas –

O'BRIEN, Kennedy–
O'ROURKE, Thomas –
ORR, Matthew –

PADY, John –
PENNY, Samuel –
PENROSE, Joseph –
PERGO – (Spain)
PETERS, Cornelius – mate of Vennick, discharged 9 December (Holland)
PHELAN, John – digger (Queen's County) Phelan was a mate of Lalor. They had been neighbours in Ireland and partners when they

The dead and the wounded

both arrived in Melbourne. Phelan was alleged to have thrown Lalor's amputated arm down an old mineshaft near what is now the corner of Princess and Mair streets, Ballarat. Sent for trial.
POHILL -
POWELL, John -
PRIAULX, Peter -

QUIN, John -

READ, Henry - sent for trial.
ROBILLARD, Henry -
RODAN, John - (Scotland)
ROMEO, Le Fronzis, digger (Corsica). A mate of Vennick and Peters. French-Corsican, Romeo's family was related to Napolean Bonaparte. He had jumped ship in Melbourne in 1851.
ROSS, Alexander -
RYAN, Martin -
RYLEY, Walter -

SEXTON, James -
SHEADY [Sheedy], Patrick -
SMITH, Arthur -
SMITH, Richard John -
SOMERVILLE, William -
SORENSON, Jacob - sent for trial
STAFFORD, William -
STEER, William James -
STEINMAN, Herman -
SWANSON, Andrew - (Sweden)

THOMPSON, George -
TIGHE [Toy], Thomas -
TRYNON, Henry -
TUOHY, Michael - digger (County Clare). Sent for trial.

WALKER, Joseph -
WHITE, Andrew -
WINKFIELD, Robert -
WINKLEY, William -
WRIGHT, William -

Five others were taken into custody, but their names are not recorded. Henry Seekamp, editor of the *Ballarat Times*, was arrested on 4 December and was charged with inciting the rebellion.

The dead, Lalor's list

DIAMOND, Martin [John*]
— County Clare, Ireland
DONAGHEY, George
— County Donegal, Ireland
EMMERMAN, William — Petersburg
GITTINS, Patrick — Kilkenny, Ireland
GREEN, Samuel — England
HAFELE, John (Henfield, Thomas?) may be the same man —
Wurtemberg
HYNES, John — County Clare, Ireland
MULLINS — Kilkenny, Limerick, Ireland
O'NEIL, Thomas — Kilkenny, Ireland
PARKER, Thomas — died 4 December
QUIN, Edward
— County Cavan, Ireland
QUINLAN, William
— Goulburn, New South Wales
ROBERTSON, John — Scotland
ROWLANDS, Llewellyn — Wales
THONEN, Edward — Elberfeldt, Prussia

Wounded and died later

BROWN, James — Newry, Ireland
CLIFTON, George —
CROWE —
FENTON —
JULIEN, Robert — Nova Scotia
M'GLYN, Edward — Ireland
MOORE, Thaddeus
— County Clare, Ireland
POWELL, Henry —
ROSS, Captain Charles — Canada

Recovered

HANAFIN, Patrick
— COUNTY KERRY, IRELAND
HANLY, Michael
— County Tipperary, Ireland
LALOR, Peter
— Queen's County, Ireland
O'NEIL, Michael
— County Clare, Ireland

*Martin Diamond, whose store straddled the stockade defences, was named John on Peter Lalor's list of those killed, and this mistake has persisted for many years.

Military list

Only one trooper died during the battle. He was Belfast-born Private Michael Roney, 40th Regiment, aged 21 years. He was shot in the head. Captain Henry WISE, 40th Regiment, died as a result of his wounds on 21 December. He was 26 years old.

Wounded

12th Regiment

ADAIR, Robert (Private)
— shot in hand.
BOYLE, Felix (Private)
— shot in nose. Died on 10 January 1855 from his wounds, Irish.
BUTTWELL, William (Private)
— severe compound fracture of his arm.
FRENCH, William (Private)
— shot in hip.
GALVIN, Timothy (Private)
— shot in neck and ear.
PAUL, William (Lieutenant)
— shot in hip.
SMITH, John (Private)
— shot in thigh.
WEBB, William (Private)
— shot in arm and back. Died the day after the battle. He was 19 years old.

40th Regiment

BYRNE, John (Private)
— wound in neck and leg.
COLLES, Henry (Private)
— shot in side.
JUNIPER, William (Private)
— compound fracture of leg caused by gunshot.
O'DONNELL, Bernard (Private)
— shot in neck.
SULLIVAN, Patrick (Private)
— shot in arm.
WALL, Joseph (Private)
— pike wound to lower abdomen. He died after the battle aged 20 years.

Treason against Victoria

ON 22 FEBRUARY 1855, JOHN JOSEPH was the first of the Eureka insurgents to stand before Judge Sir William A'Beckett in the Melbourne Magistrate's Court. The courtroom was packed. The main case against Joseph seemed to centre on the possibility that he was the man who had shot Captain Wise; several of the troopers gave evidence that they had seen Joseph fire at the time that Wise fell. Luckily for Joseph, Wise had been struck twice and no one could prove that Joseph was responsible for hitting Wise once, twice or with two shots at the same time. Police spy Goodenough gave evidence, but did not specifically refer to Joseph. Several witnesses referred to seeing a black man in the Stockade, but defence lawyer Butler Cole Aspinall played the race card when he suggested 'there were plenty of black men on the goldfields, and it is almost impossible for anybody but a slaveholder to know a negro from his fellow'.[1] Aspinall referred to Joseph in the court as 'a riotous nigger from Down South [he had in fact come from New York] who had no conception of treason in his head, or as being actuated by the eloquence of Lawler [sic] on the top of the stump, and actually prepared to defend himself, and that he had some idea, that though a negro, in any British possession he was entitled to his liberties'.[2]

The jury retired and within one hour returned with the verdict — not guilty.

1. Hayes.   2. Campbell.   3. Raphelo.   4. Sorenson.   5. Manning.   6. Phelan.   7. Dignum.

Treason against Victoria

BELOW:
'Rebels' in the dock
Wood engraving by Samuel Calvert,
published in the Age, 10 March 1855
(LA TROBE PICTURE COLLECTION, STATE LIBRARY OF VICTORIA)

John Joseph, the first to face the bench in the state treason trials against the Eureka insurgents, was set free. He was carried triumphantly from the court riding on the shoulders of the crowd.

John Manning faced the bench on 26 January. He was promptly acquitted.

Hotham was concerned at the hasty acquittals. The Crown prosecutors suggested that no jury would convict any one of the men arraigned to be brought before A'Beckett. Public sympathy was solidly behind the insurgents, in the matter of the public trials of these fighters for justice, but there was no support for the position of Hotham's prosecution at all. The trials came to a halt; everyone concerned had to wait and allow the court shorthand writer to catch up with the enormous amount of paper work to be transcribed.

The postponement of the trials gave the public time to consider the actions of the government, and public resolve in favour of the prisoners did Hotham much damage. Public opinion of the governor had hit rock bottom. On his way home one evening Hotham was jeered at by a crowd of 200 as he passed a meeting gathered by St. Paul's church to raise funds for the defence of the prisoners. Hotham was to regret his decision to continue to stand firm against the overwhelming weight of public opinion.

John Chandler, a carrier who made his living travelling backwards and forwards along the roads

Joseph.   9. Beattie.   10. Molloy.   11. Jan Vannick.   12. Tuhey.   13. Read.

167

from Melbourne to the diggings, noted a large number of 'secretly' armed men among the 3,000 strong crowd that assembled outside the courts each day. He was convinced that they were prepared to storm the courtroom and release the prisoners if any were convicted and sentenced to hang. Everyone knew that Hotham would have moved quickly to the gallows if any were convicted. To dally would have courted disaster.

Chairman of the Ballarat Reform League Timothy Hayes was next to face court. Judge Redmond Barry presided over Hayes's trial. Barry was a Protestant Irishman who had no time for the rebellious Catholic Irish. Goodenough was again called to the court, this time to give witness against Hayes. Goodenough faced defence lawyer R.D. Ireland who ran the police spy around in circles until he refused to swear that what he said at a previous trial was correct. The case for the prosecution of Timothy Hayes was in danger of collapse. Police sub-inspector Thomas Langley told the court that he had arrested Hayes two to three hundred metres from the Stockade after the battle. On that day, Lieutenant Thomas Richards of the 40th Regiment had recognised Hayes, who was an impressively tall man and easy to see, and noted that he seemed to be avoiding the troopers. When Hayes was arrested, his wife Anastasia came up to him and asked 'Have you been taken,' to which Timothy replied, simply, 'Yes'. She rounded on Richards and demanded of him, 'Why didn't you come yesterday?', clearly suggesting that if her husband, or all the men, had been stopped before the battle, none of the heartbreak that followed would have been necessary. She then snapped at Richards, snarling, 'If I had been a man I would not

ABOVE:

Timothy Hayes, Ballarat Reform League Chairman
Hayes was captured outside the Stockade, and stood trial for treason. The prosecution tried to show that he had incited others to burn their licences at the 'monster meeting' of 17 November. When he was arrested, he still had his current licence in his possession. The prosecution case fell apart. He was the third man to be acquitted.
(PROV, 12970/P0001, UNIT 1. REPRODUCED WITH THE PERMISSION OF THE KEEPER OF PUBLIC RECORDS, PUBLIC RECORD OFFICE VICTORIA, AUSTRALIA © STATE OF VICTORIA)

ABOVE:

Anastasia Hayes
Wife of Timothy Hayes, Anastasia was one of many women who shared the trials of living on the early goldfields. Ballarat had a large community of Irish-Catholic families, who were drawn together by common bonds of Irish patriotism and religion. Each of these was exactly what drove them apart from the English. Anastasia assisted Dr. Doyle at Father Smyth's Presbytery the night Lalor's arm was amputated.
(PROV, 12970/P0001, UNIT 1. REPRODUCED WITH THE PERMISSION OF THE KEEPER OF PUBLIC RECORDS, PUBLIC RECORD OFFICE VICTORIA, AUSTRALIA © STATE OF VICTORIA)

Treason against Victoria

have allowed myself to be taken by the likes of you.'³

The defence tried to prove that it was Hayes that had incited the diggers to burn their licences at the meeting on Bakery Hill on 29 November 1854. But the defence council submitted, before the court, evidence that showed when Hayes was taken prisoner he had two gold licences in his possession. Witnesses, including Father Smyth, told the court that it was Hayes who had actually tried to bring that meeting at Bakery Hill to order, and that as chairman of the Ballarat Reform League he was not even in the Stockade on the day of the battle.

During his trial a loud crack was heard emanating from the cedar canopy over Judge Redmond Barry's head. He was forced to close the court for half an hour while tradesmen were called in to add running repairs to the seat of justice.

Within half an hour of the jury retiring, Hayes was acquitted. He too walked free.

Raffaello Carboni was next to face the judge. Although he was one of the more prominent members of the league, he argued long and hard that he had taken no part in the affray. He had spent most of the battle stuck up his chimney in fear for his life. Carboni was also one of the more easily recognised of the Ballarat men, and his neck in the noose would have been a bold warning to any other foreign digger who dared to make a stand against the good and welcoming grace of the British Crown.

Just like Hayes, much of the evidence against Carboni was based upon the belief that he too had burned his licence on 27 November. This was disproved easily. Carboni had managed to keep his licence safely in his pocket.

ABOVE:
Judge Sir William A'Beckett
William A'Beckett presided over the events of the Melbourne Magistrate's Court. It is a credit to the British legal system that each man was given his day in court and, although the jury had obviously exhibited sympathy with the rebels, they did not allow the Crown to break the spirit of revolution that it seems almost all ordinary citizens supported.
(LA TROBE PICTURE COLLECTION, STATE LIBRARY OF VICTORIA)

ABOVE:
Judge Sir Redmond Barry
Redmond Barry was one of the more influential gentlemen of his day. He was responsible for the establishment of the University of Melbourne and the Public Library, among many other public amenities. His colonial career spanned three decades, from the first court on the goldfields at Castlemaine in 1851 to the trial of bushranger Ned Kelly in 1880. Barry was a Dublin-born Protestant who had little sympathy for the poorly-behaved Irishman abroad.
(LA TROBE PICTURE COLLECTION, STATE LIBRARY OF VICTORIA)

ACQUITTAL OF BALLARAT RIOTERS IN 1855.

No jury would convict the popular Italian. A much relieved Raffaello Carboni walked free — 'Great works!'

When Nederlander Jan Vennick also walked free on 22 March the *Age* ran with the headline:

THE FIFTH DEFEAT!

Vannick [sic], another of the foreign anarchists is acquitted! Go Mr Attorney! You are very hoarse, but you are doing more in a week to bring the Government into contempt than the *Age* could do in a year. [4]

Michael Touhy and James Beattie were both tried and acquitted on 23 March. By now it would have been incredible if the jury would single out one man for a conviction against all others. The prosecution had simply not called any of the key players in the affair. No Commissioner Rede, no Captain Thomas, and only a handful of contemptible spies, and troopers whose testimony had already proved to be unreliable.

The only Australian-born insurgent called before the bench on 26 March was Thomas Dignum. He was discharged without trial.

There were five trials still to be heard, and the prosecution sought leave to advise the governor to bring the prosecutions to a speedy halt. While James McFie Campbell, William Molloy, John Phelan, Henry Read and Jacob Sorenson awaited for

ABOVE:
Acquittal of Ballarat Rioters in 1855
The citizens of Melbourne kept vigil at the doors of the courthouse throughout the entire length of the trials.

This engraving from the *Illustrated Australian News* published on 25 June 1887 shows one of the 'digger rebels' being carried shoulder high from the court after he had been acquitted.

It is presumed that this is a portrait of Jan Vennick, who was arrested in his tent 300 metres from the stockade. It didn't really matter to the troopers whether the digger was in or out; just being in the vicinity, and a foreigner to boot, was enough evidence to bring the 'insurgent' to trial. Vennick was the fifth man to face the court and the fifth to be set free.
(LA TROBE PICTURE COLLECTION, STATE LIBRARY OF VICTORIA)

their day in court, Hotham was advised that to continue would hold the government 'up to to derision and mockery, and that it would be most prudent to desist'.⁵

Hotham persisted, saying that if the jury would not do their duty, he failed to see why he should not do his.

The remaining five prisoners were brought before the court on 27 March 1855 and all were acquitted.

This destroyed Hotham's command over the colony. He had refused all advice to bring the trials to an end, and now all those who had stood accused at his demand walked free. The jury had openly defied the governor. To rub further salt into his already stinging wounds, the British Secretary of State for the Colonies, Earl Grey, reprimanded Hotham with this confidential note after reading the long awaited transcript of the first trial:

> In further acknowledgement of your dispatch ... respecting the trial of the prisoners taken at Ballarat, I wish to say that although I do not doubt you have acted to the best of your judgement, and under advice, yet in question the expediency of bringing these rioters to trial under a charge of high treason, being one so difficult of proof, and so open to objections of the kind which appear to have prevailed with the jury.⁶

Poor Henry Seekamp

The only man sentenced to a term of imprisonment for complicity in the whole Eureka affair was the editor of the *Ballarat Times*, Mr. Henry Seekamp. Seekamp was arrested in his own office on 4 December 1854, tried and jailed for sedition.

After his arrest, he was taken to 'the Camp' cells where he was chained to the American digger-rebel Charles Ferguson. Ferguson recalled that Seekamp was convinced that the government was likely to go all the way and show the prisoners no mercy. Seekamp told Ferguson that the government 'had shown no mercy before and there was none to be expected [now]'.

The court, in evidence against Seekamp, used his own words against him. His comments published in the *Ballarat Times* on 18 November 1854, around the time of the 'monster meeting' at Bakery Hill and the burning of the licences, surely proved the prosecution case. He had published:

> This league is nothing more or less than the Germ of Australian Independence. The die is cast and fate has stamped upon the movement its indelible signature. No power on earth can now restrict the united might and headlong strides for freedom of the people of this country and we are lost in amazement while contemplating the dazzling panorama of the Australian future. We salute the league and tender our hopes and prayers for its prosperity.

The following article, published the day before the storming of the Stockade, would surely have tipped the balance and proved the prosecution case against him:

> 2 December 1854, the *Ballarat Times*:—
> Those men who have the power and can exercise it will take the law into their own hands and enforce their principles where the Government now little expect. Instead, therefore, of the diggers looking for remedies where none can be found let them strike deep at the root of rottenness and reform the chief government ... If they are not satisfied the gathering clouds of popular indignation will burst like a whirlwind over guilty and suspecting heads and sweep the length and breadth of the land.⁷

On the day that he was arrested Seekamp had just printed an extraordinary edition of the *Ballarat Times*, which if it had not been secured by a friend and disposed of hastily could have had Seekamp locked up for some time. All but one copy of that issue of the *Times* were consigned to the flames. The only snippet remembered from that issue

LET IT BURN, I'M ONLY A LODGER.

bore the phrase, referring to Eureka: 'This foul and bloody murder calls to high heaven for vengeance, terrible and immediate ...' If Hotham had seen that article Seekamp may have swung rather than lingered in the cells for only three months.

Seekamp had £105 on him when he was taken as he was preparing to depart for Bendigo.

The commission reports

A commission of inquiry was established after Eureka. All the principal goldfields were visited and evidence of the digger's grievances gathered.

The commission had as its members: Chairman William Westgarth, the man responsible for the migration of a large number of hard-working, industrious middle-European settlers (Wends) to the colony (Westgarth also published a *Guide to the Goldfields of Australia* in 1851); Gold Commissioner Wright, a man who had once had a digger arrested on the Forest Creek diggings for riding too quickly past him, failing to remove his hat, and disturbing him while he was reading a newspaper (Wright had also been commissioner on the Bendigo, Ballarat and Castlemaine diggings); and John Pascoe Fawkner, the highly opinionated and influential 'first man of Melbourne' who, after Eureka, voted for a letter of congratulations for 'a job well-done' to be forwarded to the military commander on behalf of the Legislative Council. Other members of the commission were John Hodgson, John O'Shanassy, and James Ford Strachan, who were also all members of the Legislative Council.

When the inquiry placed its report before the governor on 27 March 1855, the same day as the last of the digger-insurgents was acquitted, Hotham was convinced that it showed rather too plainly the hand of Fawkner in its recommendations. The day of governance by imperial decree was at an end,. The battle at the Eureka Stockade had forced the hand of government to allow governance by popular consent. Laws must first be acceptable for the good governance of all to be made good laws.

Although the commission was not directed to inquire into the Stockade affair as a reason for their deliberations, it was not possible to ignore the events leading up to 3 December 1854.

The inquiry found that as the earnings of the diggers were far less than earnings in other comparable industries; the licence fee was both inequitable and oppressive.

The inquiry recommended to the government that the licence fee be abolished. Miners' rights and a tax on the export of gold were introduced

ABOVE:
Let it Burn, I'm Only a Lodger
Wood engraving by Nicholas Chevalier,
published in Melbourne Punch, 1856

Hotham had to face his one-time adversaries Lalor and Humffray in the parliament after their election to the Legislative Council. His control over the affairs of the colony was irreparably weakened by his defeat over the Eureka trials. This cartoon shows Hotham ignoring Victoria, burning, while the Ballarat rebels rally in his head.

(LA TROBE PICTURE COLLECTION, STATE LIBRARY OF VICTORIA)

in its place. They also recommended: that commissioners be replaced with local wardens and elected mining courts; the representation of miners in the Legislative Assembly; and the miner's right to vote. All the recommendations of the commission were adopted.

On 14 July 1855, Raffaello Carboni became the first mining warden appointed to the local court in Ballarat to adjudicate on mining disputes. On 10 November 1855, Peter Lalor and John Basson Humffray were both elected to the Victorian Legislative Assembly. In a completion of the circle which begun when Lalor first arrived in the colony, he was back again working with the railways, only this time he was appointed, not as engineer, but as Minister for Railways in the Victorian government. Poor Sir Charles Hotham was about to have to face the men who had stood against him across the floor of the legislative chamber. He would have to face, daily, the men he had once sought to destroy.

Hotham's demise

Lieutenant-Governor Sir Charles Hotham died just twelve months after the attack on the Stockade — anxious as he was, about the state of public affairs, and the changes being forced on the administration of the colony, he suffered an attack of diarrhoea on 22 December 1855. He had just been informed that an attempt to form a ministry had been abandoned when he suffered an epileptic fit, followed by several more, re-occurring almost every half hour. On the last day of the year, Hotham became comatose around 11.00 in the morning and died at 12.45 in the afternoon of 31 December 1855. During his last days, he was a

ABOVE:
John Pascoe Fawkner — 'The Old Colonist', 1862
Fawkner is credited as the founder of Melbourne when he arrived in Port Phillip on 29 August 1838 ahead of any colonial governor. He was also the first to publish a newspaper in the colony. Fawkner, although fond of military affairs, was responsible for bringing down the report of the Inquiry in the Goldfields that was highly critical of Hotham, and also agreed to the 'digger-Chartists' demands for change
(ALLPORT LIBRARY AND MUSEUM OF FINE ARTS, HOBART)

ABOVE:
Peter Lalor M.L.A Speaker of the House
(REX NAN KIVELL COLLECTION, U4951
BY PERMISSION, NATIONAL LIBRARY OF AUSTRALIA)

"THE RIGHT MAN FOR THE RIGHT PLACE."

Wanted A Governor.

With his heart in the place where a true man's
  should be;
Who can feel for distress in the land where he rules,
Apart from the jargon of old-fashioned schools;
And who does, in the face of a world, what is due
To the claims of the many, and not of the few!

Wanted a governor! — not of the stamp,
That his virtues have always a touch of the cramp;
Not one who would rather his subjects rebel,
Than concede what is just, and their grievance
  dispel;
No formal red-tapist, no old party hack;
Nor one of the kind that we have at TOORAK.

Wanted a governor! — fitted to fill,
A post of some credit with competent skill;
A man of some energy, talent and sense,
To perceive what is right, and the right to dispense;
Who has learnt that the Laws of the Land are
  designed,
For a blessing, and not as a curse to mankind.

Wanted a Governor! Honest and free,
With his heart in the place where a true man's
  should be;
Who can feel for distress in the land where he rules,
Apart from the jargon of old-fashioned schools;
And who does, in the face of a world, what is due
To the claims of the many, and not of the few!

— Melbourne *Punch* (Vol. 1 1856)

disappointed and broken man. He was buried on 3 January 1856 in the Melbourne General Cemetery. The Legislative Council voted a grant of £1,500 towards his burial and the erection of a suitable monument to the man who had brought Victoria almost to a state of civil war.

Commander of the colonial military forces, Major-General Edward Macarthur, the eldest son of New South Wales founding father, sheep-farmer and squatter John Macarthur, held the post as interim governor for the following twelve months, until an appropriate appointment could be made.

Another new governor

Governor Hotham was replaced by Sir Henry Barkly, who arrived in the colony from a posting in Jamaica on 23 December 1856 and was installed the day after Christmas day. Born in London in

ABOVE:

The Right Man for the Right Place
Wood engraving by Frederick Grosse, published in Melbourne Punch, *1856*

Sir Charles and Lady Hotham stand on the quay, looking forward to departing for 'home'. With cashbox in hand and all their possessions stacked up, this image of the couple is wishful thinking on behalf of most of the citizens of Victoria. Hotham never left; he died in office on the last day of December 1856.
(LA TROBE PICTURE COLLECTION, STATE LIBRARY OF VICTORIA)

1815, Barkly was an astute businessman, with extensive estates in Guiana, where had been appointed governor before his appointment to Jamaica. He was to quickly become the first popular governor of the Colony of Victoria. This may have been partly sympathy on the part of the people of Victoria, as his life was struck by personal tragedy early in this posting.

His first wife, Lady Elizabeth, was a popular favourite amongst the colonists. Although expecting the birth of her second child she persisted in driving her pony-cart herself, unattended, as she had often done before. Driving up the slope onto Princes Bridge, an omnibus coming from St. Kilda in the opposite direction crashed into her, tipping her from the cart. The leather reins of the omnibus had snapped and the horses ran free causing the upset. Lady Elizabeth died a few days later. She had been forced into an early labour, as a result of the accident, and had given premature birth to a son. This trauma had proven too much for the popular wife of the Governor. The people of the Colony of Victoria went into mourning for the loss of the first of the imperial appointments for whom they had any affection. Sir Henry Barkly was taken into the hearts of the people over his sad loss.

Barkly made his first visit to the goldfields in 1857. On a later visit, in October 1861, when the mood of the goldfields was totally changed, Barkly played to the crowd. He donned the blue shirt and mode of dress of the miners while inspecting the underground tunnels. It appears that someone in power had, at last, learned something from Hotham's seemingly contradictory view that 'all power proceeds from the people' — that it is better to be seen amongst them than to stand defiantly against them.

The movement for democratic change (which had its beginnings on Forest Creek [Castlemaine] at the 'Great Meeting of Diggers', and spread to Bendigo, where, although the great petition had done little to sway the opinion of the governor, it had united the diggers in opposition) had seen its end-game near the gravel pits at Eureka.

Mark Twain, famed American author and journalist, visited the Australian diggings in 1895. He, like so many other Americans, was sure that the spirit of the goldfields would usher in a long awaited Australian republic when he wrote in 1897:

By and by there was a result; and I think it may be called the finest thing in Australian history.

It was a revolution – small in size, but great politically; it was a strike for liberty, a struggle for principle, a stand against oppression.

It was the Barons and John, over again; it was Hampden and Ship-Money, it was Concord and Lexington, small beginnings all of them great in political results, all of them epoch making.

It is another instance of a victory won by a lost battle. It adds an honourable page to history; the people know it and are proud of it. They keep green the memory of the men who fell at the Eureka Stockade.

ABOVE:
Sir Henry Barkly, K.C.B.E
Photograph by Batchelder & O'Neill, Melbourne, c. 1860
Sir Henry was the first of Victoria's colonial governors who was actually liked by the majority of the people. An astute businessman with a common and quiet geniality, he had also been a highly successful governor of Jamaica before he was posted to Victoria after Hotham's death in 1856.
(LA TROBE PICTURE COLLECTION, STATE LIBRARY OF VICTORIA)

BELOW:
Lola Montes[z]
Hand-coloured photograph, c. 1855
(REX NAN KIVELL COLLECTION, R10777
BY PERMISSION, NATIONAL LIBRARY OF AUSTRALIA)

Lola whips up a storm

HENRY SEEKAMP brought himself to public notice once again when, in 1857, he engaged in a public stoush with Madame Lola Montez, 'The darling of the diggers'.

Fresh from California, Lola was on a tour of the Australian diggings where she was much-loved by all who came to see her rather lascivious stage performances — except for Henry Seekamp.

While Lola had suffered criticism of her performances wherever she had appeared around the globe, her much publicised affairs with Franz Liszt, Alexandre Dumas (peré) and the King of Bavaria had made her an international curiosity, and open to much ridicule. She had even believed that, having bedded Ludwig I, she could have attained royal status. A pity that she had forgotten that she was still married to her first husband, an English army officer who was stationed in India. Ludwig abdicated his throne for the love of Lola, or was it in disgrace at the stupidity of his affair?

Seekamp wrote an article in the *Ballarat Times* which appeared on 19 February, ignoring her performance as an actress and concentrating on her past performances, for which she had earned the sobriquet 'La Belle Horizontale'. It was the detail concerning her private affairs (and there had been many) that raised the ire of Madame Montez.

Lola was in the habit of carrying a riding whip, even when she appeared on stage. She was used to whipping her audience if they failed to please her. In fact, her performances became more popular the angrier she became. At one Paris performance, furious with the reaction she was getting from the audience, she removed her garters and

ABOVE, RIGHT:
Lola Montez and Ludwig I, King of Bavaria
Lola Montez was a libertine, an unusual woman for her time; she had bedded so many great men that she earned the title 'La Belle Horizontale'; however this did not stop the King of Bavaria losing his heart, his head and his throne over his infatuation with her.

After a hasty retreat from Europe, Lola Montez settled in America and toured the Californian diggings where she had limited success; but when she kicked up her heels, and her skirts, in Ballarat and Bendigo, she also kicked up a storm.

Digger William Craig recalled an incident when a lightning bolt struck the stage when she was performing her notorious 'Spider Dance' in Bendigo. Like the great trooper she was, unperturbed, Lola simply announced to her adoring audience that 'there is to be a little thunder and lightning in the latter part of the play' and danced on.

Below:
A cartoon from *Melbourne Punch*, celebrating the other 'Battle of Ballarat', between Madame Lola and the seditious Henry Seekamp.

tossed them angrily into the crowd. They loved it. The audiences then conspired to infuriate her just so they could watch her remove her garters. This was not the kind of career she had hoped for.

Seekamp's article made her crazy. She lay in wait for him at his favourite watering hole, the United States Hotel, which stood next to the Victoria Theatre where she was performing. She attacked Seekamp with her riding crop on the stairs of the hotel. Aware that she may be in wait for him, Seekamp had brought his own whip along and the pair lashed out at each other for several minutes.

The opposition newspaper, the *Ballarat Star*, reported:

> Madame Lola entered from a side door with a short light whip in her hand, and walking quickly up to Mr. Seekamp, who it seems was not altogether unprepared for something of the sort, as soon as he recovered himself from the rapidity of the attack, used his riding whip in return, and for a short time the combat raged with more than Trojan fury.

She was so angry at the newspaperman that she decided to destroy his career. She sued him for criminal libel. He retaliated and sued for assault. She fought back, having him charged with publishing an unregistered newspaper.

While Lola Montez remained a popular figure on the Ballarat goldfields there were few who were prepared to stand up for the once-convicted Henry Seekamp. It seems that Ballarat wanted to move on from the troubled times when Seekamp was a prominent voice in the community. As a result of Lola's actions against Seekamp, the *Ballarat Times* was ruined.

His opinion of Madame Lola Montez may have been somewhat coloured by the fact that he had married a well-known actress, Clara Marie Du Val, in 1854.

THE BATTLE OF Ballarat.

[WHICH IS NOT TO BE FOUND IN THE "PERCY RELIQUES."]

God prosper long our noble selves,
Our lives and safeties all;
A woful battle once there did
On Ballarat befall.

To write the Spanish Dancer down,
Erle Seekamp did essay,
The child may rue that is not born,
The battle of that day.

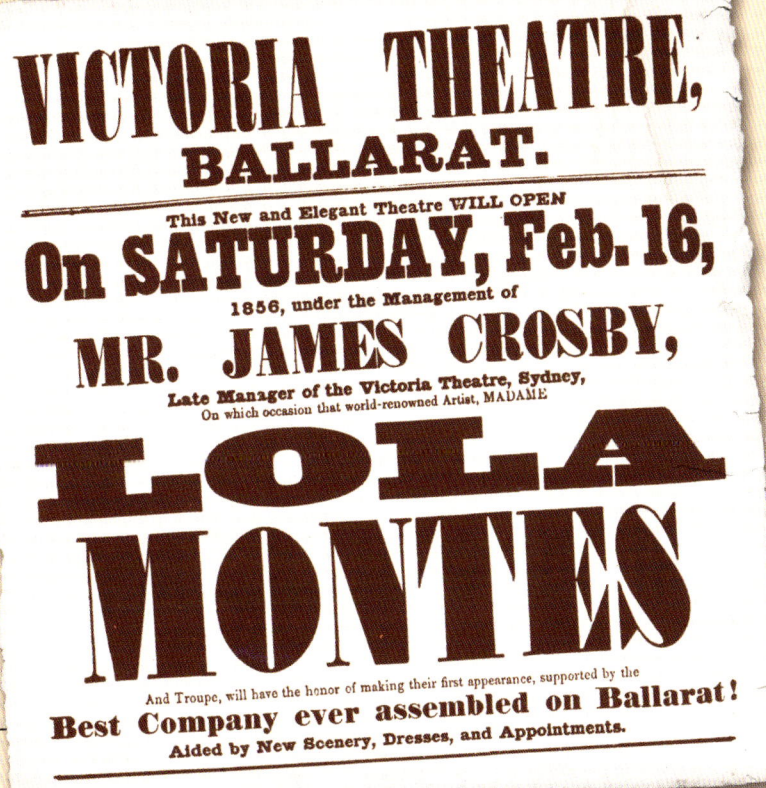

VICTORIA THEATRE, BALLARAT.
This New and Elegant Theatre WILL OPEN
On SATURDAY, Feb. 16,
1856, under the Management of
MR. JAMES CROSBY,
Late Manager of the Victoria Theatre, Sydney,
On which occasion that world-renowned Artist, MADAME
LOLA MONTES
And Troupe, will have the honor of making their first appearance, supported by the
Best Company ever assembled on Ballarat!
Aided by New Scenery, Dresses, and Appointments.

Above:
Theatre poster, Victoria Theatre, Ballarat c. 1857

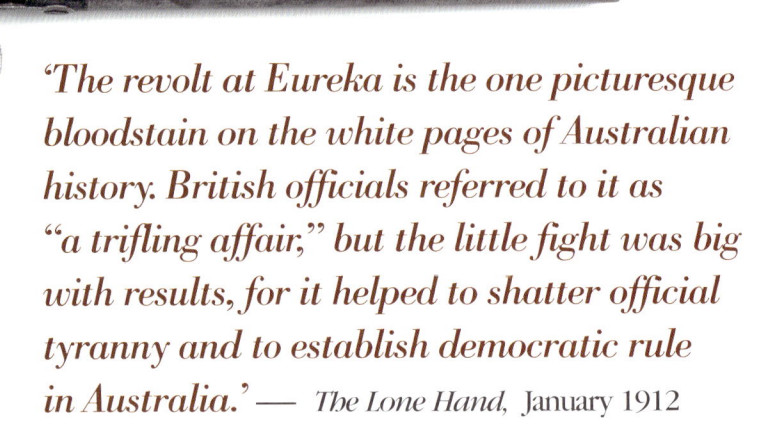

'The revolt at Eureka is the one picturesque bloodstain on the white pages of Australian history. British officials referred to it as "a trifling affair," but the little fight was big with results, for it helped to shatter official tyranny and to establish democratic rule in Australia.' — The Lone Hand, January 1912

In Memoriam

THE FOLLOWING ARE LISTED AS HAVING either being inside the Stockade at the time of the attack, having taken an active part, or as eye-witness to the battle.

Stockaders, innocent-bystanders, eye-witnesses and spies.

ABBOTT, Elizabeth Emms and James — While the battle raged Elizabeth hid behind a trunk inside their tent which was within the Stockade.

ADAMS, Charles — Arrested after the battle.

ADAMS, William — Although not living within the Stockade, William was wounded attempting to take his wife and children to safety.

ALLAIRE, Nicholas — Arrested on 3 December.

ALLEN, Richard — Arrested on 3 December.

ALLEN, Thomas — Allen operated the Waterloo Coffee House which was within the boundary of the Stockade. Once a loyal soldier who had fought with the 33rd Regiment at Waterloo, he had reported to Captain Thomas, of the 40th Regiment, prior to the battle, that he was held prisoner within the Stockade.

AMIES, Elizabeth Anne — Eighteen months old at the time of the battle, Elizabeth was lucky to survive when shots were fired on her parents' tent which had showed the light of a candle after curfew. Sandbags had been packed against the walls of the tent to protect her.

AMIES, Emma (Gloucester, England) and John (Shropshire) — Parents of Elizabeth. All three were present in their tent at the time of the battle.

ANDERSON, Carl — Arrested after the battle (Sweden).

ARNOLD, Arthur — (Bristol, England).

ASH, Joseph —

ASHBURNER, James — Stockader. Pikeman during the battle. Helped Lalor to escape outside the Stockade and hid him beneath a pile of slabs. Arrested, spent the night in 'the Camp' chained to Timothy Hayes. (Liverpool, England).

ATHERDEN, William — Inside the Stockade at the time of the battle. (England).

ATTON, Thomas — (Lincolnshire, England).

ATTWATER, William — a.k.a. Bendigo Bill and Captain Green.

AVONDALE, William — Arrested after the battle.

BAKER, Margaret — Present within the Stockade (England).

BARBERIS, Joseph — Barberis was an adventurer. He first travelled to South America, and then joined

ABOVE:
Peter Lalor's double-shot muzzle loading pistol. Lalor was taking aim with this pistol at the troops breaching the Stockade walls when he was shot in the left shoulder.
(LA TROBE PICTURE COLLECTION, STATE LIBRARY OF VICTORIA)

the '49 rush to California; from there he came to the Ballarat diggings in 1851. A spectator of the battle, he was one of the few men who knew where Lalor was hiding, and even claimed that he knew were Lalor's arm was buried. (Genoa, Italy).

BARCLAY, James — Arrested after the battle.

BARKER and HUNT — storekeepers who had flown the Eureka Flag from their store on Specimen Hill on 29 November 1854.

BARRY, Thomas — Arrested after the battle.

BATTY, N. — In the Stockade at the time of the battle.

BAZLEY, Henry — Arrested after the battle.

BEATTIE, D. — Stockade.

BEATTIE, James — Beattie was arrested by Trooper Henry Goodenough near the London Hotel, 100 metres from the Stockade, after the battle. Sent for trial, charged with treason and was acquitted (Cumberland, England).

BELL, John — Bell jumped ship at Portland in 1852 and headed for the Ballarat diggings (Enniskillen, Ireland).

BELL, William Walton — was within the Stockade at the time of the battle. (Northumberland, England).

BENJAMIN, John — Had a tent within the Stockade.

BIRD, John — Eye-witness to the battle, 13 years old at the time.

BISK, Thomas — Arrested after the battle.

BLACK, Alfred — Lalor's Secretary of War. Alfred was on the Ballarat Reform League Committee and was present when Lalor leapt upon the stump and called the diggers to join with him. Black recorded the names of Lalor's captains and their divisions, and was also responsible for drafting the 'Declaration of Independence'.

BLACK, George — Brother of Alfred. A prominent Chartist, George was also editor of the *Diggers Advocate* and a voting member of the Ballarat Reform League. He was present within the Stockade at the time of the battle.

BLACK, George — Brother of Alfred.

BOURKE, John — Stockader.

BOX, Thomas — Arrested after the battle.

BRADFORD, William — Stockader. Bradford had a piece of the flag which is displayed at the Eureka Centre.

BRADLEY, J.T. — Stockader.

BRADY, Hugh — Stockader.

BRIGGS, George — Stockader.

BROWN, Charles — Arrested after the battle.

BURNNETT, Robert — Captain of the Californian Brigade.

CAHILL, John — Stockader, arrested after the battle County Clare).

CAIL, Amy — Helped to hide Lalor (Monmouth, Wales).

CAIL, John — (Winchester, England).

CALLINAN, Bridget — present after battle. Helped her three stockader brothers, John, Michael and Patrick, to escape.

CALLINAN, John (jnr.) — Stockader (County Clare).

CALLINAN, Michael — Stockader, wounded in battle.

CALLINAN, Patrick—Stockader, wounded in battle.

CAMPBELL, James — First to enter the Stockade after battle.

CAMPBELL, James McFie — Stockader, arrested, sent for trial, aquitted (Jamaican)

CANNY, Michael — Stockader, wounded in battle (County Clare).

CANNY, Patrick — Stockader, wounded in battle, brother of Michael.

CAPUANO, Antonio — Stockader (Italy).

CARTNEY, James — Had a tent outside the Stockade. Rushed to join in the battle but was too late. Hid in a chimney until the troopers had gone. Earned nickname 'Smoking Jimmy'.

CLENDINNING, Dr. George — Donated guns to stockaders.

CLENDINNING, Martha — Wife of George. Martha had a piece of the flag given to her by Dr. Carr.

CLIFTON, William or George — Stockader, wounded in battle, died one month later (Bristol, England).

CONDON, Edmond — Stockader, escaped to Brown Hill (Tipperary, Ireland).

COSTELLO, Lancelot — Transportee. Claimed compensation for destruction of his tent which stood within the Stockade (Ireland).

COX, Thomas — Stockader, escaped and hid in a deserted mine (Chelsea, London)

COX, William and Eliza — Henry Powell died in William and Eliza Cox's tent after battle.

COXHEAD, Frederic London — Stockader, wounded in battle, died 18 months later (London, England).

CROOK, Christopher — One of first inside the Stockade after battle.

CROWE, A.W. — Stockader, wounded, died later from his wounds (Scotland).

CROWE, John — Stockader, killed in battle (Kilkenny).

CUMMINS, Stephen (Ireland) and Jane (England) — Sheltered Lalor after battle. Helped to move him to Geelong.

CURTAIN, Patrick — Stockader and captain of the pikemen. Had all his possessions destroyed when troops fired the Stockade.

DALTON, John Thomas — Stockader, helped to hide Lalor beneath slabs (Ireland).

D'ANGRI, Natale — Later was to become mining partner with Lalor, Red Streak Mine, Creswick (Naples, Italy).

DAVIDSON, George — Arrested after battle.

DAVIS, Mrs. — Eye-witness, saw trooper fire at Carboni.

DAVIS, William — Avoided capture by hiding down a mine-shaft (Truro, Cornwall).

DAWS, Charles Pearson — (Nottinghamshire, England).

DEGAN, Thomas — Arrested after battle.

DELAHUNTY, William M. — Stockader.

DELAMERE, John — Arrested after battle.

De LONGEVILLE, Harry — Stockader, claimed to have heard the bugle call and fired the first shot that awakened the diggers and started the battle.

DEVELIN, Willam — Arrested after battle.

DIAMOND, Martin (County Clare) and Ann — Had store, half in, half out of the Stockade. Martin was bayoneted by the troops in front of the store, and in front of his wife.

DIGNAM, Thomas — Stockader, pikeman, wounded, arrested, sent for trial, acquitted without trial (Sydney, Australia).

DONAGHEY, George — Stockader, killed in battle (Donegal)

DONNELLY, Catherine — Six years old at time of battle, she was among several children who were lost and were said to have been looked after by Aborigines.

DONNELLY, John — Storekeeper who lost all his possessions after the troops fired the Stockade. Claimed compensation, was rejected. Father of Catherine.

DOUDIET, Charles — Eye-witness. Helped Captain Ross to escape to the Free Trade Hotel where he died later of his wounds.

DOYLE, Dr. Timothy — Helped in the amputation of Lalor's arm.

DUKE, Anne — One of the women who sewed the stars on the Southern Cross Flag. In the Stockade at the time of the battle.

DUKE, George — Husband of Ann, and was in the Stockade at the time of the battle.

DUMBRELL, Stephan — Stockader.

DUMBRILL, W. — Stockader.

DUNLOP, John — Stockader. Veteran of the battle of Waterloo, Cavalry officer Dunlop was recruiting a mounted division for the defence of the Stockade but was too late. With James Regan discovered the first gold at Poverty Point. Close friend of Lalor and Duncan Gillies (Scotland).

DUPRAT — Carboni claimed that Duprat was within the Stockade at the time of the battle.

DYNAN, Denis — Stockader, wounded in battle. (County Clare).

DYNAN, Michael — Arrested after the battle.

DYTE, Charles — Eye-witness, close friend of Bentley.

EARLS, J. — Stockader.

EDWARDS, Nicholas — Arrested after the battle.

ELLIS, Joseph — Arrested after the battle.

EMMERMAN, William — Stockader, killed during battle (Petersburg).

EMMERSON, George and Phoebe —storekeepers. Phoebe sheltered Black, Humffray and George Scobie (brother of James) after battle. After her husband George passed away in 1857 she married George Scobie (Durham, England).

ESMOND, James Willam — Stockader, gathered arms and ammunition for the defence of the Stockade. The discoverer of the first gold at Creswick somehow managed to avoid arrest after the battle.

EVANS, J. — Stockader.

FAHEY, Mary and Phillip — Storekeepers on the Eureka diggings (Tipperary).

FAULDS, Mary and Matthew — Within the Stockade, their daughter Adeliza was born at the time the battle (Glasgow, Scotland).

FENTON — Stockader, wounded during battle, died shortly after.

FERDINAND — Arrested after battle.

FERGUSON — Arrested after battle.

FERGUSON, Charles Derius — Eye-witness. Californian Ranger who witnessed the shooting of Captain Wise. Arrested after battle, but later released due to the representation of Dr. Kenworthy, who spoke convincingly to Hotham on behalf of all the Americans — except poor John Joseph (America).

FIRMAN, G. G. — Stockader.

FISCHER, W. — Stockader.

FLYNN, Edward — Killed by soldiers as he was running from the Stockade.

FRANK, John Arnold — Was inside the Stockade at the time of the battle (Yorkshire, England).

FRANKS, Agnes — Eye-witness. In her tent within the Stockade at the time of the battle (Kilkenny, Scotland).

FRASER, Alexander — Arrested after battle (Scotland).

FRASER, John — Eye-witness (Scotland).

GALLOWAY, William — Arrested after battle. Had tent next to William Cox, witness at inquest into the death of Henry Powell.

GAVIN, Matthew and Molly — Inside the Stockade (Ireland).

GAYNOR, Thomas — Inside the Stockade, helped to conceal Lalor beneath the slabs. Brother of Anne Duke (Ireland).

GILHOOLY, Patrick — Arrested after the battle.

GILLIES, Duncan — Partner to Peter Lalor in the claim at the gravel pits (Glasgow, Scotland).

GILMORE, George — Stockader, (Coleraine, Ireland).

GITTINGS, Patrick — Killed in battle (Kilkenny, Ireland).

GLEESON, Martin — Publican, hid miners after the battle (Kilkenny, Ireland).

GLENN — Arrested as a spy by the stockaders before the battle. Glenn made so much noise the stockaders let him go.

GODDARD, G. — By-stander, wounded during battle.

GORDON — Storekeeper arrested after battle.

GOVE, Bill — Stockader.

GRAY, Joseph — Arrested after battle.

GREEN, Samuel — Stockader, killed during battle (England).

GREEN, Tom — Ex-serviceman, stood guard over Skarrat's Victoria Restaurant which was near the Stockade.

GULLEN, Martin K. — Lad who threw the stone that broke the lamp at Bentley's Hotel. The fire that ensued was the beginning of the whole Eureka inferno. Eye-witness to the battle.

HAFELE, John — Blacksmith who forged pikes for the pikemen, killed in the battle (Wurtenberg, Germany).

HALL, Captain John — Stockader. Witness to the shooting of Captain Wise.

HALL, Robert (Newcastle-upon-Tyne, England), his sons James and Thomas — Brickmaker Robert Hall sheltered his sons beneath some planking during the battle. Eye-witness to the battle.

HALL, W. R. — Stockader, a Californian Ranger during the battle.

HANLEY, Michael — Stockader, wounded in battle.

HANNAFIN, Patrick — Stockader, wounded in battle.

HANRAHAN, John — Stockader (Ireland).

HANRAHAN, Michael — Stockader, captain of the pikemen. Although he was Lalor's right-hand man he was not in the Stockade at the time of battle (Ireland).

HAPPY JACK a.k.a. George Clifton — Stockader, severley wounded in battle, died on 14 January 1855 of his wounds; said to have been a derelict nobleman.

HARDIE, William Simpson — Shot in a fusillade from 'the Camp' on 4 December 1855. Amputated leg as a result of his injury and died of typhoid on 9 January 1855.

HARTINGTON, Anna — Attended the wounded after the battle at the request of Father Smyth.

HARTLEY, George Robert — Stockader, known as the 'Stockade Poet', slighty wounded in battle (Philadelphia, United States of America).

HASLEHAM, Frank Arthur — Correspondent for the *Geelong Advertiser*, was shot in the right shoulder by police 300 metres outside the Stockade. Received £400 compensation for his injury.

HAYES, Anastasia — Wife of Ballarat Reform League Chairman Timothy Hayes; she assisted in the amputation of Lalor's arm, took the arm and threw it down a mineshaft. Helped sew the flag of the Southern Cross (Kilkenny, Ireland).

HAYES, Michael — Helped shelter Lalor in his tent at the foot of Black Hill, before Lalor could be taken to Geelong.

HAYES, Timothy — Chairman of the Ballarat Reform League who was arrested after the battle while 300 metres from the Stockade. Mining partner of Peter Lalor. Sent for trial, charged with treason (Kilkenny Ireland).

HEFFERNAN, James — Stockader, helped carry Lalor to safety.

HENDERSON, J. B. — Professional artist, witness to the battle.

HENFIELD (HEFELE), Thomas (John) — Stockader, blacksmith, killed in battle (Wurtemburg, Germany).

HEPBURN, James — Arrested after battle.

HICKEY, Patrick — Arrested after battle.

HIGGINS, Richard Sydney — Stockader. Having run out of ammunition, Higgins ran from the Stockade and was chased by a mounted trooper with sword drawn. Higgins turned and aimed the empty pistol at the trooper, who, after weighing up the situation, wheeled his horse about and galloped away (Killarney, County Kerry).

HINDS, Isaac — Arrested after battle.

HINDON, Joseph — Arrested after battle.

HOGAN, Jeremiah — Arrested after battle.

HOGGAN, James Cochran — Was at Eureka with his 16-year-old son James (Scotland).

HOLMES, Laurence Carter — Holmes was moving his horses to safety at the time of the battle. He assisted with the wounded later in the day.

HOLYOAKE, George — Prominent Chartist and member of the Ballarat Reform League. Brother of Henry (London).

HOLYOAKE, Henry — Political activist, Chartist, member of the Ballarat Reform League, Goldfields Reform League. He was on his way back from Bendigo when he heard the news that the Stockade had fallen (London).

HONISS, Edward — Was out walking early in the morning when he saw carts moving dead bodies away from the Stockade.

HOWARD, Patrick — Arrested after the battle (Dublin, Ireland).

HOWES, Charles — Stockader (Tasmania).

HOWSON, Walter — Eye-witness to the battle.

HUMPHREYS, Richard — Arrested after the battle.

HYNES, Bridget — Eye-witness. Bridget, among several other women, saved the lives of a number of stockaders when troops were bayoneting the wounded after the attack by crying out 'He's dead!'. (County Galway, Ireland).

HYNES, John — Killed during the battle (County Clare, Ireland).

HYNES, Thomas — Stockader, pikeman, husband to Bridget who was said to have hidden his trousers and pike to keep him away from the Stockade. First cousin of Patrick Hynes (soldier) and John Hynes, who was killed in battle.

JACK, 'Three Finger' — Leader of the 'Tipperary Mob'.

JACKSON, Harry — Eye-witness to the battle.

JACKSON, William — Eye-witness to the battle.

JAMES, Henry — Stockader.

JONES, Edmund — Stockader.

JONES, John — Sawyer, ordered by the military to make coffins for the dead (Wales).

JONES, William — Stockader. Arrested after the battle.

JOSEPH, John — Stockader. African-American. Arrested after the battle, sent for trial, charged with treason. Accused of shooting Captain Wise (New York, United States of America).

JUKES, Gordon — Eye-witness.

JULIEN, Robert — Stockader. Severely wounded in battle, died 14 January 1855 of his wounds (Nova Scotia, Canada).

KEDDER, Charles — Arrested after the battle.

KEENAN, John — Stockader (Kings County, Ireland).

KELLY, Catherine — Six years old at the time, she was cared for by Aborigines during the battle (Kilkenny, Ireland).

KELLY, Daniel, Jeremiah and Patrick — Present at Eureka.

KELLY, John — Stockader. Arrested after battle.

KELLY, Timothy — Refused to participate after hearing the password for the Stockade was 'Vinegar Hill'.

KELLY, Thomas — Father of Daniel, Jeremiah and Patrick, and was training others as militia for the defence of the Stockade.

KEMP, J. — Stockader.

KENNEDY, Patrick — Arrested after battle.

KENNEDY, Thomas — Prominent 'physical force' Catholic Chartist. Member of the Ballarat Reform League. Kennedy was attempting to bring diggers from Creswick to support the Stockade at the time of the battle (Scotland).

KENT, Francis — Arrested after the battle.

KIDD, Robert — Stockader.

KINNANE, Nancy — Nursed Peter Lalor after the battle (Tipperary, Ireland).

KINNEAR, Martin — Arrested after the battle.

KNIPE, John — Prominent agitator against the licence fee, Knipe was present in the Stockade as a delegate from Simpson's diggings and Bendigo. He was arrested after the battle.

LALOR, Peter — Stockader. Member of Ballarat Reform League, commander-in-chief of the Stockade. Severely wounded in battle. Charged with treason, in absentia, but avoided capture (Queens County, Ireland).

LAZARUS, Samuel — Eye-witness to the battle.
LEADLOW, John — Arrested after the battle.
LEE, Morgan — Stockader (County Galway, Ireland).
LENAN, Mrs. — A soldier took a pot-shot at her, when she stuck her head out of her tent, which was near to the Stockade.
LESLIE, Robert — Arrested after the battle.
LESSMAN, Adolfus — Stockader. Lieutenant of riflemen, slightly wounded in battle (Hanover).
LEVINSON, Hyman — Eye-witness.
LEWIS, Abbot, Benjamin and Minchin — Stockaders. Brothers (Ireland).
LIGHT, Jenny — Said to have provided fabric for the flag of the Southern Cross.
LISTER, Andrew — Stockader.
LITTLE, Joseph — Although reported in the government *Gazette* as being killed in the battle, there is no evidence that he was in the Stockade.
LIVINGSTON, Charles — Arrested after the battle.
LONG, James — Inside the Stockade at the time of the battle.
LORRIMER, Robert — Eye-witness (Scotland).
LYNCH, John — Stockader. Captain under Lalor. Helped to conceal Lalor beneath a pile of slabs (County Clare, Ireland).
McCARTNEY — Arrested after the battle.
MADDEN, James (12 years) and John (11 years) — Eye-witnesses (Armagh, Ireland).
MADDEN, John (snr.) — Stockader.
MADDEN, William John — Stockader. Father of James and John.
MAGENNIS, Duguld — Arrested after the battle.
MAINGER — Eye-witness.
MAINE, D. — Stockader.
MALCOLM, James — Eye-witness (Scotland).
MALRYEN, Thomas — Arrested after the battle.
MANNING, John — Stockader. Arrested and charged with treason, sent for trial and acquitted. Said to have written many of the articles for the *Ballarat Times* for which Henry Seekamp was convicted of sedition.
MARTIN, Michael — Eye-witness (County Fermanagh, Ireland).
MATTSON, Isaac — Stockader (California, America).
MAYHER, Thomas — Arrested after the battle.
McCULLAGH — Taken prisoner by the Stockaders as a spy.

McGILL, James Herbert — Stockader. Commander of the Californian Rifle Brigade. Second-in-command to Peter Lalor (America).
McGLYNN, Edward — Stockader. Killed in battle (Tipperary, Ireland).
McGRATH, George — Stockader.
McGRATH, Tobias — Stockader.
McINERNEY, Michael — Stockader (County Clare, Ireland).
McKEOWN, Joseph — Arrested after the battle.
McLAREN, Alexander (Sandy) — Stockader. Hid with Thomas Cox, in a deserted mine, after the battle (Lanarkshire, Scotland).
McMAHON, Edward — Arrest after the battle.
McNAB — Blacksmith who had his forge inside the Stockade.
MEADE, Patrick — Arrested after the battle.
MEAGHER, Michael — Arrested after the battle.
MELODY, Bill — Lieutenant of the Californian Brigade.
MILLMAN, Alfred — Stockader (Buckinghamshire, England).
MOLLOY, William — Arrested and sent for trial. Acquitted.
MOORE, Patrick — Stockader (County Clare).
MOORE, Thaddeus — Stockader, wounded in battle, died later in the day. Brother of Patrick (County Clare, Ireland).
MORRISON, Michael — Stockader, wounded in the battle (County Galway, Ireland).
MULLET, Lydia — Eye-witness.
MULLINS, Michael — Stockader, killed in battle. Incorrectly recorded as Thomas on the Eureka monument (County Limerick, Ireland).
MURPHY, James — Stockader. Blacksmith and pike sharpener. Helped to ferry Lalor to Geelong. On meeting Lalor years later Murphy was enraged when Peter Lalor, MLA Minister for Railways, did not remember him.
MURPHY, Thomas — Arrested after the battle.
NAYLOR, James Cooper — Stockader.
NEALSON — Stockader, one of the digger leaders.
NIDA, Antonio Francisco — One of the Creswick men who joined the Stockade. He was camped outside the Stockade at the time of the battle.
NIDSCHELM, Harold E. —
NOONAN, Mrs Michael — Assaulted at the time of the battle.

NOONAN, Michael — Arrested at the time of the battle.

O'BRIEN, John — Eye-witness to the battle.

O'BRIEN, Kennedy — Arrested after the battle.

O'BRIEN, Michael — Stockader. Father Smyth asked O'Brien to move Lalor from tent to tent after the battle.

O'DAY, Patrick — Stockader. Although he had trained the pikemen, he was absent attending to his wife at the birth of their child at the time of the battle.

O'DONOGHUE, Patrick — Stockader.

O'MAHONY, M. — Stockader.

O'NEIL, John — Stockader (Ireland).

O'NEIL, Michael — Stockader, wounded in battle (County Clare, Ireland).

O'NEIL, William — Stockader.

O'NEILL, Thomas — Stockader. Pikeman, killed in battle (County Kilkenny, Ireland).

ORAVALNO — Stockader, died as result battle wounds.

O'ROURKE, Thomas — Arrested after the battle.

ORR, Matthew — Arrested after the battle.

OSBORNE, A. — Stockader.

PARDY, John — Arrested after the battle.

PENHALLURIACK, William — Had left the Stockade before the battle.

PENNY, Samuel — Arrested after the battle.

PENROSE, Joseph — Arrested after the battle.

PERGO — Arrested after the battle (Spain).

PETERS, Cornelius — Arrested after the battle (Holland).

PETERS, Andrew — Carboni called this man a spy.

PICKUP, James — Digger at the gravel pits who witnessed police setting fire to Michael Noonan's tent.

PIERSON, — Eye-witness.

POHILL — Arrested after the battle.

POLINELLI, Antonio — Stockader (Bergamo, Italy).

POTTER, John Lishman — Stockader.

POWELL, Henry — Creswick digger who took no part in the battle. Died as a result of wounds inflicted by Sergeant Akehurst after the battle.

POWELL, John — Arrested after the battle.

POWLETT, F.A. — Bystander, wounded during the battle.

PRIAULX, Peter — Arrested after the battle.

QUIN, John — Arrested after the battle.

QUIN, Edward — Stockader, killed during battle (Ireland).

QUINANE, Patrick and Nancy — Their tent within the Stockade was detroyed by troopers. Nancy attended the amputation of Lalor's arm (Tipperary, Ireland).

QUINLAN, William — Stockader, killed in battle (Goulburn, New South Wales).

QUINN, Edward — Stockader, killed in battle (County Clare, Ireland).

RANKIN, E. —

REDMAN, G. — Eye-witness.

REED, Henry — Arrested after the battle, charged with treason, sent for trial, acquitted.

REGAN, James — With John Dunlop, Regan found the first gold at Poverty Point, Ballarat. Said to have been one of those who helped Lalor to escape from the Stockade.

RICHARDSON — Stockader who lost an arm in the battle.

RICHARDSON, J — Stockader.

ROBERTSON, John — Stockader. Friend of Carboni. Killed in battle (Perthsire, Scotland).

ROBILLIARD, Henry — Arrested after the battle.m

ROBINSON, John — Stockader (Nova Scotia, Canada).

RODAN, John — Arrested after the battle (Scotland).

ROMEO, Le Fronzis — Arrested after the battle (Corsica).

ROSS, Alexander — Arrested after the battle.

ROSS, Captain Charles — Stockader. Severely wounded in battle; died on 5 December 1854 as a result of wounds. Designed the flag of the Southern Cross (Canada).

ROWLANDS, Elizabeth and Mary — Eye-witnesses.

ROWLANDS, Llewellyn — Stockader. Killed during battle.

RYAN, James — Stockader (Tipperary, Ireland).

RYAN, Martin — Arrested after the battle. Had all his property destroyed by troopers.

RYAN, Matthew — Had his tent destroyed by troopers.

RYAN, Patrick — Had tent within the Stockade.

RYLEY, Walter — Arrested after the battle.

SCOBIE, George — Stockader. Brother of the murdered James Scobie (Auchterarder, Scotland).

SERJEANT, Robert Malachi — Eye-witness.

SEXTON, James — Arrested after the battle.

SHANAHAN, Edward (Teddy) — Had tent within the Stockade (America).

SHEADY, Patrick — Arrested after the battle.

SHEEHAN, John — Had property destroyed after battle.

SHEEHAN, Luke — Stockader. Leader of the pikemen. He was wounded in the battle (County Galway, Ireland).

SHIELDS, G. — Stockader.

SMITH, Arthur — Arrested after the battle.

SMITH, Catherine — Supposedly killed during battle.

SMITH, Richard John — Arrested after the battle.

SMITH, Thomas Henry — Stockader (England).

SMITH, William (Billy) — Stockader.

SOMERVILLE, William — Arrested after the battle.

SORANSON, Jacob — Stockader. Arrested, charged with treason, sent for trial, acquitted (Sweden).

STAFFORD, William — Arrested after the battle.

STEER, William James — Arrested after the battle.

STEINMAN, Herman — Arrested after the battle.

STURRICH, Charles Louis — Stockader (Switzerland).

SUTHERLAND, Dr. Henry — Stockader. Mate of Peter Lalor and Duncan Gillies (Isle of Skye, Scotland).

SYMMONS, James — Injured during the battle (England).

SYMONDS, Francis F. — Wounded in the battle (Cornwall, England).

SYMONDS, William Gummow — Brother of Francis. Within Stockade at the time of battle.

TAPPIN, J. — Stockader.

THOMAS, William — (Cornwall, England).

VENNICK, Jan — Arrested in his tent 300 metres from the Stockade, accused of treason, sent for trial, acquitted (Holland).

VERN, Frederick - (Hanover). Vern was one of the early leaders of the Ballarat Reform League, although there were some who suggested that he was also a spy for Governor Hotham. In a bogus farewell letter, published in the *Age* on 15 January 1855, he mourns his 'banishment' from Australia and the denial of either the 'warrior's death' or a 'patriot's grave'.

Carboni wrote that it was Vern's long legs that had denied him his place among the heroes, as he was last seen by his compatriots running hell-for-leather into the bush at the height of the battle at the Stockade.

It is believed the Vern turned up years later when, under the guise of Mr. Charles H. F. De la Vern of Forbes, he wrote to the Chief Secretary of the Government of New South Wales offering his services in the hunt for notorious bushrangers, including Ben Hall.

Vern claimed his military experience in both Hungary and America as reference in his favour, but failed to mention his 'revolutionary' experience in Ballarat. The Inspector-General of Police, John McLerie, worked against Vern, claiming that he knew his true identity and advised the governor that a reward of £500 was still being offered by the government of Victoria for his capture. Vern was not engaged for the hunt for Hall and his mates.

WALKER, Joseph — Arrested after the battle.

WALLACE, D. — Tents and clothing destroyed by troopers.

WARNER, James —Stockader. Wounded in the battle.

WATSON, Robert — Stockader (Paisley, Scotland).

WATTS, J. — Marched with 2,000 men from Creswick to join the Stockade. He was with 300 men to meet the soldiers on the Melbourne road at the time of the battle.

WEARNE, Elizabeth — Eye-witness. Six years old at the time of the battle, she witnessed the soldiers marching to the Stockade.

WEARNE, James and Patience — Eye-witnesses. Patience is said to have hidden a miner beneath her skirt after the battle.

WHITE, Andrew — Arrested after the battle.

WHITE, William R. — (Cornwall, England).

WIBURD, James — Stockader. White was also involved in the Lambing Flat Riot of 1867 (London, England).

WILLIAMS, Theo — Eye-witness. A 'Moral-force' supporter he was, nevertheless, wounded by a sabre-cut near his tent 300 metres from the Stockade.

WILSON, Elizabeth and Richard T. — Eye-witnesses who had a store opposite the Stockade. One of the diggers hid beneath her skirts to avoid capture.

WINKFIELD, Robert — Arrested after the battle.

WINKLY, George — Arrested after the battle.

WITHERS, Anastasia and Samuel (London) — Anastasia was one of the first women on the Victorian diggings. She is said to be one of the three women who sewed the flag of the Southern Cross.

WRIGHT, William — Arrested after the battle.

WYBURD, J. — Stockader.

YOUNG, Mrs. James — It is said that Peter Lalor hid under her skirt during his escape from the Stockade.

ZILLES, Conrad — Publican who was present at the time of the battle (Germany).

WHILE IT IS NOT POSSIBLE TO KNOW IF all of the following military personnel actually took part in the battle on 3 December 1854, their presence in Ballarat is known and it is highly likely that they did their duty on that fateful day.

Military

ADAIR, Robert — Private, 12th Regiment.
ADAMS — Lieutenant, 40th Regiment.
AKEHURST, Arthur — Special Constable.
ALDERTON, William — Sergeant, 12th Regiment.
AMOS, Gilbert — Gold Commissioner, Warden.
ARCHER, Edward — Private, 12th Regiment.
ARDEN, George Banks Floyer — Surgeon, 12th Regiment.
ATKINSON, Arthur — Captain, 12th Regiment.
ATTWELL, William — Private, 12th Regiment.
BADCOCK, John — Police Trooper.
BARDEN, Joseph — Private, 12th Regiment.
BARNEBY, — Commander
BIGSBY, Josiah — Soldier, 40th Regiment.
BIRCH, John — Private, 12th Regiment.
BIRD, William — Private, 12th Regiment.
BITTERLY, William — Police Trooper.
BOURNE, James — Private, 12th Regiment.
BOWDLER, George Owen — Lieutenant, 40th Regiment.
BOYLE, Felix — Private, 12th Regiment, (killed in battle).
BOZEN, John — Private, 12th Regiment.
BRADLEY, Bartholemew — Private, 12th Regiment.
BRAGG, William — Private, 12th Regiment.
BREADLEY, Thomas — Private, 40th Regiment.
BREWEN, — Sergeant.
BRIEN, Denis — Private, 40th Regiment, (killed in battle).
BROADHURST, John Edward — Lieutenant, 40th Regiment. Commanded the force who were present at the burning of Bentley's Hotel.
BROKER, Benjamin — Private, 12th Regiment.
BROWN, George — Private, 12th Regiment.
BROWN, James — Private, 12th Regiment.
BRUCE-GARDYNE, Thomas McPherson — Lieutenant, 40th Regiment.
BRYAN, John — Private, 12th Regiment.
BRYANT, George — Private, 12th Regiment.
BURGESS, Samuel — Private, 12th Regiment.
BURT, Frank R. — Private, 12th Regiment.
BURY, James — Private, 12th Regiment.
BUTLER, Patrick — Sergeant, 40th Regiment.
BUTTWELL, William — Private, 12th Regiment, (wounded).
BYERS, John — Private, 12th Regiment.
BYLORD, George — Soldier, 40th Regiment.
BYRNE, Peter — Soldier, 12th Regiment.
CALVIN, Timothy — Private, 12th Regiment.
CAMERON, John — Private, 40th Regiment.
CAMPBELL, John — Private, 40th Regiment.
CANTY, Andrew — Private, 12th Regiment.
CANTY, Timothy — Private, 12th Regiment.
CARTER, Charles Jefferies — Sub-Inspector, foot police. Carter was ordered by Captain Thomas to set fire to the Stockade after the troops had been withdrawn.
CASSERLEY, John — Sergeant, 12th Regiment.
CHAMBERLAIN, Charles — Private, 12th Regiment.
CHOMLEY, Hussey — Sub-Inspector, Police.
CHRISTIE, Edward — Private, 12th Regiment.
CLAMPERT, Samuel — Private, 12th Regiment.
CLARK, James — Police Trooper.
CLARKE, Sir Andrew — Military Engineer.
CLIFF, William — Private, 40th Regiment.
CLINTON, Patrick — Private, 12th Regiment.
COLLINS, Jonas — Private, 12th Regiment.
COLES, Edwin — Private, 40th Regiment.
COLVIN, William — Corporal, 12th Regiment.
CONCRITT, John — Mounted Policeman.
COOMBE, Richard — Private, 12th Regiment.
CORK, Willam — Private, 40th Regiment.
CORNISH, Robert — Private, 12th Regiment.
COTTES, Henry — Private, 40th Regiment (wounded).
CRESSWELL, John — Private, 12th Regiment.
CRICK, William — Private, 12th Regiment.
CROSS, Joseph — Private, 12th Regiment.
CROTHERS, William — Private, 12th Regiment.
CRUDE, Hayman — Private, 12th Regiment.
CULPECK, Thomas — Private, 12th Regiment.
CUSACK, Martin — Private, 40th Regiment.
DALEY, Martin — Private, 12th Regiment.
DAVIDSON, William — Private, 12th Regiment.
DAVIE, James — Private, 12th Regiment.
DAVIS, George — Private, 12th Regiment.

DAVIS, Samuel — Private, 12th Regiment.
DAWSON, Thomas. H. — Private, 12th Regiment.
DEWY, Thomas — Private, 12th Regiment.
DOHERTY, John — Trooper
DONEGAN, John — Private, 12th Regiment.
DONNELLY, Thomas — Private, 12th Regiment.
DICK, Dr. — Doctor, 12th Regiment.
DONEGAN, John — Private, 12th Regiment.
DONNELLY, Thomas — Private, 12th Regiment.
DONOHOE, John — Private, 12th Regiment.
DORE, John — Private, 12th Regiment.
DOWARD, John — Private, 12th Regiment.
DOWD, Peter — Private, 12th Regiment.
DOWNS, Thomas — Private, 12th Regiment.
DRURY, John — Private, 12th Regiment.
DUKE, John — Private, 12th Regiment.
DUTTON, Frederick — Private, 12th Regiment.
DWYER, Patrick — Private, 40th Regiment.
EGAN, John — Drummer boy, 12th Regiment. John Egan was reported to have been killed when the diggers fired upon the troops as they drove through the Eureka field on 28 November 1854. The truth is that Egan was shot in the groin, and survived, although a tombstone was erected after Eureka which told an entirely different story.
FENNELLY, William — Private, 12th Regiment.
FERGUSON, Adam — Private, 12th Regiment.
FERGUSON, Owen — Private, 12th Regiment.
FINNESS, John — Private, 12th Regiment.
FINN, John — Private, 12th Regiment.
FISCHER, Henry — Private, 12th Regiment.
FITZGERALD, Thomas — Private, 40th Regiment.
FLYNN, Daniel — Private, 12th Regiment.
FLYNN, John — Private, 12th Regiment.
FORD, James — Private, 12th Regiment.
FORSYTH, Joseph — Private, 12th Regiment.
FOSTER, Henry — Police inspector. Foster arrested Timothy Hayes outside the Stockade after the battle.
FRENCH, William (Norm) — Private, 40th Regiment, (severely wounded).
FRIEND, William — Private.
FROST, Thomas — Private, 40th Regiment.
FULLER, George — Private, 12th Regiment.
FURGIS, William — Private, 12th Regiment.
FURNELL, Samuel — Police sub-inspector. Furnell was in charge of mounted police in the attack on the Stockade.

GALVIN, Timothy — Private, 12th Regiment, (severely wounded).
GAFFENEY, Patrick — Private, 12th Regiment.
GARDENER, William — Sergeant, 40th Regiment.
GARDINER, Willam — Private, 12th Regiment.
GARDNER, James — Private, 12th Regiment.
GARDYNE, Thomas McMahon Bruce — Lieutenant, 40th Regiment.
GARVEY, Thomas — Private, 12th Regiment.
GARWOOD, Joseph — Private, 12th Regiment.
GATES, Alfred — Private, 12th Regiment.
GAY, Michael — Private, 12th Regiment.
GIBSON, Joseph — Sergeant, 12th Regiment.
GLADING, George — Private, 12th Regiment.
GLANCEY, James — Private, 12th Regiment.
GODDARD, Henry — Private, 12th Regiment.
GOODENOUGH, Henry — Police under-cover agent. After the battle, Goodenough arrested James Beattie and Raffaello Carboni.
GORE, James — Private, 40th Regiment. Gore was one of the first military men into the Stockade.
GRANT, Robert — Private, 12th Regiment.
GREEN, William — Private, 12th Regiment.
GRIFFIN, Robert — Private, 12th Regiment.
GRIMSTONE, Bryan — Private, 12th Regiment.
GRIMWOOD, Thomas — Private, 12th Regiment.
HACKETT, Charles Prendergast — Police Magistrate. Hackett was at the Stockade before the battle. He was to read the Riot Act, but events went too quickly for him to do his duty.
HADDON, William T. — Private, 12th Regiment.
HAGERTY, Daniel — Sergeant, 40th Regiment. He was standing beside Captain Wise when Wise was shot.
HALES, Israel — Private, 40th Regiment.
HALL, Charles Henry — Private, 40th Regiment.
HALL, Henry — Private, 12th Regiment.
HALL, John — Private, 12th Regiment, (wounded in battle, died 31 December 1854).
HALL, William — Private, 12th Regiment.
HAMMOND, James — Hammond died on the return journey to Melbourne after the battle.
HAMMOND, Walter — Private, 12th Regiment.
HARDING, John — Private, 12th Regiment.
HARDING, George — Private, 12th Regiment.
HARE, John — Private, 12th Regiment.
HARGREAVES, Richard — Private, 12th Regiment.
HARRIS, Charles Henry — Sergeant.

Opposite:
A pattern 1842 percussion musket. Manufactured in London by 'Tower of London' this type of musket was the last of the smooth bore arms to be issued to British regiments.
The 12th Foot (East Suffolk Regiment) and the 40th Foot (2nd Somersetshire Regiment) both used the Pattern 1842 in the battle at the Eureka Stockade.
(AUSTRALIAN WAR MEMORIAL COLLECTION)

HARVEY, John — Private, 40th Regiment.
HARVEY, Patrick —
HAWTHORNE, David A. — Private, 12th Regiment.
HAYMAN, George — Private, 12th Regiment.
HEARN, John — Private, 12th Regiment.
HEGARTY, Daniel — Sergeant, 40th Regiment.
HEWITT, Absalom — Private, 12th Regiment.
HILL, James — Private, 40th Regiment.
HODGSON, John L. — Private, 12th Regiment.
HOGAN, Thomas — Private, 12th Regiment.
HOGGETT, John — Private, 12th Regiment.
HOLDRED, John — Private, 12th Regiment.
HUNT, John — Private, 12th Regiment.
HURSTWAITE, John — Private, 12th Regiment.
HUSTABLE, William — Private, 12th Regiment.
HUXLEY, James — Private, 12th Regiment.
HYNES, Patrick — Soldier. Patrick Hynes's first cousin Thomas Hynes was a pikeman during Eureka.
JACKSON, Robert — Private, 12th Regiment.
JEFFREY, James — Private, 12th Regiment.
JEWELL, William — Private, 12th Regiment.
JOHNSTONE, Robert — Private, 12th Regiment.
JOHNSTONE, William — Private, 12th Regiment.
JONES, John — Private, 12th Regiment.
JONES, Richard — Private, 12th Regiment.
JUBB, Joseph — Private, 12th Regiment.
JUG, Finnes — Private, 12th Regiment.
JUNIPER, William — Private, 40th Regiment, (severely wounded in battle).
KEANE, John — Shoemaker for the army.
KEEBLE, James — Private, 12th Regiment.
KEEBLE, John — Private, 40th Regiment.
KEEFE, Francis — Private, 12th Regiment.
KEEGAN, James — Private, 12th Regiment.
KEEN, Thomas — Private, 12th Regiment.
KEEN — Military commander.
KEETHE, Francis — Private, 12th Regiment.
KELLY, James — Private, 40th Regiment.
KELLY, Laurence — Private, 40th Regiment.
KELLY, Richard — Police constable.
KENNEDY, John — Private, 12th Regiment.
KENWOOD, William — Private, 12th Regiment.
KING, George — Sergeant.
KING, Hugh — Private, 40th Regiment.
KING, John — Police constable. John King tore down the Eureka flag and kept it as a souvenir.
KNIGHT, John — Private, 12th Regiment.
KNIGHT, Edward — Private, 12th Regiment.
KNOWLES, John — Private, 12th Regiment.
LACKEY, John — Private, 12th Regiment.
LADBROOK, Charles — Private, 40th Regiment.
LANG, William — Private, 12th Regiment.
LANGAM, John — Private, 12th Regiment.
LANGHAM, Francis — Private, 40th Regiment.
LANGHAM, John — Private, 40th Regiment.
LANGLEY, Thomas — Police sub-inspector Langley was one of the men who arrested Timothy Hayes 300 metre outside the Stockade.
LAWLER, Michael — Police trooper.
LAWRENCE, William — Private, 12th Regiment.
LEEKEY, John — Private, 12th Regiment.
LEGGATT, William — Private, 12th Regiment.
LITTLEHALES, George Richard — Captain, 12th Regiment (Littlehales died in 'the Camp', from dyssentry, two months after the fall of the Stockade).
LOUGE, James — Private, 40th Regiment.
LUMBER, William — Private, 12th Regiment.
LYNCH, James — Private, 12th Regiment.
LYNESS, Joseph — Private, 12th Regiment.
MacCARRON, William — Soldier, 40th Regiment.
MACOBOY, John — Private, 40th Regiment.
MAHONEY, Michael — Private, 12th Regiment.
MANELLA, William — Corporal, 40th Regiment.
MANNING, John — Private, 40th Regiment.
MARKSAND, John — Private, 12th Regiment.
MARTIN, Willam — Private, 12th Regiment.
McADAM, Michael — Private, 40th Regiment.
McADAM — Private.
McARDELE, John — Private, 12th Regiment.
McARTHUR, John — Private, 12th Regiment.
McCABE, Peter — Private, 40th Regiment.
McCAMMON, James — Private, 12th Regiment.
McCOMISH, Edward — Private, 12th Regiment.
McDERMOTT, Henry — Private, 40th Regiment.
McDERMOTT, Thomas — Private, 12th Regiment.
McGARRY, John — Private, 12th Regiment.
McGORRIGLE, Peter — Private, 12th Regiment.
McGRATH, Patrick — Private, 12th Regiment.
McGURK, John — Private, 40th Regiment.
McIVOR, — Mounted police constable who was wounded in battle.
McNEIL, John — Sergeant.

In Memoriam

MEACHAM, Charles — Private, 40th Regiment.
MEDGLEY, Edward — Private, 12th Regiment.
METHAM, John — Private, 12th Regiment.
MILLS, Robert — Private, 12th Regiment.
MILNE, Robert — Sergeant major of Police.
MINER, Charles — Private, 12th Regiment.
MITCHELL, Patrick — Private, 40th Regiment.
MOORE, Jacob — Private, 12th Regiment.
MORAN, Michael — Private, 40th Regiment.
MULLEN, Lot — Private, 40th Regiment.
MURRAY, Alfred — Private, 12th Regiment.
MUST, Charles — Private, 40th Regiment.
MYERS, Samuel — Private, 12th Regiment.
NAVEL, Jeremiah — Private, 12th Regiment.
NEILL, John — Private, 40th Regiment.
NEILL, John Martin Bladen — Major.
NELSON, Captain — Private, 40th Regiment.
NEWELL, Jeremiah — Private, 12th Regiment.
NOBLE, Mark — Private, 40th Regiment.
NORRISH, John — Private, 12th Regiment.
NOWLAN, James — Private, 12th Regiment.
NUNN, George — Private, 12th Regiment.
O'CONNEL, Michael — Private, 40th Regiment.
O'DELL, Edward — Private, 40th Regiment.
O'DONNELL, Bernard — Private, 40th Regiment.
O'DONNELL, James — Private, 12th Regiment.
O'GREADY, James — Sergeant, 12th Regiment.
O'KEEFE, Daniel — Private, 12th Regiment.
O'NEIL, John — Private, 40th Regiment.
PARKER, Samuel — Private, 12th Regiment.
PARRY, James — Private, 12th Regiment.
PASLEY, Charles — Assistant Engineer, 12th Regiment, second-in-comand to Captain Thomas.
PATCHETT, Henry — Private, 40th Regiment.
PAUL, William Henry — Lieutenant, 12th Regiment, (severely wounded in battle).
PAWSEY, William — Sergeant, 12th Regiment.
PEARCE, William F. — Private, 40th Regiment.
PERCY, William — Private, 12th Regiment.
PIKE, Thomas — Private, 12th Regiment.
PINDER, Michael — Private, 12th Regiment.
PRIESTLEY, — Military undercover agent.
PRINCE, Henry — Private, 12th Regiment.
PYM, Henry — Private, 12th Regiment.
QUINN, William — Private in the 12th Regiment.
RAFFERTY, Edward — Private, 12th Regiment.
RAWSON, Terence — Private, 12th Regiment.
RAYNOR, Joseph — Private, 40th Regiment.
RAYNOR, Joseph — Private, 12th Regiment.
REED, John — Private, 12th Regiment.
REED, Thomas — Soldier, 40th Regiment.
REID, Robert — Private, 12th Regiment.
REILLY, Edward — Private, 12th Regiment.
REILLY, James — Private, 12th Regiment.
REILLY, Patrick — Sergeant.
REVEL, William — Soldier, 40th Regiment.
REYNOLDS, James — Private, 12th Regiment.
RICHARDS, Bailey — Lieutenant, 40th Regiment.
RICHARDSON, William — Corporal, 40th Mounted Division.
RILEY, Edward — Private, 40th Regiment.
RONEY, Michael — Private, 12th Regiment, (killed in battle).
ROOTS, Charles T. — Private, 12th Regiment.
ROW, Benjamin — Private, 12th Regiment.
RYAN, John — Private, 40th Regiment.
SERGEANT, John — Private, 12th Regiment.
SHANAGHAN, Garret — Private, 12th Regiment.
SHANAHAN, Patrick — Private.
SHARKEY, James — Private, 12th Regiment.
SHARLAND, John — Private, 40th Regiment.
SHARPE, Edward — Private, 12th Regiment.
SHARPE, George — Private, 12th Regiment.
SHAW, William — Private, 12th Regiment.
SHEPPEARD, William — Private, 12th Regiment.
SHOVLIN, John — Private, 12th Regiment.
SINNOTT, Patrick — Private, 40th Regiment.
SKINNER, William — Private, 12th Regiment.
SMITH, John — Private, 12th Regiment, (wounded in battle).
SMITH, Peter Henry — Police Inspector.
SMITH, Thomas — Private, 12th Regiment.
SMITH, William — Private, 40th Regiment.
SORRELL, Cornelius — Private, 40th Regiment.
SPOONER, Willam — Private, 12th Regiment.
STEWART, James — Private, 12th Regiment.
STEWART, John — Private, 12th Regiment.
STOREY, William — Private, 12th Regiment.
SULLIVAN, John — Private, 12th Regiment.
SULLIVAN, Patrick — Private, 40th Regiment, (slightly wounded in battle).
SUTCLIFFE, William — Private, 12th Regiment.

Author's Note: The names reproduced here are taken from the *Eureka Research Directory, 1999 Edition,* compiled by Ballarat Heritage Services, Ballarat. This edition has a much more comprehensive description of each person, wherever information does exist, and includes other personnel such as government officials, storekeepers, doctors, publicans, etc., and other persons known to be in Ballarat but not involved in the Stockade. Also referenced are persons involved in other events pre-Eureka, such as the fire at Bentley's Hotel, arrest of Gregorius and the 'monster' meetings.

SWAN, William — Private, 40th Regiment.
SYMS, Henry — Private, 12th Regiment.
SYNOTT, Patrick — Soldier.
TAYLOR — Police sub-inspector, in command of police at the Stockade.
THOMAS, John Wellesley — Captain, 40th Regiment, Military commander of the attack on the Stockade.
THOMPSON, Alfred — Private, 12th Regiment.
THOMPSON, Henry — Private, 12th Regiment.
THOMPSON, John — Private, 12th Regiment.
THOMPSON, William — Police constable.
TIMMONS, Henry — Private, 12th Regiment.
TOTTERDELL, Thomas — Private, 12th Regiment.
TURNER, James — Private, 40th Regiment.
TURNER, William — Private, 12th Regiment.
UNDERWOOD, William — Private, 12th Regiment.
VALIANT, — Lieutenant colonel in the Military.
WAGSTAFF, James — Private, 12th Regiment.
WALKER, Andrew — Private, 12th Regiment.
WALL, Joseph (John) — Private, 40th Regiment, (mortally wounded during the battle. Died later of pike wound to the lower abdomen).
WALLACE, William T. F. A. — Soldier, Grenadier Guards.
WALSH, Patrick — Private, 40th Regiment.

WARD, George — Private, 12th Regiment.
WARNER, George — Private, 12th Regiment.
WATSON, Robert — Private, 12th Regiment.
WEARER, Richard — Private, 12th Regiment.
WEBB, William — Private, 12th Regiment, (mortally wounded during battle, died on 5 December 1854 from gunshot wounds).
WEBSTER, Richard — Private, 12th Regiment.
WHELAN, Cornelius — Private, 12th Regiment.
WHITE, John Warren — Captain, 40th Regiment.
WILKINSON, William — Private, 12th Regiment.
WILSON, William — Private, 12th Regiment.
WISE, Henry Christopher — Captain, 40th Regiment (mortally wounded during battle, died on 21 December 1854 from gunshot wounds and flesh wound to the thigh).
WOOLEY, William — Private, 12th Regiment.
WRIGHT, James — Private, 12th Regiment.
WRIGHT, John — Private, 12th Regiment.
XIMENES, Maurice Frederick — Police sub-inspector, commander of foot police at Ballarat.
YALDEN, Charles — Private, 12th Regiment.
YOUNG, Richard — Private, 12th Regiment.

MONUMENT IN THE BALLARAT CEMETERY TO THOSE WHO FELL AT THE EUREKA STOCKADE

In Memoriam

THE EUREKA STOCKADE inspired a plethora of artists and writers to offer their impressions of the battle most saw as a struggle of the working man against the establishment. Such is the stuff that legends are born of; gore spread on Australian soil gave the burgeoning nation its bloodied crusade, and the Southern Cross its rallying cry.

Flag of the Southern Cross

Sons of Australia, be loyal and true to her—
    Fling out the flag of the Southern Cross!
Sing a loud song to be joyous and new to her—
    Fling out the flag of the Southern Cross!
Stained with the blood of the diggers who died by it,
Fling out the flag to the front, and abide by it—
    Fling out the flag of the Southern Cross!

See how the toadies of Austral throw dust o'er her—
    Fling out the flag of the Southern Cross!
We who are holding her honour in trust for her—
    Fling out the flag of the Southern Cross!
See how the yellow-men next to her lust for her,
Sooner or later to battle we must for her—
    Fling out the flag of the Southern Cross!

Beg not of England the right to preserve ourselves,
    Fling out the flag of the Southern Cross!
We are the servants best able to serve ourselves,
    Fling out the flag of the Southern Cross!
What are our hearts for, and what are our hands for?
What are we nourished in these southern lands for?
    Fling out the flag of the Southern Cross!

Shall we in fear of the Dragon or Bruin now
    Keep back the flag of the Southern Cross?
Better to die on a field of red ruin now,
    Under the flag of the Southern Cross.
Let us stand out like gallant Eureka men—
Give not our country the sorrow to seek her men—
    Fling out the flag of the Southern Cross!

See how the loyal are storing up shame for us
    Under the light of the Southern Cross.
Never! O never be coward a name for us—
    Fling out the flag of the Southern Cross!
England's red flag will bring hatred and worse to it,
Murder and rapine hath brought a black curse to it;
    Fling out the flag of the Southern Cross!

Have we not breasts for the bullets of thunderers?
    Fling out the flag of the Southern Cross!
Have we not steel for the bosoms of plunderers?
    Fling out the flag of the Southern Cross!
Prove ourselves worthy the land we inherit now,
Feed till it blazes the national spirit now!
    Fling out the flag of the Southern Cross!

Let us be bold, be it daylight or night for us—
    Fling out the flag of the Southern Cross!
Let us be firm—with our God and our right for us,
    Under the flag of the Southern Cross!
Austral is fair, and the idlers in strife for her
Plunder her, sneer at her, suck the young life from her!
    Fling out the flag of the Southern Cross!

Fling out the flag to the front, and abide by it—
    Fling out the flag of the Southern Cross!
Stand by the blood of the diggers who died by it—
    Fling out the flag of the Southern Cross!
Fling out the flag to the front, and be brave for it.
Liberty! Light! or a battle-field grave for it!
    Bonny bright flag of the Southern Cross!

— published in *Truth*, 9 August 1891.

Victoria's Southern Cross
To the tune of 'The Standard Bearer'

I.

When Ballarat unfurled the 'Southern Cross,'
Of joy a shout ascended to the heavens;
The bearer was Toronto's Captain Ross;
All frightened into fits red-taped ravens.

Chorus

For Brave Lalor —
Was found 'all there',
With dauntless dare:
His men inspiring:
To wolf or bear,
Defiance bidding,
He made them swear —
Be faithful to the Standard, for victory or death.

II.

Blood-hounds were soon let loose, with grog imbued,
And murder stained that Sunday! Sunday morning;
The Southern Cross in digger's gore imbrued,
Was torn away, and left the diggers mourning!

Chorus

III.

Victoria men, to scare, stifle or tame,
Ye quarter-deck monsters are too impotent;
The Southern Cross will float again the same,
United Britons, ye are *omnipotent*.

Chorus.

OPPOSITE:
Monument in Ballarat cemetery to those who fell at the Eureka Stockade.
    The inscription on this memorial at Ballarat reads 'In this place with other soldiers and civilians of the military camp then in Ballarat were buried the remains of the British soldiers Henry Christopher Wise, Captain, Michael Roney and Joseph Wall, Privates of the 40th Regt. and William Webb, Felix Boyle and John Hall, Privates of the 12th Regt. who fell dead or fatally wounded at the Eureka Stockade in brave devotion to duty on Sunday, 3rd December 1854 whilst attacking a band of aggrieved diggers in arms against what they regarded as a tyrannous administration.'
(BY PERMISSION, NATIONAL LIBRARY OF AUSTRALIA)

Eureka - a Fragment by Henry Lawson, 1889.

Roll up, Eureka's heroes, on that grand Old Rush afar,
For Lalor's gone to join you in the big camp where you are;
Roll up and give him welcome such as only diggers can,
For well he battled for the rights of miner and of man,
And there, in that bright, golden land that lies beyond
     our sight,
The record of his honest life shall be his 'miner's right'.
Here, many a bearded mouth shall twitch, and many a tear
     be shed,
And many a grey old digger sigh to hear that Lalor's dead.
But wipe you eyes, old fossickers, o'er worked out fields
     that roam,
You need not weep at parting with a digger going home

Now from the strange wild seasons past, the days of
     golden strife,
Now from the Roaring Fifties comes a scene from Lalor's life:
All gleaming white amid the shafts o'er gully, hill, and flat
Again I see the tents that form the camp at Ballarat.
I hear the shovels and the picks, and all the air is rife
With the rattle of the cradles and the sounds of digger-life;
The clatter of the windlass-boles, as spinning round they go,
And then the signal to his mate, the digger's cry, 'Below!'
From many a busy pointing-forge the sound of labour swells,
The tinkling at the anvils is as clear as silver bells.

I hear the broken English from the mouth at least of one
From every state and nation that is known beneath the sun
The homely tongue of Scotland and the brogue of Ireland
     blend
With the dialects of England, from Berwick to Land's End;
And to the busy concourse here the West has sent a part,
The land of gulches that has been immortalised by Harte*;
The land where long from mining-camps the blue smoke
     upward curled;
The land that gave that 'Partner' true and 'Mliss' unto the
     world;
The men from all the nations in the New World and the Old,
All side by side, like brethren here, are delving after gold;
But suddenly the warning cries are heard on every side
As, closing in around the field, a ring of troopers ride;
Unlicensed diggers are the game, their class and want
     are sins,
And so, with all its shameful scenes, the digger-hunt begins;
The men are seized who are too poor the heavy tax to pay,
And they are chained, as convicts were, and dragged in
     gangs away;
While in the eye of many a mate is menace scarcely hid -
The digger's blood was slow to boil, but scalded when it did.

But now another match is held that sure must light the
     charge,
A digger murdered in the camp! his murderer at large!
Roll up! Roll up! the pregnant cry awakes the evening air,
And angry faces surge like waves around the speakers there.
'What are our sins that we should be an outlawed class?'
     they say,
'Shall we stand by while mates are seized and dragged, like
     'lags', away?
Shall insult be on insult heaped? Shall we let these things go?'
And on a roar of voices comes the diggers' answer - 'No!'
The day has vanished from the scene, but not the air of night
Can cool the blood that, ebbing back, leaves brows in anger
     white.
Lo! from the roof of Bentley's inn the flames are leaping high;
They write 'Revenge!' in letters red across the smoke-
     dimmed sky.
Now the oppressed will drink no more humiliation's cup;
Call out the troops! Read martial law! — the diggers' blood is up!

'To arms! To arms!' the cry is out; 'To arms if man thou art;
For every pike upon a pole will find a tyrant's heart!'
Now Lalor comes to take the lead, the spirit does not lag,
And down the rough, wild diggers kneel beneath the Diggers'
     Flag,
And, rising to their feet, they swear, while rugged hearts beat
     high,
To stand beside their leader and to conquer or to die!
Around Eureka's stockade now the shades of night close fast,
Three hundred sleep beside their arms, and thirty sleep their
     last.

Around about fair Melbourne town the sounds of bells are
     borne
That call the citizens to prayer this fateful Sabbath morn;
But there, upon Eureka's hill, a hundred miles away,
The diggers' forms lie white and still above the blood-stained
     clay.
The bells that ring the diggers' death might also ring a knell
For those few gallant soldiers, dead, who did their duty well.
There's many a 'someone's' heart shall ache, and many a
     someone care,
For many a 'someone's darling' lies all cold and pallid there.
And now in smoking ruins lie the huts and tents around,
The diggers' gallant flag is down and trampled in the ground.

The sight of murdered heroes is to hero hearts a goad,
A thousand men are up in arms upon the Creswick road,
And wildest rumours in the air are flying up and down,
'Tis said the men of Ballarat will march upon the town.
But not in vain those diggers died. Their comrades may rejoice,
For o'er the voice of tyranny is heard the people's voice;
It says: 'Reform your rotten law, the diggers' wrongs make right,
Or else with them, our brothers now, we'll gather in the fight.'
And now before my vision flash the scenes that followed fast —
The trials, and the triumph of the diggers' cause at last.

'Twas of such stuff the men were made who saw our nation
     born,
And such as Lalor were the men who led their footsteps on;
And of such men there'll many be, and of such leaders some,
In the roll-up of Australians on some dark day yet to come.

HENRY LAWSON
— *published in the* Bulletin *2 March 1889.*

---

* In the third verse of this poem Lawson refers to the popular poet and short-story writer of the American West, Bret Harte. Born in New York in 1839, Harte worked as a compositor, and was later editor of the widely-read San Francisco weekly newspaper *The Golden Era*. It was there that he first met the young writer Sam Clemens, better known as Mark Twain, who also had something to say about Eureka. Harte's story almost parallels Lawson's own, and it is easy to see why he honours Harte, the author of 'Luck of Roaring Camp' and 'The Outcasts of Poker Flat', and 'Mliss', the story of a motherless child from the Sierra Nevada trying to find her place in the world.

In Memoriam

The Eureka Stockade by George Hartley, Stockade Poet, 1893.

I tell of famed Eureka,
In the year of fifty-four,
To desperation the diggers
   Now were driven.
They treated us as convicts,
Until at length we swore
As a birthright to us
   Freedom shall be given.

Third December, Sunday morning,
Night, as yet, upheld a cloud,
We heard the soldiers' bugle
   Shrill and clear.
'Fall in, pike men, fall in,'
Thonen's voice rang out aloud,
We all knew that the troops
   Were drawing near.

Brave Lalor held the centre post,
Scarce awake his mates stood round.
   'For God's sake men,
   now do your duty,'
Was his command.
From our ranks a shot was fired,
And its not a venture lost,
That this first shot was by
Some traitor's hand.

'California rangers
To the fence,'
Captain Burnnett sternly cried,
   Bill Melody the first man to obey.
The bullets fast now flying,
The rangers quick replied;
Stood up, and boldly
   Mingled in the fray.

The 'forlorn hope', at 'double quick',
Came up in 'single file',
Their arms, now carried,
   At 'the trail'
With bayonets fixed, full ready,
The diggers for to stick.
'Brown Bess', at this work,
   Never yet did fail.

The 'Slogan' now was ringing
A wild, unearthly shriek:
The diggers all now
   Manfully did cheer,
For it was now quite evident,
That 'Greek had now met Greek',
And the 'tug of war'
   In its full sense was here.

The diggers' fire was drawn,
As Captain Thomas meant,
On to the 'forlorn hope',
   Who got it reeling back.
The main body, well extended,
Now quickly coming up,
For they well knew
   The diggers' fire was spent.

They quickly breeched the timber
That formed the Stockade fort;
Blood flowing freely now
   From bayonet stabs.
To them, this fierce blood letting
Seemed only hellish sport;
The blood lay round in sickening
   clots and dabs.

This hand to hand encounter
Of course could not last,
As the soldiers numbered
   Nearly four to one.
For I was an eye-witness, and
Remember well the past,
Although the years are many
   That have gone

They rushed the 'Southern Cross',
Near Tom, the blacksmith's shop,
A sabre stroke poor Tom got
   Through the skull.
Our ensign quickly down,
Treated as worthless 'slop';
All through the dust our flag
   Got many a pull.

Revere the memory of those
   diggers,
Who fought in a good cause;
On Eureka so bravely
   Stood their ground.
   to arms to put down tyranny,
Died to crush bad laws,
Of their comrades now
   Few only can be found.

Poem and portrait of George Hartley (inset) from 'From Tent to Parliament. The Life of Peter Lalor' by James Vallens, produced by Mr James Oddie on the occasion of the 50th Anniversary of the Eureka Stockade in 1903. In the collection of the Ballarat City Library.

Veteran of the Stockade, Philadelphian George Hartley, was living at Mt. Egerton in Victoria when he penned this poem to his fallen comrades on 2 January 1893.

He mentions the first shot fired into the air, and suggests that it was not fired in anger at the troopers at all, but fired from within the Stockade by a traitor to the cause. This single shot started the battle, and the troopers responded with a barrage of musket-fire, followed by a decisive, and brutal, bayonet charge.

The death of Tom the blacksmith, from a sabre slash to the skull, is described here, as is Thonen's call to those who defended the Stockade with pikes made the day before by the unfortunate pikeman.

Hartley wanted to list the names of Captain Robert Burnnett and Lieutenant Bill Melody of the California Rangers Company, as he felt that they had been overlooked in Wither's *History of Ballarat*. The Americans were hardly recognised at all after the dust had settled on the Eureka field. Doctor Charles Kenworthy, an American who had once acted as a spy among the insurgents, even toasting the 'Diggers of Victoria' at a dinner given on 20 November 1854, had interjected on behalf of his fellow countrymen, pleading with Hotham to turn a blind eye to the Californians and let them go free.

The only citizen of the United States taken into custody, charged and sent to face trial was the African-American James Joseph.

A Ballad of Eureka by Victor Daley.

Stand up, my young Australian,
   In the brave light of sun,
   And hear how Freedom's battle,
   Was in the old days lost—and won.
   The blood burns in my veins, boy,
   As it did in years of yore,
   Remembering Eureka,
   And the men of 'fifty-four.

The old times were the grand times,
   And to me the past appears,
   As rich as seas at sunset,
   With its many-coloured years;
   And like a lonely island,
   Aglow in sunset light,
   One day stands out in splendour—
   The day of the Good Fight.

Where Ballarat the Golden
   On her throne sits like a Queen,
   Ten thousand tents were shining
   In the brave days that have been.
   There dwelt the stalwart diggers,
   When our hearts with hope were high . . .
   The stream of Life ran brimming
   In that golden time gone by.

They came from many countries,
   And far islands in the main,
   And years shall pass and vanish,
   Ere their like are seen again.
   Small chance was there for weaklings,
   With these men of iron core,
   Who worked and played like giants
   In the year of 'fifty-four.

The tyrants of the goldfields,
   Would not let us live in peace;
   They harried us and chased us,
   With their horse and foot police.
   Each man must show his licence
   When they chose, by fits and starts:
   They tried to break our spirits,
   And they almost broke our hearts.

We wrote a Declaration
   In the store of Shanahan,
   Demanding Right and Justice,
   And we signed it, man by man,
   And unto Charles Hotham,
   Who was then Lord of High,
   We sent it; Charles Hotham
   Sent a regiment in reply.

There comes a time to all men,
   When submission is a sin;
   We made a bonfire brave, and
   Flung our licences therein.
   Our hearts with scorn and anger,
   Burned more fiercely than the flame,
   Full well we knew our peril,
   But we dared it all the same.

On Bakery Hill the Banner,
   Of the Southern Cross flew free;
   Then up rose Peter Lalor,
   And with lifted hand spake he:
   'We swear by God above us,
   While we live to work and fight,
   For Freedom and for Justice,
   For our Manhood and our Right.'

Then, on the bare earth kneeling,
   As on a chapel-floor,
   Beneath the sacred Banner,
   One and all, that oath we swore;
   And some of those who swore it,
   Were like straws upon a flood,
   But there were men who swore it,
   And who sealed it with their blood.

We held a stern War Council,
   For in bitter mood were we,
   With Vern and Hayes and Humffray,
   Brady, Ross, and Kennedy,
   And fire-eyed Raffaello,
   Who was brave as steel, though small—
   But gallant Peter Lalor,
   Was the leader of us all.

Pat Curtain we made captain,
   Of our Pikemen, soon enrolled,
   And Ross, the tall Canadian,
   Was our standard-bearer bold.
   He came from where St. Lawrence,
   Flows majestic to the main;
   But the River of St. Lawrence,
   He would never see again.

Then passed along the order,
   That a fortress should be made,
   And soon, with planks and palings,
   We constructed the Stockade.
   We worked in teeth-set silence,
   For we knew what was in store:
   Sure never men defended,
   Such a feeble fort before.

All day the German blacksmith,
   At his forge wrought fierce and fast;
   All day the gleaming pike-blades,
   At his side in piles were cast;
   All day the diggers fitted,
   Blade to staff with stern goodwill,
   Till all men, save the watcher,
   Slept upon the fatal hill.

The night fell cold and dreary,
   And the hours crawled slowly by.
   Deep sleep was all around me,
   But a sentinel was I.
   And then the moon grew ghostly,
   And I saw the grey dawn creep,
   A wan and pallid phantom,
   O'er the Mount of Warrenheip.

When over the dark mountain,
   Rose the red rim of the sun,
   Right sharply in the stillness,
   Rang our picket's warning gun.
   And scarce had died the echo,
   Ere, of all our little host,
   Each man had grasped his weapon,
   And each man was at his post.

The foe came on in silence,
   Like an army of the dumb;
   There was no blare of trumpet,
   And there was no tap of drum.
   But ever they came onward,
   And I thought, with indrawn breath,

This ballad was one of Victor Daley's best-known works.
   Born in Ireland in 1858, Daley immigrated to Australia in 1878 and wrote under the pen-name 'Creeve Rowe'. He died in 1905.

The Redcoats looked like Murder,
  And the Blackcoats looked like
    Death.

Our gunners, in their gun-pits,
  That were near the palisade,
  Fired fiercely, but the Redcoats,
  Fired as if upon parade.
  Yet, in the front rank leading,
  On his men with blazing eyes,
  The bullet of a digger,
  Struck down valiant Captain Wise.

Then 'Charge!' cried Captain Thomas,
  And with bayonets fixed they
    came,
  The palisade crashed inwards,
  Like a wall devoured by flame.
  I saw our gallant gunners,
  Struggling vainly, backward reel,
  Before that surge of scarlet,
  All alive with stabbing steel.

There Edward Quinn of Cavan,
  Samuel Green the Englishman,
  And Haffele the German,
  Perished, fighting in the van.
  And with them William Quinlan,
  Fell while battling for the Right,
  The first Australian Native,
  In the first Australian fight.

But Robertson the Scotchman,
  In his gripping Scottish way,
  Caught by the throat a Redcoat,
  And upon that Redcoat lay.
  They beat the Scotchman's head in,
  Smiting hard with butt of gun,
  And slew him—but the Redcoat
  Died before the week was done.

These diggers fought like heroes,
  Charged to guard a kingdom's gate.
  But vain was all their valour,
  For they could not conquer Fate.
  The searchers for the wounded
  Found them lying side by side.
  They lived good mates together,
  And good mates together died.

Then Peter Lalor, gazing
  On the fight with fiery glance,
  His lion-voice uplifted,
  Shouting, 'Pikemen, now advance!'
  A bullet struck him, speaking,
  And he fell as fall the dead;
  The fight had lost its leader,
  And the pikemen broke and fled.

The battle was not over,
  For there stood upon the hill,
  A little band of diggers,
  Fighting desperately still,
  With pistol, pike, and hayfork,
  Against bayonet and gun.
  There was no madder combat,
  Ever seen beneath the sun.

Then Donaghey and Dimond,
  And Pat Gittins fighting fell,
  With Thaddeus Moore, and
    Reynolds:
  And the muskets rang their knell,
  And staring up at Heaven,
  As if watching his soul's track,
  Shot through his heart so merry,
  Lay our jester 'Happy Jack'.

The sky grew black above us,
  And the earth below was red,
  And, oh, our eyes were burning,
  As we gazed upon our dead.
  On came the troopers charging,
  Valiant cut-throats of the Crown,
  And wounded men and dying
  Flung their useless weapons
    down.

The bitter fight was ended,
  And, with cruel coward-lust,
  They dragged our sacred banner,
  Through the Stockade's bloody dust.
  But, patient as the gods are,
  Justice counts the years and waits—
  That banner now waves proudly,
  Over six Australian states.

I said, my young Australian,
  That the fight was lost — and
    won—
  But, oh, our hearts were heavy
  At the setting of the sun.
  Yet, ere the year was over,
  Freedom rolled in like a flood:
  They gave us all we asked for—
  When we asked for it in blood.

God rest you, Peter Lalor!
  For you were a whiteman whole;
  A sword blade in the sunlight,
  Was your bright and gallant soul.
  And God reward you kindly,
  Father Smith, alive or dead:
  'Twas you that give him shelter
  When a price was on his head.

Within the Golden City,
  In the place of peace profound,
  The Heroes sleep. Tread softly:
  'Tis Australia's Holy Ground.
  And evermore Australia,
  Will keep green in our heart's core,
  The memory of Lalor
  And the men of 'fifty-four.

— VICTOR DALEY (1858–1905)

THE EUREKA STOCKADE MONUMENT (FROM THE DESIGNS).

Sketcher

MELBOURNE, SATURDAY, MAY 22, 1880.

BALLARAT BROKERS: A "CORNER" SKETCH.

Ballarat after the Battle

THE DISCOVERY OF GOLD and the subsequent development of extensive mining infrastructure brought an immediate change in the economy of any region; most of the early squatters were virtually forced to abandon their holdings, as first the alluvial gold-seekers swarmed across their properties, to be followed soon after by the company men. The deep-lead mining companies constructed tall steel winding platforms, steam-driven wheel-houses and quartz-crushing mills, and soon devoured all the timber for kilometres around the diggings and spread grey sand and mullock across the landscape.

For almost a century after the end of the golden days, centres such as Ballarat and Bendigo still bore the scars of this type of company mining. Lines of poppet legs were strung out across the hills and gullies; sand dumps, like ancient tors, marred the skyline and refused to revegetate for years. The legacy of this mining forced many the pastoralist to abandon his flocks ahead of the machine, after Ballarat had unfurled the flag of the 'Southern Cross'.

Between the years of 1853–60, a total of 4,806,477 ounces of gold was won from the Ballarat mines. This was rivalled only by the Bendigo field that also saw in excess of 4,000,000 ounces won in the same period. The gold from these great centres laid the foundations on which colonial Victoria was built.

INSET:
H.R.H. The Duke of Edinburgh visits the Band of Hope Gold Mine in Ballarat on 10 December 1867.

The first royal visitor to the colony, Prince Alfred, was one of hundreds of celebrities who travelled to Ballarat to marvel at the industry that had prospered since the days of insurrection.

Only 13 years earlier, revenge was taken on the diggers in the name of his mother, Queen Victoria. While he was enjoying a picnic at the Clontarf Sailor's Home in Sydney, Alfred was attacked and shot in the back by a failed Ballarat mining investor. The prince survived but his would-be assassin, the disaffected Irishman Henry James O'Farrel, was hanged in Darlinghurst gaol five weeks later.

Carte-de-visite by Roberts Bros. Sturt Street Ballarat, 1867
(AUTHOR'S COLLECTION)

ABOVE:
Queen Quartz Gold-Mining Claim, Ballarat, c. 1880
(BY PERMISSION, NATIONAL LIBRARY OF AUSTRALIA)

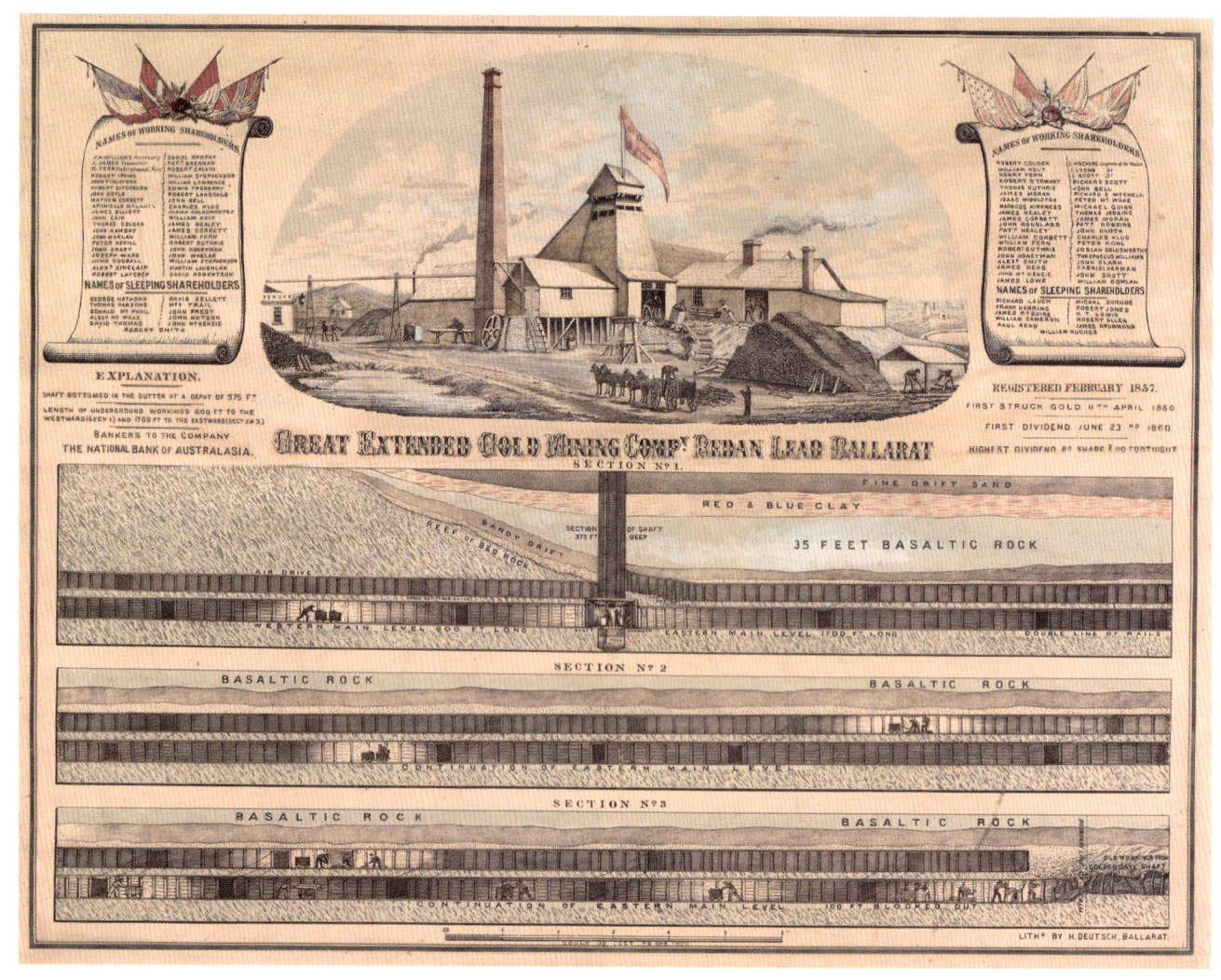

ABOVE:

Great Extended Gold Mining Company. Redan Lead, Ballarat
Lithograph by Hermann Deutsch, Ballarat, c. 1863

Items such as this printed sheet showing the mining infrastructure, underground workings of the mine and lists of shareholders were used to indicate the bona-fides of the company and to encourage capital investment.

(REX NAN KIVELL COLLECTION, U4951
BY PERMISSION, NATIONAL LIBRARY OF AUSTRALIA)

ABOVE:

Great Northern Freehold Gold Mining Company, Ballarat
Wood engraving published in Illustrated Australian News, *18 July 1868*

(REX NAN KIVELL COLLECTION, U4951
BY PERMISSION, NATIONAL LIBRARY OF AUSTRALIA)

Ballarat after the Battle

TOP:
Sergeants Freehold Quartz Gold Mining Company's Claim, Redan, Ballarat, 1881
Watercolour by T. G. Moyle

(BY PERMISSION, NATIONAL LIBRARY OF AUSTRALIA)

ABOVE:
Quartz Crushing, Base of Black Hill, Ballaarat
Lithograph by James Blundell & Co., Melbourne, 1855.
From a drawing by S. T. Gill

(REX NAN KIVELL COLLECTION NKNK6290/11.
BY PERMISSION, NATIONAL LIBRARY OF AUSTRALIA)

BELOW:
Nelson & Wellington Gold Mining Company, Sebastopol
Lithograph by Herman Deutsch, Ballarat c. 1860
(BY PERMISSION, NATIONAL LIBRARY OF AUSTRALIA)

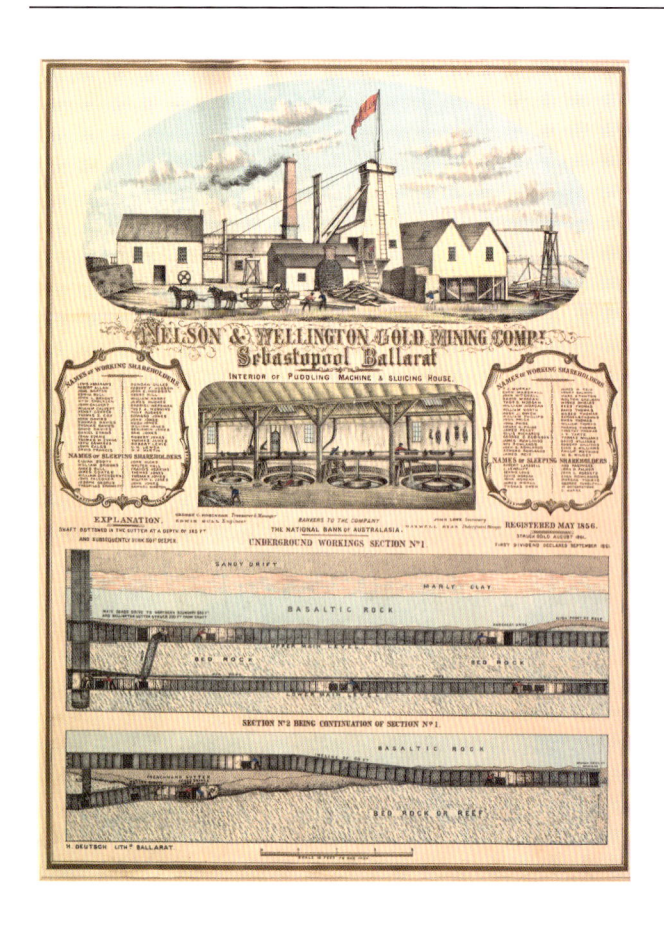

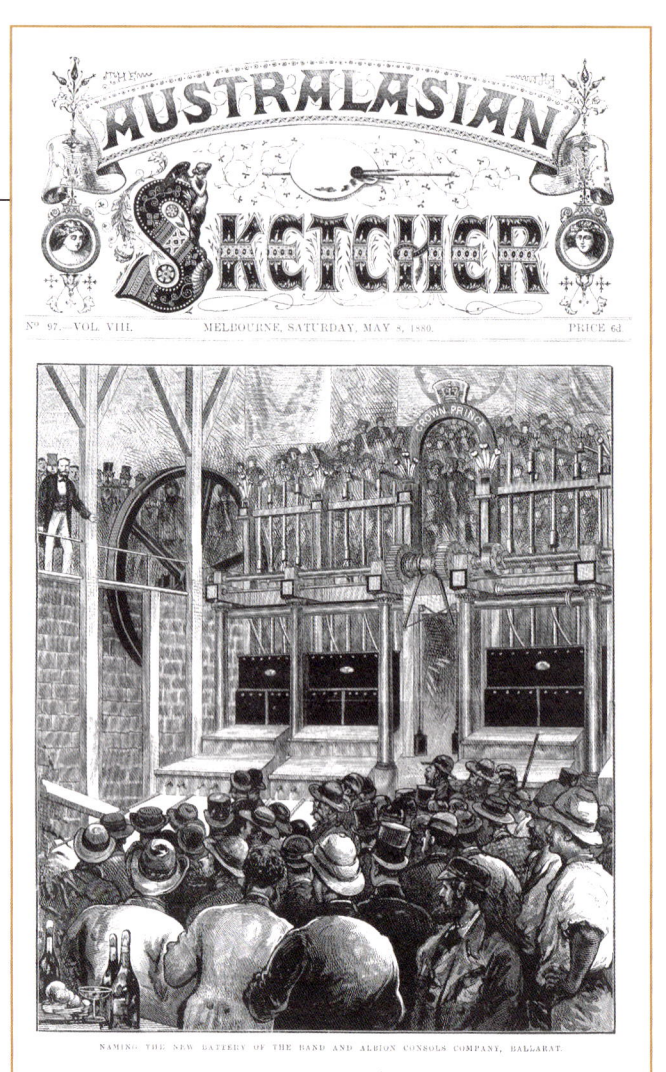

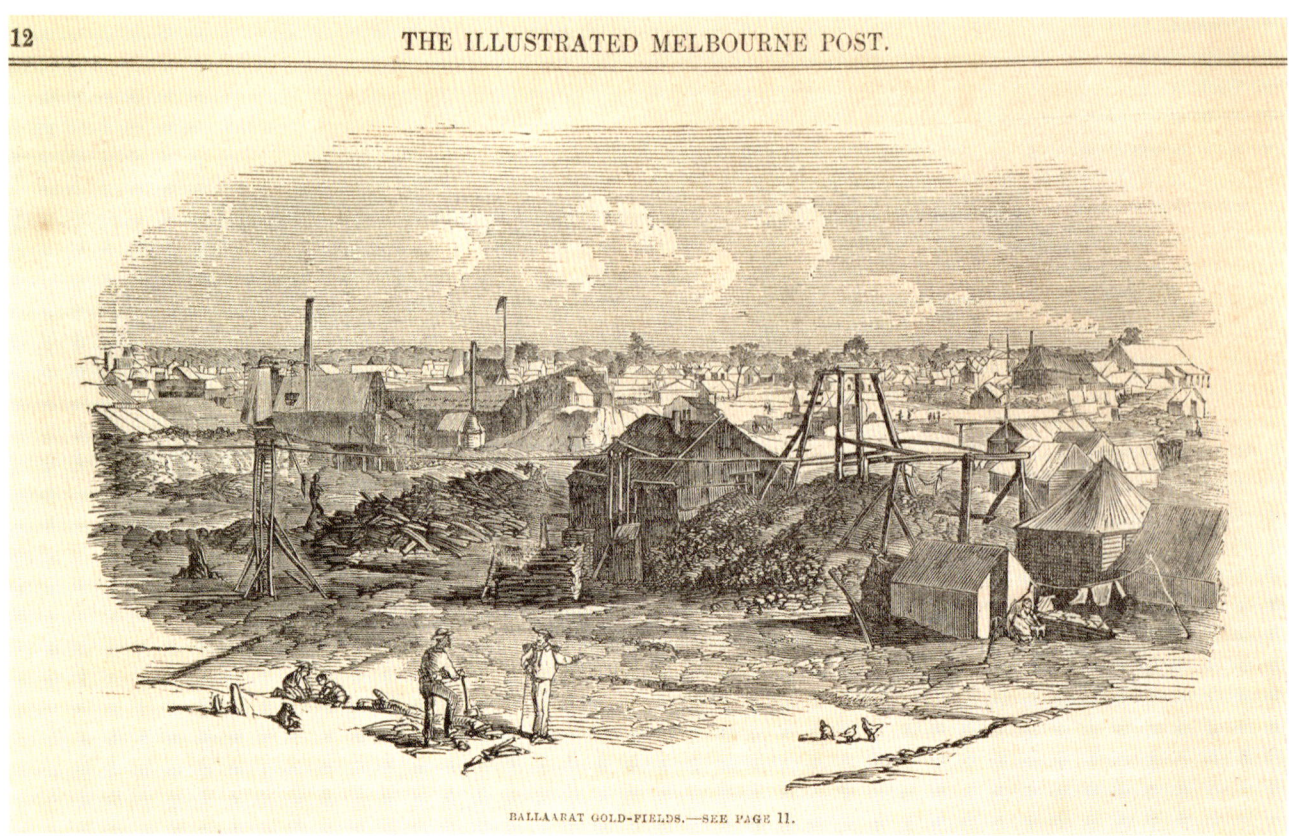

200

Ballarat after the Battle

ABOVE:

Black Hill, Ballarat
Photograph by Richard Daintree, c. 1861

(LA TROBE PICTURE COLLECTION,
STATE LIBRARY OF VICTORIA)

OPPOSITE PAGE, TOP RIGHT:

Naming the New Battery of the Band and Albion Consols Company, Ballarat
Published in the Australasian Sketcher *on 8 May 1880*

BOTTOM:

Ballarat Gold Fields, 1873
Wood engraving published in Victoria, exhibited by the commissioners of the International Exhibition, 1873

Such was the international reputation, and investment in the central Victorian goldfields that engravings such as these shown opposite played a vital role in promoting opportunities for capital in the colony.

(BY PERMISSION, NATIONAL LIBRARY OF AUSTRALIA)

ABOVE:

The Black Hill, Ballarat
Photograph by William Bardwell, c. 1870

The Black Hill certainly suffered more than its fair share of mining activity as the mining companies literally tore it apart in search of gold. Both of these photographs show the progress of degradation over a decade.

(LA TROBE PICTURE COLLECTION, STATE LIBRARY OF VICTORIA)

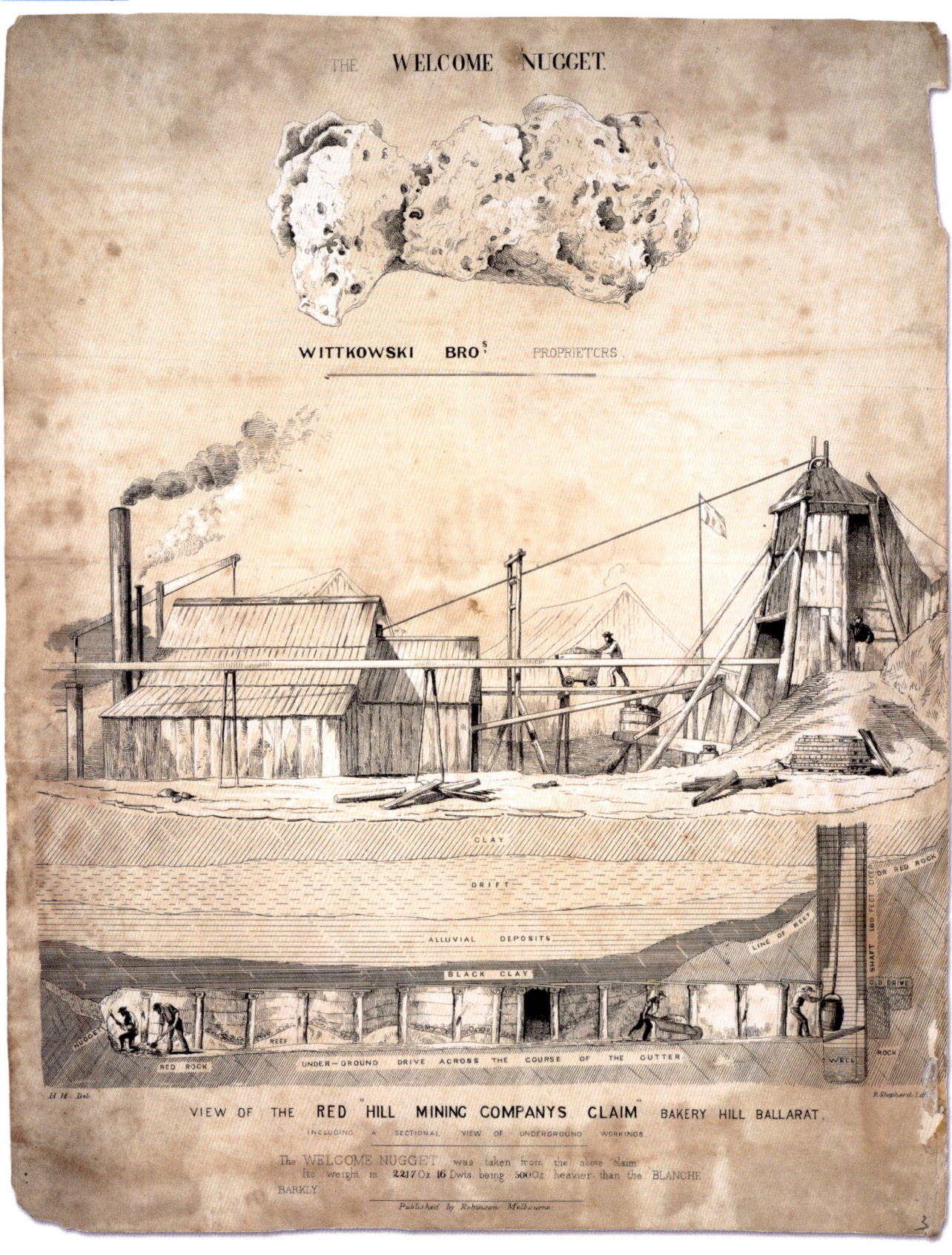

ABOVE:
The Welcome Nugget, Wittkowski Bros.
View of the Red Hill Mining Company's Claim
Lithograph by R. Shepherd, 1870, from a drawing by H. Huyghe

An inscription accompanying this drawing reads: 'The Welcome Nugget was taken from the above Claim on the 9th June 1858 at twenty minutes past eight PM. Its weight is 2217 Oz 16 Dwts / being 500 Oz heavier than the Blanche Barkly. It has been Assayed by Wm Birkmyre Esqr of the Port Philip Gold Co. / & contains 99.20 per Cent of pure Gold — 23 Carats 3 1/8 Grains being the purest Mass of Native Gold on record.'

The 'Blanche Barkly' weighed 1,743 ounces and was uncovered in Kingower on 27 August 1857. The 'Welcome Nugget', valued at £10,500, was taken to London where it went on display at the Crystal Palace; it was later melted down into gold sovereigns.

(BY PERMISSION, NATIONAL LIBRARY OF AUSTRALIA)

BELOW:
Star of the East Gold Mining Co., Ballarat
Coloured postcard, c. 1907
(LA TROBE PICTURE COLLECTION, STATE LIBRARY OF VICTORIA)

BELOW:
Golden Point as it was in 1857
Engraving published in the Australasian Sketcher
(LA TROBE UNIVERSITY, BENDIGO, LIBRARY COLLECTION)

The big nuggets

There were a number of 'notable nuggets' found on the Ballarat diggings that won fame, and considerable wealth, for those lucky diggers who unearthed them.

The first, a nugget weighing 2,112 ounces called 'Sarah Sands', found in 1852, is the 'monster nugget' described by Antoine Fauchery on page 45.

The next was found at Canadian Gully on 2 January 1853; it weighed in at 1,011 ounces. Another nugget found in the same gully was 'The Canadian'. It weighed 1,319 ounces and was found on 31 January 1853.

The 'Lady Hotham', 1,177 ounces, was found at Dalton's Flat on 8 September 1854.

The 'Welcome Nugget', found on Bakery Hill on 9 June 1858, weighed 2,217 ounces.

The 'Kohinoor', weighing 834 ounces, was found in August 1860, and the 'Lady Don', 606 ounces, was found on 12 November 1866.

Bibliography

ANDERSON, HUGH, *Eureka. Victorian Parliamentary Papers. Votes and Proceedings 1854-67.*

BLAIR, DAVID, *The History of Australasia.* McGready, Thomson and Niven, Glasgow, 1879.

BRIDE, THOMAS FRANCIS, *Letters from Victorian Pioneers.* Published for the Trustees of the Public Library, Public Library, Museums and National Gallery of Victoria, Melbourne 1898.

CARBONI, RAFFAELLO, *The Eureka Stockade.* Melbourne University Press, Melbourne, 1963; first published 1855.

CHANDLER, JOHN, *Forty Years in the Wilderness*, ed. Michael Cannon. Loch Haven Books, 1990; first published by the author, 1893.

CLARKE, C. M. H., *Select Documents in Australian History, 1851—1900.* Angus and Robertson, Sydney, 1955.

CRAIG, WILLIAM, *My Adventures on the Australian Goldfields.* Cassell & Co., London, 1853.

CURREY, C. H., *The Irish at Eureka.* Angus and Robertson, Melbourne, 1954.

CUSACK, FRANK, *Bendigo: A History.* Heinemann, Melbourne, 1973.

FABIAN, SUZANE, *Mr. Punch Down Under*, Greenhouse Publication, Richmond, 1982.

FAUCHERY, ANTOINE, *Letters From a Miner in Australia.* Georgian House, Melbourne, 1965; first published in French 1857.

HARVEY, JACK, *Eureka Rediscovered. In Search of the Site of the Historic Stockade.* University of Ballarat, Ballarat, 1994.

HORNE, R. H., *Australian Facts and Prospects.* London 1859.

HOWITT, WILLIAM, *Land, Labour & Gold, or Two Years in Victoria with Visits to Sydney and Van Diemen's Land.* Lowden, Kilmore, Vic., 1972; first published 1855.

IRVING, J., *A Journal of Events, Social and Political, Home and Foreign. From the Accession of Queen Victoria — June 20 1837. Annals of our Time.* MacMillan & Co., London, 1870.

KIMBERLY, W. B., *Bendigo & Vicinity*, F.W. Niven & Co., Printers and Publishers, Melbourne and Ballarat, 1895.

MACFARLANE, IAN, *Eureka, From the Official Records.* Public Record Office of Victoria, Melbourne, 1995.

MCKILLOP, FRANK (ed. Geoff Hocking), *Early Castlemaine. A Glance at the Stirring Fifties.* New Chum Press, Castlemaine, 1998. First published *The Mount Alexander Mail*, 1908-9.

MACKAY, GEORGE, *The Annals of Bendigo.* Mackay & Co., Bendigo, 1867.

MACKAY, GEORGE, *The History of Bendigo.* Mackay & Co., Bendigo, 1891.

Oddie, J., *Peter Lalor, and History of the Stockade.* Berry, Anderson & Co., Ballarat, 1904.

ROSS, JOHN (ed.). *Chronicle of Australia.* Viking Books, Penguin, Ringwood, 2000.

SERLE, GEOFFREY. *The Golden Age. A History of the Colony of Victoria, 1851-1861.* Melbourne University Press, Melbourne, 1963.

SUTHERLAND, GEORGE. *Tales of the Goldfields.* George Robertson, Melbourne, 1880.

SUTHERLAND, ALEXANDER. *Victoria and its Metropolis: Past and Present. Vol. 1.* McCarron, Bird & Co., Melbourne, 1888.

WICKHAM, DOROTHY, *Shot in the Dark. A Pre-Eureka Incident. Being the Compensation Case of Benden S. Hassell.* Goldfield Heritage Books, Ballarat Heritage Services, Ballarat, 1998.

WICKHAM, DOROTHY; GERVASONI, CLARE; PHILLIPSON, WAYNE, *Eureka Reminiscences*, Ballarat Heritage Services, Ballarat, 1998.

WICKHAM, DOROTHY; GERVASONI, CLARE; PHILLIPSON, WAYNE, *Eureka Research Directory*, Ballarat Heritage Services, Ballarat, 1999.

WICKHAM, DOROTHY; GERVASONI, CLARE; PHILLIPSON, WAYNE, *The Eureka Flag. Our Starry Banner*, Ballarat Heritage Services, Ballarat, 2000.

WITHERS, WILLIAM BRAMWELL, *History of Ballarat, and some Ballarat Reminiscences.* Ballarat Heritage Services, Ballarat, 1999, first published 1895.

WRIGHT, DAVID MCKEE, *Poetical Works of Henry Lawson.* Angus and Robertson Publishers, Sydney, 1925.

Notes

Introduction
1. G. Serle. *The Golden Age. A History of the Colony of Victoria, 1851-1861.* Melbourne University Press, Melbourne, 1963, p. 173.

Before the Ballaarat Field
1. T. F. Bride, *Letters from Victorian Pioneers.* Published for the Trustees of the Public Library, Public Library, Museums and National Gallery of Victoria, Melbourne 1898, p. 55.
2. Ibid.
3. W. B. Withers, *History of Ballarat, and some Ballarat Reminiscences.* Ballarat Heritage Services, Ballarat, 1999, first published 1895, p. 9.
4. Op. cit., p. 9.
5. Op. cit., p. 8.

The Journey Begins
1. E. H. Hargraves, *Australia and its Gold Fields.* H. Ingram & Co. London, 1855. pp. 114-5.
2. J. Ross, *Chronicle of Australia.* Viking Books, Penguin, Ringwood, 2000, p. 300.
3. J. Bonwick, *Notes of a Gold Digger and Gold Digger's Guide*, Melbourne, 1942 (first published 1852), p. 25.

Gold in the Ballarat Hills
1. W. B. Kimberley, *Bendigo and Vicinity.* F.W. Niven & Co., Printers and Publishers, Melbourne and Ballarat, 1895, p. 12.
2. Ibid.
3. G. Sutherland, *Tales of the Goldfields.* George Robertson, Melbourne, p. 44.
4. Ibid.
5. D. Blair, *The History of Australasia.* McGready, Thomson and Niven, Glasgow, 1879, pp. 417-8.
6. Ross. Op. cit., p. 301.
7. Ibid.
8. Ibid.
9. A. Fauchery, *Letters From a Miner in Australia.* Georgian House, Melbourne, 1965; first published 1857, p.51.
10. Ibid.
11. Op. cit., p. 52.
12. Op. cit., p.53.
13. Ross. Op. cit., p. 302.
14. Op. cit., p. 283.
15. Fauchery. Op. cit., pp.79-80.

The Road to Sedition
1. McKillop (ed. Hocking), *Early Castlemaine.* New Chum Press, Castlemaine, 1998, p. 64.
2. Kimberley. Op. cit., p. 18.
3. G. Mackay. *The History of Bendigo.* Mackay & Co., Bendigo, 1891, p. 9.
4. *Mount Alexander Mail*, 13 May 1854.
5. McKillop. Op. cit., p. 64-5.
6. Mackay. Op. cit., p. 8.
7. Blair. Op. cit., p. 430.
8. McKillop. Op. cit., p. 35.
9. W. Howitt, *Land, Labour & Gold, or Two Years in Victoria with Visits to Sydney and Van Diemen's Land.* Lowden, Kilmore, Vic., 1972; first published 1855, p. 130.
10. McKillop. Op. cit., p. 35.
11. G. Mackay, *The Annals of Bendigo.* Mackay & Co., Bendigo, 1867, p. 21.
12. McKillop. Op. cit., p. 71.
13. Blair. Op. cit., p. 432.
14. Loc. cit.

Red Ribbon Rebellion
1. *Melbourne Morning Herald*, quoted in G. Serle. *The Golden Age. A History of the Colony of Victoria, 1851-1861.*

Melbourne University Press, Melbourne, 1963, p. 109.
2 Howitt. Op. cit., p. 224.
3 G. Mackay, *The Annals of Bendigo*. Op. cit., p. 21.
4 Ibid.
5 F. Cusack, *Bendigo: A History*. Heinemann, Melbourne, 1973, p. 89.
6 Kimberley. Op. cit., p. 20.
7 Cusack. Op. cit., p. 93.
8 Blair. Op. cit., p. 433.
9 Op. cit., p. 434.
10 *Argus*, 10 September 1853.

A New Governor
1 *Bendigo Advertiser*, 29 August 1854.
2 Ibid.
3 A. Sutherland, *Victoria and its Metropolis: past and Present*. Vol. 1. McCarron, Bird & Co., Melbourne, 1888, p. 360.
4 Ibid.
5 Ibid.
6 G. Mackay, (1) p.36.
7 Ibid.
8 A. Sutherland. Op. cit., p.360.
9 Howitt. Op. cit., pp. 405-6.

Joe! Joe! Joe!
1 Blair, p. 431
2 Ibid.
3 Withers. Op. cit., pp. 50-1.
4 D. Wickham, G. Gervasoni, W. Phillipson *Eureka Reminiscences*, Ballarat Heritage Services, Ballarat, 1998, p. 9.
5 Withers. Op.cit., pp. 51-2.
6 Op. cit., 48.
7 Howitt. Op. cit., 238
8 McKillop. Op. cit., 66-7.
9 Ibid.
10 R. H. Horne. *Australian Facts and Prospects*. London 1859, pp. 28-9.
11 Howitt. Op. cit., pp. 262-3
12 Op. cit., pp. 236-7.
13 McKillop. Op. cit., p.62.
14 Howitt. Op. cit., 237.
15 Withers. Op. cit., p. 49.
16 Wickham, Gervasoni, Phillipson. Op. cit., p. 21.
17 Op. cit., p. 20.

The Troubles Begin
1 Withers, Op. cit., p. 89.
2 Op. cit., p. 90.
3 *Ballarat Times*, 14 October 1854.
4 Ibid.
5 *Ballarat Times* 11 October 1854.
6 Withers. Op. cit., p. 51.
7 Ibid.
8 Blair, Op. cit., p. 443.
9 I. MacFarlane, *Eureka, From the Official Records*. Public Record Office of Victoria, Melbourne, 1995, p. 50.
10 Op. cit., p. 52.
11 *Ballarat Times*, 28 October 1854.
12 MacFarlane. Op. cit., p. 87.
13 Serle. Op. cit., p. 165.
14 MacFarlane. Op. cit., p. 91.
15 Withers. Op. cit., p. 61.
16 Serle. Op. cit., p. 166.
17 The *Argus*, 10 April 1855.
18 Withers. Op. cit., p. 70.
19 J. Oddie, *Peter Lalor, and History of the Stockade*. Berry, Anderson & Co., Ballarat, 1904, p. 28-9.
20 Op. cit., p. 19.

3 December 1854
1 Wickham, Gervasoni, Phillipson, Op. cit., p. 29-33.
2 W. Craig. *My Adventures on the Australian Goldfields*. Cassell & Co., London, 1853, 266-7.
3 Ibid.
4 Howitt. Op. cit., p 227.
5 Serle. Op. cit., p. 173.
6 R. Carboni, *The Eureka Stockade*. Melbourne University Press, Melbourne, 1963, p. 101
7 A. Sutherland. Op. cit., p. 371.
8 Blair. Op. cit., p. 448.

9 J. Irving. *A Journal of events, Social and Political, Home and Foreign. From the Accession of Queen Victoria — June 20 1837. Annals of our Time*. MacMillan & Co., London, 1870, p. 42.

Treason against Victoria
1 MacFarlane. Op. cit., p. 140.
2 Ibid.
3 Op. cit., p. 145.
4 Op. cit., p. 148.
5 Op. cit., p. 149.
6 Ibid.
7 Op. cit., p. 159.

Picture details:
Ballarat Fine Art Gallery Collection

Pages 96-7
Eugene von Guerard
Old Ballarat as it was in the Summer of 1853-54,
oil on canvas, 750 x 1386 mm
Gift of James Oddie on Eureka Day, 1885

Pages 106-7
Charles A. Doudiet
Eureka Riot 17th October, 1854
watercolour on paper, 168 x 237 mm
Purchased by the Ballarat Fine Art Gallery
with the assistance of many donors, 1996

Pages 122-3
Swearing allegiance to the 'Southern Cross'
watercolour, pen and ink on paper, 167 x 232 mm
Purchased by the Ballarat Fine Art Gallery
with the assistance of many donors, 1996

Pages 105-7
Eureka Slaughter 3rd December, 1854
watercolour, pen and ink on paper, 163 x 239 mm
Purchased by the Ballarat Fine Art Gallery
with the assistance of many donors, 1996

Pages 148-9
Unknown
Eureka Flag, 1854
wool, cotton, 2600 x 3240 mm (irregular)
Gift of the King Family, 2001

Acknowledgements

Thanks go to the keepers of the nation's picture collection, who render invaluable assistance in the preparation of books such as this. In particular I would like to acknowledge the generous assistance of the Ballarat Fine Art Gallery; La Trobe Picture Collection, State Library of Victoria; National Library of Australia, Canberra; Public Records Office, Victoria and Ballarat; Mitchell Library, State Library of New South Wales; Mortlock Library, State Library of South Australia; and the State Library of Tasmania.

I would also like to thank Clare Gervasoni and Dorothy Wickham from Ballarat Heritage Services, whose own research and published works had given me so much valuable background material; Bendigo publisher James Lerk, who is always generous with advice and assistance with Bendigo pictures; and Castlemaine author Peter Cuffley, who generously read through the manuscript and offered some valuable, and timely, insights.

I would like to offer special thanks to the Ballarat Fine Art Gallery, and to the Ballarat Eureka Stockade Museum; the gallery for their support through the generous loan of the flag and the excellent Charles Doudiet sketches and the museum who have supported my books in the past and were eager for this one.

I would also like to thank a fellow I had met only once, at the ABC in Melbourne, Paul Murphy, a descendent of 18-year-old stockader Michael Canny. Murphy was so enthusiastic about the whole saga that I was greatly encouraged to tell this story of the battle in which his great-grandfather was wounded, and honour all those ordinary men and women whose enthusiasm for their adopted country, Australia, changed the onward march of our history. They ushered in our Australian democracy, under that glorious blue flag — the flag of the 'Southern Cross'.

Index

A'Beckett, Sir William 166, 169
aborigines
  shepherd boy 20
Agitation Hill, Castlemaine 63, 72
Aitken, Mr. 12
Akehurst, Arthur 150
Americans 116, 119, 130, 161, 171, 193
Anderson, Henry 10
Anderson's Creek, Vic., 33
Anti Gold Licence Association
'Anti-Licence Agitation' 72
Armstrong, Commissioner 31
Arnold, Arthur 150
Arnot, Thomas 102
arrest of Gregorious 102
Ashburner, James 143
'Australia Felix' 17
Australasian Anti-Transportation League 24

Bakery Hill 103, 117
  meetings 103, 114, 120
  'Red Hill Mining Company' 202
Balla[a]rat, Vic., 10, 23, 27, 36, 81
Ballarat Art Gallery 148
Ballarat goldfields 201
Ballarat Reform League 113, 117, 121, 160, 169
Ballarat Star 15
'Band and Albion Consols Company' 201
'Band of Hope' mine 197
Bank of Victoria 104
  robbery 138
Barker, Dr., 23, 32, 58
Barkly, Sir Henry 174
  Lady Elizabeth 175
Barry, Sir Redmond 168-9
Bassar, George 101
Bathurst, NSW, 18, 19, 20
Bellpost Hill, Vic., 10
Bendigo, Vic., 32, 74, 80, 154
Bendigo Government Camp 69
'Bendigo Mac', see McLachlan
Bentley, James 100
Betts, John 12
Bird, John 95-6
Black, Alfred 126
  George 75, 116, 125-6
  Thomas 138
Black Hill, 199, 201
Blair, David 158
Bolton, John 104
'Bonan Yong', Buninyong, Vic 14
Bridgewater Bay, Vic., 17
Brown, Captain Edward 65, 73
Bull, Lieut. Col., J. E. N. 66
Buninyong, Vic., 10, 23, 27, 38
Buninyong Hotel 19
Burnette, Robert 138, 193
Burrumbeet, Lake 10

California, U.S.A., 8, 18, 20, 24
California Rangers Company 193
Californian Rifle Brigade 130, 138, 150
Callinen, Thomas 144
Campbell, James 146
  William 19
Campbell's Creek, Vic., 19
'campites' 88
Canny, Michael 143
  Patrick 143
Carboni, Raffaello 117, 126-7, 142, 150-1, 169, 173
Carr, Dr., 100, 150
Castlemaine, Vic 62, 154, 159
Chandler, John 167
Chapman, Thomas 19
Chartists 76, 80, 113

Chewton, Vic 51, 58
Chinese 76, 125
Chisholm, Caroline 159
Christian, Trooper 62
Clarke, Rev. W. B., 19
Clunes, Vic. 19, 23, 28
Cobb & Co. 130, 162
Cockburn, Mr., 47
Coleman, George 14
Comerford, George 12
Commission of Inquiry 172
Commissioners 90
Connor, Mr. 33
Corio Bay, Vic 10
Cox, William 150
Coxhead, Frederick 144

D'Arcy, Mr. 10
D'Ewes, John 100, 115
Dalton, John 143
Dane, Captain 47
deaths at Eureka 164
deep lead mining 197
Denovan, W. D. C. 76, 152
Derwent Co. 10
Dexter, Mr., 69, 75
Diamond, Martin 130, 144
digger hunts 92-3
'Diggers' Advocate' 75
diggers' banner 69
Diggers' Congress Movement 75
Dignum, Thomas 12
Donaghey, George 144
Doudiet, Charles 151
Duke, Anne 146
Duke of Edinburgh (Prince Alfred) 197
Dunlop, John 31, 134
Dunne, Alicia 125

Embling, Dr. 154, 158
Emmerman, William 144
Esmond, James 19, 22, 24, 27, 128
Eureka Hotel 99
  arrests 108
  compensation claim 130
  fire 105
Eureka flag 146, 148
Eureka lead 126

Farrell, John 100
Farrell, Mrs. 23, 32
Fauchery, Antoine 37, 203
Fawkner, John, MLC 117, 158, 172
Fenton & Gibson 23, 32
Ferguson, Charles 171
first discovery of gold
  in Australia 19
  in Victoria 23
first protest on diggings 33
first shipment of gold 24
Fisher, David 10
FitzRoy, Sir Charles 20, 28, 76
Fletcher 114
Forest Creek, Vic. 32, 35, 51, 57
Foster, Col. Sec., John 74, 114, 159
Free Trade Hotel 151
Frencham, Henry 23, 32, 157
Fulton, Thomas 158

Gab, George 14
Gad, Edward 101
Garrett, Henry 104
Geelong, Vic. 15, 22, 28
Gipps, Gov. George 19
Glenmona Station, Vic. 19
Gold Discovery Committee 22
gold escort 65

gold licence 88
Golden Point, Ballarat 31, 33-4, 203
Goldfields Reform League
  formed 104
Goodenough, Henry 133
Goold, Bishop 120
gravel pits 121, 128
'Great Extended Gold Mining Company' 198
'Great Meeting of Diggers' 51
'Great Northern Gold Mining Company' 198
Gregorious, Johann 102, 113
Grey, Earl 75, 129, 171

Hafele, John 142
Hance, Hervey 100
Hardy, Commissioner 60
Hargraves, Edward Hammond 18, 19
Harrison, Captain 57, 59
Harte, Brett 192
Hartley, George 193
Hartley, NSW 19
Hassell, Bendan 119
Hastie, Rev., Thomas 15
Hayes, Timothy 121, 168
  Anastasia 168
Heffernan, James 143
Henty 17
Hepburn, Capt. John 12, 162
Hepburn Springs, Vic 12
Hermiston, Andrew 95
Hiscock, Thomas 19, 23, 37
Holyoake, Henry 114-5, 152
Hotham, Lieut-Gov., Sir Charles 98
  arrival in Victoria 76
  death 173
  visits goldfields 79
    Bendigo 81
    Forest Creek 82
Howitt, William 69, 161
Humffray, John Basson 113, 116, 121, 161
  elected to parliament 173
Hurd, Albert 116

Innes, George 14
Irwin, Samuel 120

Johnstone, Captain 102
Jones, Dr. 65
Joseph, John 162, 166, 193

Kennedy, Margaret 23, 32
  Thomas 114, 116, 125-6, 129
Kentworthy, Dr. Charles 193
Kerr, Dr. 20
King, John 144
  Isabella 144

Lalor, Peter 121, 125
  address meeting for the first time 121
  arm amputated 153
  elected to parliament 173
  marriage 125, 153
  proclaims 'Southern Cross' 121
  takes charge of Stockade 138
land purchase 75
La Trobe, Sir Charles Joseph 18, 29
  recalled to England 76
  receives Bendigo petition 70
  visits Ballarat 37
Learmonth, Somerville 12
  Thomas 10, 22
Lewis Ponds Creek, NSW 20
licence fee
  Bendigo petition 65, 71
  first protests 33, 63

Index

hunts 85
inspection 52
introduction 31
last licence hunt 113, 121
Red Ribbon Rebellion 63, 65
reduced NSW 76
removal NSW 99
sliding scale 74
Sofala protest 60
storekeeper's licence 74
suspension 73
thirty shilling fee 47
Lister, John 20
logs, the 31, 95
Longville, Henry 134
Lonsdale, Captain 17, 22
Lord, Trooper 103
Lothair Mining Company, Clunes, Vic 125

Macarthur, Maj-Gen. Edward 174
McIntyre, Andrew 109
    letter to his brother 109
Mackay, Angus 59, 65
Management of the Goldfields Act 74
Mangan, Trooper 62
Manning, John 129
Marriott, Henry 104
Marshall, James 8, 18
martial law 158
Martin, Peter 100
McGill, James 130, 150, 162
McIvor diggings 65
McLachlan, Police Magistrate Lachlan 79
McMahon, 62
Melbourne Magistrates Court 168
Melbourne meeting 154
    second meeting 158
Melody, Bill 193
Michel, Louis John 22-3, 33
Mitchell, Chief Comm. of Police 72
Mitchell, Major, Thomas, Livingston 10, 17, 24
'monster meeting' 120
'Monster Nugget' 44, 202
Montez[s], Lola 176
Mooney, Tom 100
Moore, Teddy 143
Moore, Thadeus 151
Mouat, James 'Bendigo' 32
Mt. Aitken 12
Mt. Alexander 12, 17, 23
Mt. Macedon 12, 17, 23
Myers, Assistant. Comm. 59

'Nelson & Wellington Gold Mining Company' 200
Nickle, Major 138, 152, 157, 160, 162
nuggets
    'Blanche Barkly' 202
    'Kohinor' 203
    'Lady Don' 203
    'Lady Hotham' 203
    'Sarah Sands' 203
    'The Canadian' 203
    'The Welcome Nugget' 202

Oddie, James 35, 148
O'Farrel, Henry James 197
O'Niell, Thomas 144
Ophir Creek, NSW 20
Ovens River diggings, Vic. 59
Owens, John Downes 59

Panton, Commissioner, J. A. 66, 74, 79, 82, 87
Peters, Andrew 133
petition 65-6

Piddington, Rev. 61
pikeman's terrier 146
Poverty Gully (see Golden Point)
Powell, Henry 150
Power, Dr. 14
prisoners 164
protests
    Sofala, NSW 60
    storekeepers' 160
Provisional Anti-Licence Committee 85
Pyrenees Ranges, Vic. 22

quartz crushing 198
'Queen Quartz Gold-Mining Claim' 197
Quinlan, Will 144
Quin, Thomas 104

'Red Hill Mining Company', The 202
Red Ribbon Agitation 72
Red Ribbon Rebellion 63, 65, 71
Redan Lead, Ballarat 198, 199
Rede, Commissioner Robert 100, 105, 114, 121, 133
Regan, James 31
Regiments
    40th. 72, 114, 118, 133, 146, 157
    99th. 58, 74, 118, 133, 146, 157
Richards, Lieut. 142, 168
Roney, Michael 146
Ross, Captain 126, 138, 146, 151
Royal Commission into the Goldfields 116

Sacramento, USA 8, 18
Sandhurst (see Bendigo)
San Francisco, USA 8, 192
Scobie, James 99
Sebastopol, Vic. 12, 200
Seekamp, Henry 165, 171, 176
seperation of the colony 17
'Sergeants Freehold Quartz Gold Mining Company' 199
Serjeant, R. M. 94
shepherding 87
shipping
    Europa 8
    Great Britain 44
    HMS *Rattlesnake* 17
sly-grog 53, 62, 88-9
Smyth, Father Patrick 102, 113, 120, 161, 169
Sofala, NSW 60
'Southern Cross' flag 121, 125, 142, 144, 146
'Star of the East Gold Mining Company' 203
Star Hotel, Ballarat 113, 125
Stawell, Attorney-General. W. F. 118
Stockade 126
    attack 133
    map 132, 134-5
    spies 129
Strzelecki, Count Paul de 19
Sutherland, George 34
Sutter, John 8
Swindells, Herbert 34
Tambaroora diggings, NSW 60
Tarleton, Mr. 119
terrier 146
Thomas, Captain 114, 133
Thompson, Dr. 10
Thomson, G. E. 65, 71, 88
Thonen, Edward 142
Tolpuddle martyrs 8
Tom, Charles 20
    William 20
Train, G. F. 130, 162
trials

Eureka rebels 166
    McIntyre, Fletcher, Westerby 115
troops arrive 118
Turon River diggings, NSW 60
Twain, Mark 175, 192

Van Demonians 104
Vennick, Jan 150, 170
Vern Frederick 114, 121, 142
'Vinegar Hill' 131

Wall, Mr. 85
Wendouree, Lake 12
Welch, Lawrence 100
    Mary Anne 101
'Welcome Nugget', The 202-3
Wentworth, William Charles 18, 20
Westerby, 'Yorkie' 114
Westgarth, William 172
White Horse Range 31
Wilson, John 146, 148
Wise, Captain (40th Reg.) 138, 150, 152
Withers, Anastasia 146
Withers, William Bramwell 15
Wittowski Bros. 202
Wright, Chief Commissioner of Goldfields 73, 172

Ximenes, Sub-Inspector Maurice 105

Yarrowee Creek 12, 31
Yuille, Archibald Buchanan 12
Yuille, William Cross 10, 22
    Ballarat Station 31
Yuille's swamp 12

The Eureka Stockade Memorial
'Stereoscope' postcard photographed by George Rose c. 1910.
(LA TROBE PICTURE COLLECTION, STATE LIBRARY OF VICTORIA)

'On to the field, our doom is sealed,
To conquer or be slaves;
The sun shall see our country free,
Or set upon our graves.'
(Great Works)

— RAFFAELLO CARBONI, 1855